Life in the Spirit!

Experiencing the Fullness of Christ

Paul J. Bucknell

Books by Paul J. Bucknell

Allowing the Bible to speak to our lives today!

Overcoming Anxiety: Finding Peace, Discovering God

Life in the Spirit! Experiencing the Fullness of Christ

The Lord Your Healer: Discover Him and Find His Healing Touch

Reaching Beyond Mediocrity: Being an Overcomer

The Life Core: Discovering the Heart of Great Training

The Godly Man: When God Touches a Man's Life

Redemption Through the Scriptures and *Study Guide*

Godly Beginnings for the Family

Principles and Practices of Biblical Parenting

Building a Great Marriage

Christian Premarital Counseling Manual for Counselors

Relational Discipleship: Cross Training

Running the Race: Overcoming Sexual Lusts

The Bible Teaching Commentary on Genesis

The Bible Teaching Commentary on Romans

Life Transformation: A Monthly Devotional on Romans 12:9-21

A Spiritual Map for Unity

Book of Romans: Bible Studies

Book of Ephesians: Bible Studies

Abiding in Christ: Walking with Jesus

Inductive Bible Studies in Titus

1 Peter Bible Study Questions: Living in a Fallen World.

Take Your Next Step into Ministry

Training Leaders for Ministry

Satan's Four Stations: The Destroyer is Destroyed

Study Questions for Jonah: Understanding the Heart of God

Our Digital Libraries include these books as well as slides, handouts, audio/videos, and much more at: www.foundationsforfreedom.net

Life in the Spirit!

Experiencing the Fullness of Christ

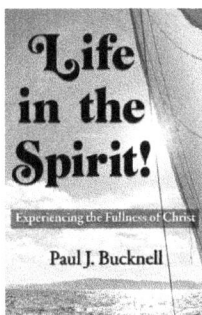

Paul J. Bucknell

Book Information

Life in the Spirit! Experiencing the Fullness of Christ

Copyright © 2018 by Paul J. Bucknell

Paperback
ISBN-13: 978-1-61993-066-7

Also in Digital eBook
ISBN-13: 978-1-61993-068-1

www.foundationsforfreedom.net
Pittsburgh, PA 15212 USA

Map contribution by Hugo Cheng.

Tribute

We magnify the Lord for His excellent ways of deeply moving in His people to cooperate with Him in His mighty redemptive work through the Holy Spirit and humbly seek that He further draws us closer to Him. Just like the air that brings life and oxygen to our lives, so the Holy Spirit excels at bringing spiritual life, desires, hopes, love, and power into our lives, bringing us into further conformity with Christ.

"Bless the LORD, O my soul, and forget none of His benefits" (Psalm 103:2).

Appreciation

Special thanks to Rev. Hugo Cheng for the map designs and to each of the four teachers who worked so closely with me when first teaching these resources: Dr. Ridge Orr, Jessie McLaughlin, and Calvin Chiang. It always means so much to me when my own daughter, Allison Bucknell-Herrera, can assist me with her willingness to edit my books, including this one!

Preface

Several things fascinated me on my first sailing event back in college, which took place on a small sailboat. I was amazed at how our fearless leader managed to swing the sail back and forth, confidently guiding the boat, gliding across that Florida lake. I was also pleasantly surprised at how speedily we traveled, being that we were powered only by the wind. Altogether, it became a special experience that provided a wonderful picture of what God's Spirit wants to do in each believer's life: not consigning us to drift listlessly about in the hot sun but empowering us to live a Christ-filled life by His powerful Spirit.

On a physical level, in order to be like my navigator friend, Jess, who masterfully sailed the boat so long ago, I would have to master many things. The same is true for experiencing and learning from the Spirit. My life and, indeed, all of the lives of those who genuinely know the Lord are all embarked on this spiritual journey. Looking back over the decades of my life spent in Christian fellowship and ministry, I can see how the Spirit of God interestingly and wisely guided and strengthened me, not just on a superficial level but by excursions deep in my heart, using unfamiliar experiences to instigate deep expectations. In the end, I have found that the Spirit has not only given us faith to believe but faith to desire, want, obey, and accomplish all that the Father wants for us. I trust, as you read this book, that you too can fully, like that boat captain, learn how to wonderfully master your spiritual boat under the powerful leadership of the Holy Spirit.

Experiencing the Fullness of Christ

There are several ways to teach about the Holy Spirit. Some teach from a top down perspective, first teaching "high theology" that eagerly tackles theological concepts like the Trinity, while others focus on relevant topics like "Being filled with the Spirit." We appreciate both of these goals, but we seek to equip you with a solid Biblical perspective of the Holy Spirit that helps you walk closely with the Spirit so that we can do His works. *Life in the Spirit!* uses the bottom-up methodology, which introduces the Holy Spirit using the developing experiences and growing knowledge of God's people of the Spirit throughout their Christian lives. Just as a newborn gradually grows in his or her awareness, so do believers in their understanding and experience of the Holy Spirit. Theology can be dangerous if learning occurs without spiritual apprehension. Our goal is to combine experience with knowledge, creating the desired powerful encounter with the Holy Spirit that results in His greater involvement in our lives and ministries.

Perhaps I can explain a bit how the Lord has impressed on me the importance of this approach. These various approaches were reintroduced to me in a flash when I discovered a 45-year-old syllabus. Soon after I was saved, about 13 years old, I started learning from a theologian who conducted a Sunday afternoon Bible study. I learned much from this great teacher and had a great amount of Biblical teaching implanted deep into my young mind. But alongside these memories, another memory exists—one of his waywardness when he later discarded his wife for a "spiritual woman." What good is doctrine when truths do not wash our hearts with faith that keeps our straying feet on the path? Like my Dad told my brother on our hikes, "Stay on the path." In the same way, we need to imbibe biblical truths so deeply that they thoroughly lead and affect our hearts.

I fully believe that God wants every believer to be filled by His Spirit just as Jesus was. Of course, our work and responsibilities differ, but the way we live out our lives will largely be the same by exuding Christ's person. May the Holy Spirit help us maximize our lives so that we can faithfully follow the path that Jesus sets before us! A good pastor friend has provided a map by which we can, island by island, navigate into the likeness of Christ through the powerful work of the Holy Spirit:

Island #1: Christian Beginnings: Life & Belief
Island #2: Christian Growth: Strength & Dedication
Island #3: Christian Service: Faith & Filling
Island #4: Christian Doctrine: Questions & Theology

Join us in this adventure of experiencing the fullness of Christ's Spirit!

Our approach will help us carefully discern and apply the more fundamental truths necessary to fully grasp the later, more conceptual truths.

Life in the Spirit! has slides and an audio/video teaching companion that is found in the D3 (BFF Discipleship #3 Digital) Library online.[1]

Paul J. Bucknell

Pittsburgh, PA, USA 15212

2018

---

[1] www.foundationsforfreedom.net/Help/Store/Intros/DLibrary-D3.html

Table of Contents

Section 3: Christian Service: Faith and Filling

Section 4: Christian Doctrine: Questions and Theology

Section 1: Christian Beginnings: Life & Belief

"So is everyone who is born of the Spirit" (John 3:8).

Christians are designed to regularly experience the presence and empowerment of the Holy Spirit and, like Jesus, to constantly rely on Him for growth in their spiritual life and for service. But what is the Holy Spirit? How does one learn about Him and rely on Him? How does He lead believers? These are some critical questions that have troubled Christians for many years. *Life in the Spirit!* navigates us through an exciting journey of learning about the Holy Spirit, island by island, so that we might constantly walk fully blessed by the Spirit's presence and power.

The first stop takes us to the island of Christian Beginnings where we explore a Christian's new life and initial belief. By starting off with sound understanding, the new believer can leap forward in his or her new life in Christ, powered by the Holy Spirit.

#1 The Path of the Spirit (Gal 5:25)

Life in the Spirit!
Experiencing the Fullness of Christ

"If we live by the Spirit, let us also walk by the Spirit" (Gal 5:25).

Jesus and the apostles said a lot about the Holy Spirit—many times referring to Old Testament passages. Though there are many confusing aspects of the Holy Spirit, ignorance of such teachings will only keep us from becoming a vibrant Christian believer. We want to focus on gaining what God has promised and given to each genuine believer. Imagine God's Spirit filling each believer in a church to the extent that Christ's life is lived out through their words, attitudes, and decisions, which then results in local churches filled with His Spirit that allow Christ to powerfully rule through their lives (Revelation 2–3).

This book is designedly quite differently than the many books out there on the Holy Spirit. Instead of first introducing complex theological concepts of the Holy Spirit, we trace the path that allows new believers to become aware of and attentive to the Holy Spirit. While we do retain a firm grasp on biblical instruction, we also acknowledge the diverse paths believers are led on, though they are still shaped by similar chronological learning experiences of God's Spirit.

All genuine believers are saved, and yet their experiences greatly differ. There are innumerable paths on the journey as each of our varying life experiences clearly testifies. However, it is helpful to look at our spiritual development as more of a path of continuous learning experiences than a road stand where we, rather predictably, pick up what we think we need. It is unfortunate that we sometimes treat one experience or lesson as the pinnacle of our lives rather than emphasizing the more significant ongoing part where the Spirit Himself leads and teaches us (John 14:26). Behind the scenes, the Holy Spirit persistently carries out His special saving work that is common to all Christians. Only after we understand our common salvation and sanctification experiences can we move forward to steeper and more challenging paths of learning regarding the Holy Spirit. Many believers, perhaps even yourself, have been very hurt by wrong teaching on the Holy Spirit or carried away with certain aspects of His gifting. We want to present and follow the good path that Jesus Himself so wonderfully modeled for us.

A. Defining the Spirit

One of the first points of confusion regarding the Spirit comes from the difficulty there is in understanding the word "Spirit." The words "Spirit" and "spirit" in the English Bible need to be distinguished. The capitalized "Spirit" refers to God Himself, whereas the lowercase "spirit" describes a person's mood or inner being. Although we enjoy the easy scheme of capitalization, it was not present in the original manuscripts, either in the Old or New Testaments. It is, however, appropriate and necessary for translators to make an educated guess at whether the 's' should be large or small. Knowing this fact will help us better understand the differences that we might find and appreciate with increasing clarification the Spirit as we progress through the Scriptures.

$$\text{Spirit} <> \text{spirit}$$

The word "spirit," regardless of capitalization, is used 519 times in the Bible, 200 (80 with the addition of "of God") times in the Old Testament and 319 (223 with "of God") times in the New. Without capitalization in the original languages, the meaning and whether it is best noted with a capital or small "s" is determined by the context alone. Usually, the context is quite clear and so it is not hard to discern whether it should be a capital 'S' in reference to God. (Note: **Exercise #1** in the Appendix provides training to help you discern accurately.)

Summary

Meanwhile, let us understand that God, through the Bible, is making clear what we otherwise would not be able to understand at all. His Spirit is actively working in this world. The Spirit and His work is often counterfeited by our sinful and selfish desires, but if we seek the Lord, then we will find that He and His works are characterized by righteousness and love. God has given us sufficient understanding to rightly detect the contours of the path, the determination to stay on it, and the necessary aid, provided by His Spirit, to walk upon it.

B. Detecting the Path of the Spirit

There is a lot of confusion when it comes to the meaning of "spirit" (or "Spirit"), so I consider it best to use actual examples to clarify the many ways the same word can be understood but should be differently translated depending on the context.

> And the earth was formless and void, and darkness was over the surface of the deep; and the **Spirit of God** was moving over the surface of the waters (Gen 1:2).

The first use of "spirit" in the Bible is in reference to the Spirit of God, which is interestingly the 16th word in the Hebrew Bible. Because of its association with God ("Spirit of God"), we capitalize the word, acknowledging it in association to God Himself rather than the air or wind. From this verse onward, we wonder, "Who is the Spirit of God and what is He doing?" We will refrain from taking a distracting (but interesting) detour in trying to explain what it means to be "moving over the waters" and instead focus on what this verse states, which is that this world is comprised of more than atoms and molecules and that the Spirit and the spirit worlds play a crucial role in the universe—a complete contrast to the tenets of popular materialism.

At times, the Spirit of God is set against an evil spirit, "The Spirit of the LORD departed from Saul, and an evil spirit from the LORD terrorized him" (1 Sam 16:14-15). Even though this evil spirit was from the Lord, it is not capitalized because it is an evil spirit. It is not stating God created the evil spirit as evil but that the Lord, having created the vacuum of righteousness by leaving Saul, made it so that an evil spirit could rush into the void, just as darkness always fills the void when light disappears.

Many times, 'spirit' (small 's') refers to a person's inner being, which includes the soul, the part that cannot be touched, such as in "and he ate; then his spirit revived" (1 Sam 30:12). This is clearly referring to a person's being rather than a spiritual being. It is important to remember for our study that there are many other original words that could mean spirit, as well as many different English words for those translations such as air, wind, and breath. The Greek and Hebrew languages simply use the same word for them. This will be pertinent when we study Nicodemus' encounter with Jesus in John 3, in which the wind is likened to the Spirit of God. The metaphor for this book is a fully extended and handsome sail, which reflects the way in which the Spirit often works, like the wind or air currents; everything works when we are "filled with the Spirit" (Eph 5:18).

The word 'spirit' can be used not only in reference to a person's being (i.e., 'her low spirit') but the nature or essence of anything like the world in the following verse. "Now we have received, not the **spirit of the world**, but the **Spirit who is from God**, that we might know the things freely given to us by God" (1 Cor 2:12). Notice here that both a small and capital 's' are used here in one verse, but they are the same Greek word (*pneuma*). The first 'spirit' refers to the essence of the world, almost personifying the world, while the latter clearly identifies itself as the "Spirit who is from God." This will be discussed more in the next chapter.

God the Spirit powerfully works in our lives.

Finally, let's note that the Spirit of God works in the lives of believers. The very person of God is dwelling in our lives. For example, the phrase, "Received...the Spirit who is from God" teaches us that believers are to be intimately acquainted with God, but there is another verse, that assumes that intimacy with God: "But the one who joins himself to the Lord is one spirit with Him" (1 Cor 6:17). He is with us, but perhaps His presence crosses our comfort zones. God is out there, yes, but He seeks a deeper influence on our lives that they may be joined and not separated.

God the Spirit, then, seeks to powerfully work in our lives. We might be unsure of how or what He does, but we can fully trust this to be an important part of how the Almighty Creator works in our lives.

C. Confusion Over False Spirits (1 John 4:1)

> Beloved, do not believe every spirit, but test the spirits to see whether they are from God; because many false prophets have gone out into the world (1 John 4:1).

We need to be ultra careful of the false spirits that seek to commune with us and attempt to lead us astray. John has some astonishing advice for any person who thinks it is good to be open to any positive vibe or spirit out there. John gives us two commands and one explanation in this one short verse.

Command #1: His command to "not believe every spirit" is straightforward: do not trust just any spirit. The most susceptible people are those who are open to whatever spirit is out there, naively believing all spirits are good. We should not assume that all spiritual beings are good because there are truly evil spirits that exist in the world. A biblical perspective holds that there are good and bad spiritual beings, hence John's warning.

Perhaps it would be helpful to clarify the distinction between the two groups of spiritual beings: the good spiritual beings include the Holy Spirit and angels, while the evil spiritual beings include the Devil and his demons, which are fallen angels. During John's time, there was a strong belief, originating from Greek philosophy, that spiritual things were good and material things were evil. Many today are involved in all sorts of 'spiritual' pursuits under the assumption that all such interactions are good. Even Christians are blinded when they succumb to using or practicing Christian yoga. They believe in the spirit of yoga and bring it into their lives and church despite its strong Hindu background that associates it with the worship of false gods. As a result, one sister who finds the need to pray with believers who have indulged in yoga and were negatively influenced by their participation in yoga, unaware that each posture is associated with a particular demon.

We need discernment to evaluate the spirits out there. What spirits are out there? Which ones have you exposed yourself to?

Command #2: "Test the spirits" is the second command that is instructing us to supplement our caution with real testing. Evidently, we cannot trust others to guard us, for after all, we need to advance to the level where we can, throughout the day, discern between evil spirits and the Holy Spirit. Learning about the Holy Spirit, then, should be a basic skill for the believer. Dangers are so commonplace that every believer needs to learn how to be diligent.

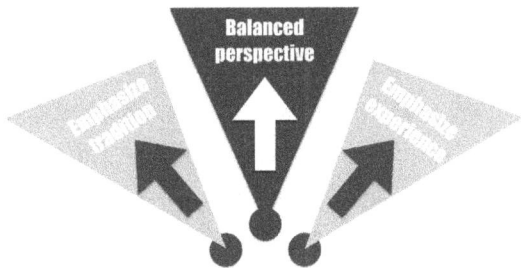

John himself provides three tests in 1 John that we can use to test the spirits: the test of love, light (purity), and proper teaching.

- Test of love: look for signs of pride, bitterness, selfishness, or anger.
- Test of light: look for hints of seduction, a spirit of deceit, and lies.
- Test of teaching: look for exaggerated claims rather than a true focus on the scriptures and Jesus Christ.

If another person speaks excitedly about what he or she has learned aside from the scriptures, then beware and reject the things they try to pass on. The Holy Spirit will always follow the Word of God, whereas elements of secrecy and fear give away the association with the dark world. The scriptures give us many tests that help us discern the spirits, that is, examining people or thoughts and the conclusions they lead us to.

Explanation: The phrase "Many false prophets have gone out into the world" shows us why we must be cautious. Just as the Holy Spirit proceeds from God, so false spirits and their accompanying false prophets issue from the evil one. Teachings, doctrines, religions, and even philosophies have a sponsor. If we indiscriminately believe what a certain person teaches, will we not mimic this false prophet? There are many cult leaders who should be called false prophets. Notice Jesus' penetrating analysis of the Pergamum church:

> But I have a few things against you, because you have there some who hold the teaching of Balaam, who kept teaching Balak to put a stumbling block before the sons of Israel, to eat things sacrificed to idols, and to commit acts of immorality. Thus you also have some who in the same way hold the teaching of the Nicolaitans. Repent therefore; or else I am coming to you quickly, and I will make war against them with the sword of My mouth (Rev 2:14-16).

Some people were spreading the teachings of Balaam while others followed a false prophet, who was perhaps called Nicolas, the followers of who were called Nicolaitans (possibly related to Acts 6:5). When a person lives or teaches wrong teaching and, to some degree, systemizes it so that it can be passed on, great deception seeps in. John says many, not a few, false prophets went into the world.

The evil one does everything to keep God's children from walking in the fullness of the Spirit because he greatly fears the spread of 'little' Christs (the literal definition of 'Christians') across the earth! Believers should not fear the Spirit but greatly desire His companionship, knowing that it is only God's growing kingdom that can bring salvation, joy, and love to this world.

D. Understanding Our Differing Beliefs

"There is one body and one Spirit" (Eph 4:4).

Each believer has grown up under the influence of one or more Christian traditions, even if the church claims not to be a tradition or denomination! What a child is exposed to greatly influences his/her approach to life—language, conversation, eating habits, etc. One's habits will shape one's mindset. A study of our beliefs, therefore, necessitates an honest assessment of our Christian lives evaluated against the scriptures. Believers, understandably, evaluate what they see in one church based on what they have experienced, so they can easily find comfort in familiarity and therefore don't judge beyond what they know at the risk of missing moral and significant issues.

When the teaching of the Holy Spirit is mentioned, many people are stirred up by past troubles, perhaps divisive situations, and harmful splits in churches. The first thing to pay attention to from this verse is that there is only "One Spirit." Though there be many varied experiences and understandings of God's Spirit among God's people, there remains one Spirit. The many divisions that supposedly came from the One Spirit—for each claims to be led by God—evidently were not from the Holy Spirit. We should refuse to quickly justify man's actions as God's leading because the Holy Spirit does not guide in this manner.

Equally important is the second teaching of being "one body." This, of course, refers to the church, the people of God. Yes, there are many denominations and many more churches, most possessing their own pastors, but there is one Bridegroom who is readying His one bride: His people. There is a great need for God's people to live in harmony, learning from and appreciating each other but not removing their discernment. There are many extreme movements that have not been properly critiqued or investigated. Often, leaders in charge of such movements that are connected to the Holy Spirit's revival, healing, or gifting end up tolerating and propagating many objectionable behaviors and teachings.

Let me provide a practical example of what it looks like to follow the Holy Spirit's leading in regard to preserving unity in the church. We know the church and Christ should possess the same unity as married couples (Eph 5:21-33). The problem is that spiritual leaders do not trust that God will lead the congregation in harmony as they resolve disagreements. The leaders may pronounce to all that they are following the Spirit, but when we discern the divisive spirit that surrounds them and their teachings, we find that they are resistant to the Spirit.[2]

---

[2] For further exploration on this topic, read my book, *"A Spiritual Map for Unity."*

Exercise #2

In order to get a better picture of what the Holy Spirit does and does not do, we need to return to the Bible. The Bible verses in Exercise #2 (Appendix 2) highlight the various activities of the Spirit of God.

While completing that assignment, you will quickly discover that the Spirit of God is in no way a tame horse, allowing us to predict the way He will work. God's genius is too great, His power too awesome to restrain His activities to a trite and predictable set of actions. The Lord loves to display His love and power, and so uniquely works through many impossible circumstances to interweave His miracles with our daily lives. For example, the call to register each person in one's hometown, as in Joseph and Mary's case, is a key part of the Christmas story, combining a number of clearly improbable circumstances into a scene that displays God's glory, inspiring the onlookers to exclaim, "Only God could do that!" On one hand, it reminds us to respect the Lord's ways of doing things—patiently waiting—but it also is great to know that at any moment the Lord might again have His Spirit perform another one of His awesome miracles. I have been waiting on the Lord for revival for decades now, and I remain poised for action.

We should not be hasty in stating whether the Holy Spirit does one thing or another. But one thing we can be sure of is the necessity of testing the spirits because there are false prophets out there—and it just might be your favorite speaker or singer!

Although precious time can be spent probing your past understandings of the Holy Spirit, it is more beneficial to catch up to the place where God wants you to be now. As we go, chapter to chapter, along the path of learning about the Holy Spirit, we need to constantly monitor the thoughts going through our mind in order to make the most of this study. For example, if some past sin, such as an adulterous thought, comes to your mind, confess it! Think of this as the Holy Spirit bringing it to your attention so that you can properly repent from it and get back on the path of learning. Conviction is one way the Holy Spirit works. We do not need to fear His penetrating work because it leads to forgiveness and freedom.

A balanced perspective is a biblical perspective because God has revealed His truth in the scriptures.

E. Experiencing the Fullness of Christ

Learning from the Holy Spirit is a lifelong process. Although we gain the Holy Spirit at one point in time at salvation (Eph 1:13 "having also believed, you were sealed in Him with the Holy Spirit of promise"), learning the ways of the invisible Spirit is another. Our goal is to be sensitive as to how the Holy Spirit leads us along the path of life while we're here on earth. This, as said above, can be tricky because He is spirit, and truth about the Holy Spirit is spread out from Genesis to Revelation. But, as we walk along this path of learning, the Holy Spirit will personally and actively increase your knowledge and experience through this exciting relationship with Him that touches upon all of your life experiences. Here are six important factors to keep in mind throughout the development of this relationship:

- A Biblical mindset is needed. There is no way we can discern the spirits' temptations without a good understanding of both the Old and New Testaments. The Holy Spirit works with the Word of God, so separating our learning from the scriptures, whether purposeful or in ignorance, is plain foolish.
- Simple to complex. The journey to understanding should begin with the basic learning blocks of salvation and proceed into

sanctification and only then into the deeper mysteries of the Holy Spirit. This is the way God teaches us in life and the practical way to study the Spirit. They are all important, but proper learning at each stage will speed your spiritual development.

- New life is meant for empowered service. Let us not be deluded into thinking that God works in our lives to simply give us fun experiences or deep understanding. He equips us to serve Him in obedience. Yes, our stories will become spectacular events to retell in eternity, but the fact of God's higher purposes carried out through our humble lives should not be forgotten.

- Balance experience with knowledge. Experience and knowledge grow together and should not be separated. Plan on getting involved in people's lives (1 Cor 13:1) and living out a Spirit-filled life.

- Action accompanies the Spirit's presence. The greatest changes always take place when the Spirit is actively working, but be careful not to solely focus on the activity but remember your relationship with the Lord through the Spirit.

- Ongoing learning requires constant reliance. That is the delight of this journey—intimacy with God. No matter the glory of past experiences, whether visions or miracles, keep looking forward at what more the Lord will do.

Summary

Being filled with the Spirit's presence should result in the goal of living out Christ's purposes for our lives for His glory and the benefit of those around us. The way to remain upon the optimum path only comes from being constantly sensitive to the Holy Spirit's leading, which, in turn, allows us to find the extra faith and knowledge needed to keep going. May the Holy Spirit help us maximize our lives so that we can follow the path that Jesus sets before us each day!

Life in the Spirit!

Discussion Questions

1. After doing Exercises 1 and 2 (in the appendix), note one thing you learned about the Holy Spirit from each.

2. Why is it important to "test the spirits"? What spirit seems to trouble you the most?

3. What is one thing you learned as a young believer regarding the Holy Spirit that has positively or negatively affected you to this day?

4. How is false teaching related to false prophets or spirits?

5. Do you tend to seek experiences or the opportunity to meet the Lord?

6. What expectations do you have for the Holy Spirit in your life? How might this shape the way you seek Him?

Life in the Spirit!

#2 The Network of the Spirit (1 Cor 2:10-16)

Life in the Spirit!
Experiencing the Fullness of Christ

"The thoughts of God no one knows except the Spirit of God."

Early on in our Christian lives, we become aware that everything is distinctly different. I suppose the most radical descriptions would be the accounts of the blind recovering sight, the deaf suddenly able to hear, or someone "falling in love." Although the change, for the most part, happens suddenly, we might not be able to understand the significance at first. A personal example I want to share happened back at the time my family got our first color television set. Before that, we only had black and white televisions; we couldn't even imagine colored screens until suddenly we had it before our eyes and could see the amazing colors spread out on a shot of a peacock's tail. Although we immediately noticed and appreciated the color, it took effort to scrutinize the difference. I remember several times asking myself, "What is different?"

Something Radically New

Paul in 1 Corinthians 2 explains the basic difference in life for the new believer; and, believe it or not, this is connected to what happened at the first Pentecost after Jesus rose from the dead. Each time the Spirit of God comes to individuals who believe in Jesus, wherever they live in the world, He takes up a key role in their lives. The whole experience is awesome, though subtle. It is not like a robotic arm that enables a person to lift heavier objects, but a completely new operating system. Perhaps the best illustration is found in the way our computer devices are enlivened, so to speak, when they connect to the internet (and alternately frustrated when not). The Spirit's presence introduces a whole new network, bringing special powers to our lives so that we can learn from God.

The teaching on the awareness of the Holy Spirit is desperately needed in our modern age, where secularism runs wild and brazenly denies any existence of the spiritual world, including the existence of God Himself (which is rather comical because man depends on God to live). This section provides important information on how the Holy Spirit works in the world and, especially, how He works in believers by way of a powerful new network that delivers a radical newness to our lives.

> It is personal.
>
> It is communicative.
>
> It is spiritual.

Paul in 1 Cor 12:11–14 refers to the existence of the spiritual world in many ways. Let's start where the passage begins—with the existence of the spiritual world as seen in human beings and in God.

A. The Natures of Man and God (1 Cor 2:11)

For who among men knows the *thoughts of a* man except the spirit of the man, which is in him? Even so *the thoughts of* God no one knows except the Spirit of God (1 Cor 2:11, NASB).

(1) Man's Personal Nature

In verse 11, Paul refers to the spirit of the human being, which has a special inner network with the ability to intertwine with one's brain and one's soul. Our thoughts do not live apart from our existence but are somehow united with our bodies.

Paul gave a basic description of this unity in verse 11, "The thoughts of a man except the spirit of the man, which is in him."[3] "The spirit of the man" then refers to the inner person—not the body—and uses 'spirit' (*pneuma*) to identify that mysterious invisible network between the soul, mind, and thoughts (i.e., self-awareness) that comprise the person. I am not the same as my thoughts, but my thoughts serve as an essential part of knowing who I am.

Human

MAN'S SPIRIT WORLD

Thoughts and Mind

A person's spirit can perceive his own thoughts. For example, I might be smiling at a neighbor and even waving at him, but I could be speaking thoughts to myself about how I detest the very sight of him. Only the person knows his thoughts unless he reveals them. This is a simple description of the spirit-body network operating inside of a person, more often called the soul.

---

[3] The phrase "the thoughts of" is not in the original Greek text, but it is inferred. Literally, it says, "Knows man" and knows "God." Whether a human or God, a person is signified by the personal thoughts that are usually hidden from others.

The secular world, largely tainted by heavy doses of materialistic philosophy, denies much of this, especially if we were to describe a picture of God's own person. They would explain these aspects in terms of electronic pulses and so forth. But, if we carefully examine people, however, they are not merely thinking, but apprehending these thoughts and evaluating them. This soul capability of ours sets us apart from other creatures, like squirrels and dogs, because we are made in God's image (Gen 1:27). Of course, we must also admit that this soul network has been hacked with a deadly virus (i.e., sin), breaking us off from the full power of God's great network; nevertheless, the basic function remains.

Interestingly, a person can communicate with another by simply projecting his thoughts (often through words). As we share our inner thoughts, we get to know a person as it says in verse 11. Knowing a person entails being able to understand not only a person's thoughts but why he or she thinks a certain way. Some things can be ascertained from a person's actions, but their communication by way of spoken or written words help them know other people; therein lies the popularity of social apps. Because we share much more than words, we typically do not admit we know someone until we have actually met them in person and assembled our gathered ideas about them.

But this is in regard to humans. What about God? How is He the same or different?

(2) The Spirit's Personal Nature

Before we go on, we must insist on a basic functional definition for the word "spirit"; otherwise, each reader could understand the word differently. In verse 11, note the two times the word "spirit" is used. An observant person might object and say "spirit" is used only once and insist that "Spirit" is used the second time. This is a good observation, but this also produces confusion. Actually, in the original Greek language, the words for "spirit" and "Spirit" are exactly the same. In English, we have rightly capitalized the second because it refers to God, but this does not give us the freedom to differentiate a person's spiritual nature to be different from God's.

The Spiritual Network

το πνευμα του ανθρωπου (the spirit of *the* man)

το πνευμα του θεου (the spirit of *the* God)

Paul uses the exact same word (*pneuma*, 2nd word from the left in the box above) to emphasize the possibility and commonality of the function of networking between two or more people. But let's save this topic of communication between God and people for later.

There is a huge difference between God's Spirit and man's spirit, but we are emphasizing the commonality of the network. This is Paul's major point here, and it's very important to remember that many people deny or try to define this function of man otherwise.

It would be tempting to conclude that, because of this, spirituality is a communion of thoughts within a person or with others, but that would be premature and would lead us to the wrong conclusion that man can naturally commune with God. Paul will write about that later, but for now, it is important to establish the fact that people and God can be aware of the thoughts of others.

(3) Brokenness Between Man and God

Let us take one step further before moving on to focus on the topic of true spirituality. Notice how in this verse God's thoughts are on a different level, or network, than man's: "Even so the thoughts of God no one knows except the Spirit of God" (1 Cor 2:11). Man can understand his thoughts (spirit dialogue), but God has His own thoughts that only He can understand. Apart from the Holy Spirit's aid, people are locked out from God's thoughts.

Whether a person is aware of this or not, this missing ability creates a deep tension and dissatisfaction within the soul (Romans 1:20–21) because mankind was originally part of this network, as seen in Genesis 1–2 by Adam and Eve's conversations with God. It was only after the fall that man became spiritually dead and unable to relate to God on the same level. Without knowing God's thoughts, people cannot know God. There is no spiritual communication and therefore no accurate knowledge. Without the Spirit (and Jesus), people and God cannot connect. People are aptly described as being spiritually dead partially because they cannot know God (Eph 2:1–2).

A broken spiritual network is evidenced by religion, philosophy, decisions, and worship that exclude God. The plethora of religions, beliefs, and diversity of thought regarding a greater being do not affirm man's spirituality and his connectedness to His spiritual Creator, but instead, reveal his separation from God because he does not accept the truths of God and therefore seeks and believes other things.

*"For all have sinned and fall short of the
glory of God" (Romans 3:23).*

Without knowing God's thoughts, we cannot know God. Without the Spirit of God, we cannot know God. And, because people do not know God, they cannot benefit from knowing Him, which significantly hampers proper relationship building with others.

The problem is not simply a lack of understanding, however, because Paul elsewhere has stated that the absence of shared values sets people in animosity against God. They reject thoughts of God, as seen in general creation and in the conscience even if they could know them.

> For the mind set on the flesh is death, but the mind set on the Spirit is life and peace, because the mind set on the flesh is hostile toward God; for it does not subject itself to the law of God, for it is not even able to do so; and those who are in the flesh cannot please God (Romans 8:6-8).

People have a spiritual nature, an inner invisible network, wiring them together and therefore are able to observe what they think and share their thoughts with others (i.e., self-expression). A person, for example, can share his thoughts, or a selfie, with others on Facebook or in personal conversations, but we should not consider them spiritual because God is not part of that network. They simply do not have the Spirit that allows them to commune with God.

Being locked out from God's thoughts keeps people from knowing Him. The Christian life, on the contrary, is described as connecting with God's own network through Jesus Christ as well as with others who have joined the same network. This results in the possibility of a personal relationship between God and the individual and a group network called the church.

We need to guard ourselves against thinking of this as something private or exclusive—as if it is only between you and God. This is one danger that stems from the other side of modernism: individualism. In fact, God has opened Himself and knowledge of Himself with all of His people so that we, as a huge family, can all know Him and share the same spiritual network. This is the church, God's people—the family. God our Father openly shares comfort, guidance, and knowledge of Himself with us through the Holy Spirit.

This shared knowledge is the basis of what is called *koinonia,* translated as fellowship, the fellowship between believer and believer with God and His Son Jesus Christ: "What we have seen and heard we proclaim to you also, that you also may have fellowship with us; and indeed our fellowship is with the Father, and with His Son Jesus Christ" (1 John 1:3). This is the reason we have an instant rapport with other believers, even if we have never met them before.

B. The Knowledge of God (1 Cor 2:10-13)

> For to us God revealed them through the Spirit; for the Spirit searches all things, even the depths of God. 11 For who among men knows the thoughts of a man except the spirit of the man, which is in him? 12 Now we have received, not the spirit of the world, but the Spirit who is from God, that we might know the things freely given to us by God, which things we also speak, not in words taught by human wisdom, but in those taught by the Spirit, combining spiritual thoughts with spiritual words (1 Cor 2:10-13).

The All-Knowing Spirit of God

There is a lot of apprehension among some people regarding governments, Facebook, or Google spying on what they do.

Interestingly, though these larger companies can watch what we watch and hear our words, they cannot know our minds. They can only guess at what we are thinking by drawing conclusions from our activities, like what we search, how much time we spend viewing certain types of video, what words we write, or by tracking the images that we invite into our minds. This is not knowing our minds but it is close to it. (They even want to trace what your eyes are actually looking at on a screen!) The Spirit of God, however, does penetrate our minds, "For the Spirit searches all things, even the depths of God." The "all things" definitely includes our thoughts, and God's judgment will be based on this knowledge. Note how the Psalmist asks God to know His heart.

> Search me, O God, and know my heart; Try me and know my anxious thoughts; And see if there be any hurtful way in me, and lead me in the everlasting way (Psalm 139:23–24).

Through the Spirit, God searches "all things," including the minds of all the people He created. His knowledge of the hearts and minds of mankind forms the basis for God's judgment and treatment of them. There is no hiding what we are doing. Yes, we can hide our minds from others because it's hard to know people's genuine motives. But "The Spirit searches all things" (10), which reveals how the Spirit knows the inner thoughts of human beings and "even the depths of God" (from simple to complex).

A great example of this is the way the Lord noticed Sarah laughing to herself behind a tent curtain when He made the promise of her having a son in her old age.

And the LORD said to Abraham, "Why did Sarah laugh, saying, 'Shall I indeed bear a child, when I am so old?' Is anything too difficult for the LORD? At the appointed time I will return to you, at this time next year, and Sarah will have a son." Sarah denied it however, saying, "I did not laugh"; for she was afraid. And He said, "No, but you did laugh" (Gen 18:13–15).

Knowing the Mind of God

The Spirit of God knows not only man's thoughts but the very mind of God: "even the depths of God." This leads us to a very important conclusion.

Although this seems self-evident, we do not know the thoughts of God (because of our sinful nature); we are ignorant of God. Rarely do people claim to know God's thoughts. Their problems are usually more basic as to whether they know if God exists. They have minimized their responses to the point that they cannot see the evidence of God in the creation around them (Rom 1:20–21).

Not a few people call themselves agnostic. They simply do not know about the things of God and have given up trying. Agnostic literally means "without knowledge." This is a biblically attested position of the unbeliever and the heart problem of religions and philosophies. They are guessing what God/god might be like, but they don't really know. Siddhartha Gautama started his journey toward what would later be called Buddhism in ignorance. He admitted his total lack of knowledge or enlightenment. Zen Buddhists and certain Hindu devotees practice meditation or yoga in an attempt to connect with the spirit world. They are all searching because they rightly sense something there! However, without the Spirit of God, mankind cannot know the things of God.

Receiving the Thoughts of God

Paul's words, "For to us God revealed them" (10) identifies how God reveals His thoughts to a select group—"to us." They "have received... the Spirit who is from God" (12). God's network is spiritual because it intertwines man's thoughts with God's thoughts through the Spirit, allowing us to know Him through the Spirit. "Received" probably means that the Spirit of God has been intimately immeshed in our nature rather than just added on. This is the reason that regeneration, the giving of new life, is so dynamically wrapped around the receiving of the Holy Spirit in the second birth (i.e., born again).

Religions and philosophies encompass only acquiring knowledge of God rather than being wholly changed by having God "move in." All people are born with a conscience that shines a little light on how this works, but, because, of our sinful nature, it malfunctions. For example, as a nonbeliever I could often discern right from wrong or, when doing wrong, be knowledgeable of my guilt. When we receive the Spirit, we do not merely have the teaching of God distributed throughout the conscience but the actual presence of the Spirit of God. Because the Spirit is not limited to a body, He can be everywhere at once and thus fully dwells in every genuine believer. This is the ideal network indeed! This is the reason Jesus went above so that we could all live in God's presence through the Holy Spirit in us.

The amazing thing is not that the Spirit of God knows the things of God but that He is willing to pass them onto us! At the end of verse 12, Paul adds, "that we might know the things freely given to us by God." How awesome! The Spirit of God takes the things of God (mentioned in verse 13) and passes them onto us: "Which things we also speak, not in words taught by human wisdom, but in those taught by the Spirit, combining spiritual thoughts with spiritual words." The "we" shows us that Paul is no longer only speaking with reference to what he or we know on our own but also the intertwining of the Spirit's words with our own.

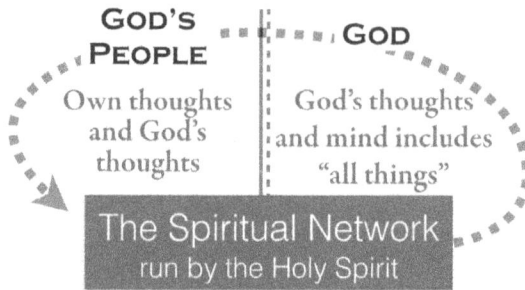

I recently was preparing for a trip, and I needed to get some files from my desktop computer to my laptop. Fortunately, my computer now has an easy way to do this through a function called AirDrop. Once Airdrop is enabled on each computer, the network can be recognized and the user can easily transfer files from one to the other. The spiritual network is like this because the Spirit of God resides in us. He is both the network and the one who knows God's person, so nothing can impede the communication because the language and network *are* the Spirit.

I remember when I discovered prayer as a new believer. Wow! I could talk to God. I'm not talking about the meaningless prayers of those who do not know God. I remembered the drab repetitious prayers in church before I came to know Him, and I knew those prayers were not worth anything. People were religious, but most of the congregants did not know God. But prayer comes alive when a person becomes a true believer. I was so excited about talking with the Lord. The Almighty

God was there listening to me, and He would be communing with me, letting me know different things.

Note two things here, each of which will later be described in more detail. First, Paul is teaching us that the spiritual network is more than just a network; it is "the Spirit who is from God." The Holy Spirit is not to be likened either to a computer search robot or a forceful power but as an extension of God Himself. The scripture here states "from God," insinuating much about the nature of the Holy Spirit, namely, that He is not just a function but a person. This will become even clearer with other passages that we explore. We have received **the** Spirit (the article "the" articulates a specific person). This passage might not verify the Holy Spirit is a person, but it certainly does speak of His function and nature. He discloses God's person to us and convinces us that the Holy Spirit is not the latest revelation of God Himself but the means by which He reveals Himself.

Second, the purpose ("that we might...") for which God reveals Himself is that we as His people can have unlimited communion with Him, where He will openly share knowledge of Himself. The word for this, linking us back to Ephesians, is that God has graced us or openly and kindly shared these things with us. The root word comes from *charis*, which is significant because it can be said that all believers—not select ones—to be "graced." God's purpose, then, is to communicate freely in such a way that we might know Him. God does not want to just pass on knowledge but rather knowledge of Him, which brings about knowledge and wisdom. This knowledge of God's deeper purpose should stir all believers to desire to know God more (2 Peter 3:18). These are the truths that will enable us to consistently walk in the Spirit and pray in the Spirit, to experience the abiding experience of His holiness, and to always be in communion with God—"pray without ceasing" (1 Thes 5:17).

Application

If you find that your heart is dull toward Him, when you're having a hard time communicating with Him, you should check for sin in your life (Isaiah 59:2), or for other hangups that hinder your communion with Him. The problem is not the "network" but always yourself. Of course, if you don't know Jesus Christ, then this network has yet to be set up.

Summary

True spirituality, then, not only includes being known of God, which is true of all people, but knowing God through the Spirit. Through Christ, God has powerfully reinstituted the spiritual network that we lost through Adam's fall. The disconnect between God and man serves as a reminder of what once was a catalyst to cause out hearts to need its initiation and sustenance through Christ and the Spirit—a renewed spiritual network where God and man are linked together, which is made evident by prayer and biblical meditation.

C. The Natural Versus the Spiritual (1 Cor 2:14-16)

> But a natural man does not accept the things of the Spirit of God; for they are foolishness to him, and he cannot understand them, because they are spiritually appraised. 15 But he who is spiritual appraises all things, yet he himself is appraised by no man. 16 For who has known the mind of the Lord, that he should instruct Him? But we have the mind of Christ (1 Cor 2:14-16).

The apostle boldly starts differentiating the natural from the spiritual in these verses. In prior verses, he explained how the key component of what makes spirituality spiritual is the Holy Spirit, so it is obvious that the natural man is he or she who does not have the Holy Spirit. It is the Spirit of God who makes one spiritual. "However, the spiritual is not first, but the natural; then the spiritual" (1 Cor 15:46).

The word "spiritual" is almost always used positively in relation to that which is affected by the Holy Spirit. Interestingly, one time in Ephesians 6:12, "spiritual forces of wickedness" is mentioned.

> For our struggle is not against flesh and blood, but against the rulers, against the powers, against the world forces of this darkness, against the spiritual forces of wickedness in the heavenly places (Eph 6:12).

We cannot say spiritual is always referring to the Holy Spirit because even the Bible speaks of spiritual beings inferior to God. These forces can be seen as a negative spiritual force, or dark ones, who gave up their holy spiritual bearings and rebelled against God. The natural man is often linked to these dark beings, which are controlled by Satan (Heb 2:14-15).

Natural Man

"Natural man" refers to people devoid of the Spirit of God. They are not spiritual and have not been born from the Spirit. Paul states four things about the natural man (1 Cor 2:14):

- The phrase "Does not accept the things of the Spirit of God" links the ability of man to do the Lord's will with his desire to do God's will. In this case, the natural man is not inclined to do God's will and therefore does not care to do what God wishes, being that he is focused on his own desires, which are in opposition to God.

- The natural man has no ability to appreciate the wisdom or goodness in the "things of the Spirit of God for they are foolishness to him" (14). It is like offering a person money in a foreign currency. Even when told that the value is high, they, because of a lack of discernment, reject the offer. And so, there is a natural distaste in society and family for God's rules, which bring blessings.

- "He cannot understand" the "things of the Spirit" (14). The things of God look foolish and therefore go unappreciated, but here Paul announces their inability to even comprehend these things.

- "They are spiritually appraised" (14). Similar in meaning to the above, people without the special saving work of the Spirit lack the ability to apprehend the things of the Spirit.

Paul openly states natural man's incapability to understand and appreciate the ways of God. The desire to do God's will is simply not there. The natural man has a will but does not willingly submit to doing God's will! Society will, at times, enforce laws to make it more profitable not to steal than to steal, but people have no inward appreciation for these things. This is why a society will tend to move downward because the forces that brought law and order will in themselves turn selfish and deteriorate.

Spiritual Man

While "natural man" describes people who are devoid of the Spirit of God—for they have not received the Spirit of God (12)—spiritual individuals do have the Spirit. Paul makes four statements about these people:

- "But he who is spiritual" (1 Cor 2:15) describes the believer in Christ having and being influenced by the Spirit. Paul in the very next chapter says that, at times, believers can act "fleshly," as if they do not have the Spirit of God, even though they do. "And I, brethren, could not speak to you as to spiritual men, but as to men of flesh, as to babes in Christ" (1 Cor 3:1). The foundational change of being spiritual people is complete when they have received the Spirit of God.

- In complete contrast to the natural man, the spiritual person "appraises all things" (15), which refers to his new ability to know the things God has told him. We must insist on the truth that this difference is an upgrade stemming from the Holy Spirit, not a learned matter. People have nothing to boast about regarding their spirituality because any and all growth comes from God's grace through the Spirit's working in him.

- He who is spiritual is marked by having "the mind of Christ" (16) through the presence of the Holy Spirit. Verse 15 speaks of the spiritual communion between God and man, but verse 16 shares the great benefits of knowing God; we have Christ's very mind, and it is for this very reason we can become His disciples. The chapter on John 16 will speak more in depth on this matter, but for now, let us remember the foundation: Knowing God comes by knowing Christ. This knowledge is brought to us by the person of the Holy Spirit.

- Paul injects a statement that does not directly describe the spiritual man but, interestingly, his humble vessel. "For who has known the mind of the Lord, that he should instruct Him?" (16). The apostle reminds us that though we have received the ability to know God and have the mind of Christ, it does not mean that we are God or can direct God. It is a humbling observation that should strike our faces when any pride comes to the door of our mind, for the archenemy fell because of his false belief that he could instruct the Lord. Spirituality is not due to our goodness or cleverness but only because of the presence of the Holy Spirit.

The new spiritual network should be highly valued as it provides for us "the mind of the Lord." It is wrong to use "spiritual" to distinguish mature believers (e.g., He is a spiritual person), for all genuine believers are spiritual because they have the Spirit of God. However, there are times when some believers better reflect the presence of the Spirit in their lives.

Conclusion

True spirituality, then, is not only being known of God, which is true of all people, but knowing God through the Spirit. Through Christ, God has powerfully reestablished the spiritual network that we lost because of Adam's fall. The disconnect between God and man serves as a pointer to what once was and now again can be established and sustained through Christ—a renewed spiritual network where God and man are linked together, evidenced by activities like prayer and biblical meditation. Through Christ and the Spirit's work, man can find restoration of the communion man previously had with God before the fall.

Summary Points
- Although everyone has a person-to-person "spiritual" network, they cannot connect to God (God—natural man).
- True spirituality (only God's people) is what describes those who have received the Spirit of God, enabling them to have the mind of Christ and commune with God—the church.

- As believers, we are potentially able to know all we need from God (includes a warning, encouragement, knowledge, etc.) in order to live out His will for our lives, just as Christ did.
- Satan will attempt to hack into this spiritual network, to block God's signal by getting us to listen to him (i.e., other spirits).
- Faith describes the confidence we have in the truths that God has revealed to us through the Spirit.

Discussion Questions

1. Can we learn things about God without the Holy Spirit? Explain your answer in light of the verses above.

2. Do you want to be connected to friends, God, or the web more? Why?

3. List at least three differences between the natural and spiritual man.

4. What is true spirituality?

5. Do you remember coming to know the Lord and making your first prayers where you knew He heard you? What was it like?

6. What can help us prevent pride in our hearts when we're called spiritual?

7. God knows everything you do, including the reasons you do them (i.e., motivations). Is there anything you need to repent from? God will eventually disclose your darkest side; it is better to gain Christ's forgiveness now.

8. This spiritual network where God communes with us and us with Him must be kept free from interference. What are the things that tend to interfere with either God speaking to you or you with God?

#3 The Conviction of the Spirit (John 16:7-11)

Life in the Spirit!
Experiencing the Fullness of Christ

EVIDENCE OF BELIEF

The Holy Spirit has touched the hearts of millions of people, first working through Jesus' life and now through His people to reach the ends of the earth. The Spirit of God is still powerfully working today perpetuating the love and truth of God.

It is crucial that we gain a deep appreciation of the Holy Spirit's work in the life of unbelievers because this is the first place most people will sense His largely invisible work. These verses from John 16 are famous for how Jesus used the last precious moments of His life on earth to convey how He would continue to minister through the Holy Spirit. Who is the Holy Spirit? What does the Holy Spirit do? How does Jesus relate to the Holy Spirit? All of these questions will be answered in this book, but it all starts with an understanding of the Spirit here in this chapter's discussion. Jesus would still be present as a companion but in a different way than he had been.

A. The Holy Spirit's Conviction (John 16:7–8)

> But I tell you the truth, it is to your advantage that I go away; for if I do not go away, the Helper shall not come to you; but if I go, I will send Him to you. And He, when He comes, will convict the world concerning sin, and righteousness, and judgment (John 16:7–8).

In verse 7, Jesus explained what would happen after His departure. He didn't avoid talking about His departure or even the way He would leave this world, but did focus on the disciples' needs after His departure. Somehow his leaving would actually become an advantage to them! The Helper (Greek: *parakletos*; Paraclete) could only come if He left them. (This is an insightful theological point that will later be investigated.) As a result, the Gospel spread into the world, touching a multitude of disciples in a matter of months from the time Jesus said those words; Jesus, limited to a body, could not properly accompany all the disciples when they went their separate ways. But He could if, through the Spirit, He made His presence and voice known: "And He, when He comes" (16:8). Jesus fully understood that the Holy Spirit would have a powerful and desirable impact on our spiritual lives, so He spent those significant hours before His death to expound on the Spirit's work.

The Spirit actively works in the spiritual sphere of the world, which includes our souls. He does the work of conviction, reproof, and teaching. This verse specifically speaks of the work among unbelievers, that is, the world, which would at some point include us all, even those brought up in Christian families.[4] This is good because it shows that God can and desires to work in us who, from our birth, are devoid of His Spirit. Jesus died for our sins, but this work would go without impact if it was not brought to the minds and hearts of the lost because, in the end, our knowledge of our sins and the Gospel must be believed. If it sounds confusing, just read through the Gospels and notice how Jesus interacted with those around Him when walking the dusty Israelite roads, which were then part of the Roman Empire. Jesus' personal ministry would continue after the cross, but only through the Spirit of God working in our lives and in the lives of unbelievers. Our Lord speaks of three kinds of conviction, but let us first consider the Spirit's work in general.

Conviction starts in the conscience but leaps forward when the Spirit reveals God's standards, making us quickly aware of our failures and guilt. However, this is only the first part of the Spirit's conversion process. (We should properly note that true conversion comes from the Spirit and not from people.) There is much more to the process! "Conviction" describes God's way of heightening the unbelievers' awareness of His moral expectations and, in turn, revealing their moral brokenness, and only then leading them to salvation through repentance. This convicting work becomes predominant for a period and generally leads the lost to the path of eternal life where Christ the Door is discovered. Even if individuals were brought up in a conservative church that preaches the Gospel, they still need to start at the entrance. It is not the church that saves the world but faith in the

---

[4] Some Christians will want to debate this, but is it not Jesus who told us that we need to be born again of water and Spirit (John 3)? Of course, I raised good children, but until they are saved, though their evil may be contained, they are still sinners who need to be saved. To have them think otherwise leads to confidence in their good works or association rather than in Jesus' work.

Lord. From the outside, we can appear to be a Christian-looking worshiper, but our hearts can remain unchanged and unwelcoming to the Holy Spirit's words of conviction.

The Spirit of God does at least some initial saving work in unsaved people. All our confidence in preaching the gospel, all types of evangelism, church planting, and missionary work are based on the primary willingness of the Spirit of God to work in the lives of people who originally are not searching for Him (Rom 3:11). This is the reason we see God, through the Spirit, imparting gifts that enable God's people to spread the Word of hope.

Let us now turn our minds to Jesus' important words about the Holy Spirit: "The Spirit of truth, comes, He will guide you into all the truth" (John 16:13). This verse introduces three specific ways that the Holy Spirit coaxes unbelievers to salvation: "He, when He comes, will convict the world concerning sin, and righteousness, and judgment" (John 16:8).

Summary

Paul summarizes Jesus' enlightenment of the world (John 1:5,9) in 2 Corinthians 4:6: "For God, who said, 'Light shall shine out of darkness,' is the One who has shone in our hearts to give the light of the knowledge of the glory of God..." (2 Cor 4:6). The Spirit of God works among unbelievers—the world. We should anticipate His work and plead with the Spirit to powerfully work in the unbelievers around us.

B. The Holy Spirit's Conviction of Sin (John 16:9)

The first aspect of conviction identifies a person's personal sin (16:8). Jesus emphasizes each aspect starting with the first one in verse 9, "Concerning sin, because they do not believe in Me" (16:9).

This particular Greek word for sin (*harmartia*), used in both verse 8 and 9, refers to missing the mark, and is used similarly in Romans 3:23. This concept can be illustrated by an arrow missing its target. The Spirit, then, points out the ways a person has not done what God demanded. He or she has missed God's expectations. This missed expectation refers both to a person's awareness of failing to keep his or her own standard (Rom 2:14-15) as well as God's standard, which is what the Holy Spirit points out.

The Spirit starts where a person is at, but this highlighting of one's failures, often over time, develops a full conviction that enables the Holy Spirit to lead the person to the next step. Conviction of sin is the sharp awareness of failure to obtain a certain confessed standard and the realization of one's moral inadequacy and failure before God. This conviction accentuates the feelings of guilt because, even though one may have disguised their sin before, they must acknowledge the violation of the standard, thus their guilt becomes very apparent. This is the "burden" that Christian carries in the classic book, *The Pilgrim's Progress*.

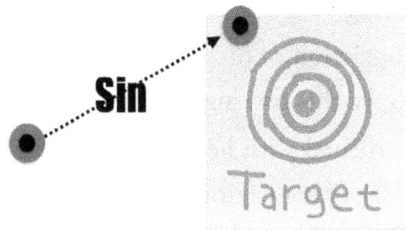

Interestingly, Jesus presents this conviction of sin not in isolation but links it to other actions of the Holy Spirit. In this sense, conviction of sin can rightly be looked upon as a process. Although we might be satisfied to see such a change, the Lord knows the full power of conviction can only be reached with the three-fold process pointed out here.

This emphasis on sin focuses on certain actions that a person has not properly completed. They have failed to keep God's standards. For example, perhaps a child says to himself that he should call his parents every Sunday night but finds that three weeks have passed before he calls them.

> The conviction of sin is the sharp awareness of failing an owned standard.

Let me apply this to how it works out with little children brought up in a church. Christian parents are rightly eager to see their children come to know the Lord, but that eagerness can blind them. Christians are often wrongly told to look for a raised hand or confession in a child to indicate saving faith; they look for these outward expressions rather than the child's heart convicted of sin. Instead of a teacher or parent trying to get a child to raise a hand, we should closely look for this conviction of the heart. With eight children, I have regularly been able to see this first sign of the Spirit's work. My youngest recently was very burdened with her guilt, and only when seeing the result of the Spirit's work of conviction did I follow up, leading her to the Lord. It is perilous for parents or youth workers to stress outward changes like baptism when the heart has not changed. This has greatly confused many children brought up in the church and leads to dead churches because that vital change of heart has not taken place. As parents, we need to carefully be on the lookout for this burden of sin and guilt that weighs upon the child, or on anyone for that matter. Just like one sees the wind blow the leaves on a tree, so this burden of sin is often a sign of the Spirit's work.

This conviction is the realization that one has fallen short of God's righteousness, but it says nothing of what the standard should be regarding this set of expectations that God has for us. This is the second aspect of righteousness that Jesus spoke of in verse 10.

C. The Holy Spirit's Conviction of Righteousness (John 16:10)

> Concerning righteousness, because I go to the Father, and you no longer behold Me. (John 16:10)

Verse 8 continues to speak on the Spirit's three-staged work of conviction but more specifically on the particular sphere of righteousness. Many of us have not carefully thought of the specific work of the Spirit in an unbeliever's heart. God is clearly the initiator, properly preparing man's heart to rightly respond to God through the Spirit's work. Guilt does not save nor does making a person aware of God's righteous standards. This work is not to be equivocated with salvation but only part of the process.

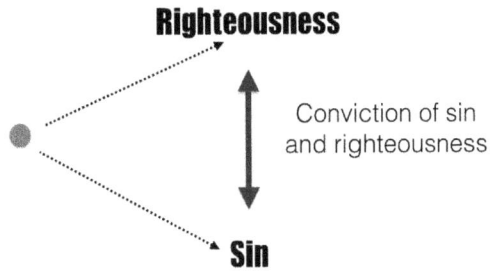

Righteousness is the second level of the triad of the Holy Spirit's work in the unbeliever. Will the unbeliever be aware of this work? Perhaps not, at least not consciously, but the person will be very aware of an inner struggle. He or she might ask, "What's happening to me?" "Why am I feeling this way?" "Why do I feel so bad about myself?" This struggle stands in opposition to what has become the popular teaching of self-esteem, that is, every person should think well of him or herself, no matter the truth.

This second aspect of conviction raises a person's awareness of where he or she should be. While the first step pointed out one's inadequacy, the presence of righteousness heightens this awareness of inadequacy by pointing out how far one has missed God's standard. While the conviction of sin projects a list of failures, the conviction of righteousness allows the Spirit to reveal a higher standard, God's standard. This, of course, intensifies the burden of guilt, making it very uncomfortable.

The teaching of good works emphasizes the lie that one's good acts can outweigh one's bad acts, and so individuals might be able to ignore the accusation of guilt regarding their sin by focusing on what they have obtained. This is one of the fundamental teachings of all religions; however, many are taken completely by surprise by this whole new standard of righteousness of which they had formerly been totally unaware. Thus, the Spirit continues to break down pride by revealing the impossibility of good works to make up for bad actions. A possible bad has become evil when seen before God's standards. The standard of righteousness becomes a looming mountain that can no longer be ignored.

An example of the heightened standard can be found in Jesus' words in the Sermon of the Mount (note how the Holy Spirit continued Jesus' ministry of clarifying God's righteous standards). Not only are we to refrain from murdering, but Jesus says it is wrong to even get angry toward others (Matt 5:21–22). Where once we could justify our meanness towards others, now the covers are pulled off and our sin— our anger—is exposed. The proud man boasts that he has not killed anyone like those horrible murderers out there, but the humble man realizes that he has fallen short simply by being angry with those made in God's image, and thus he deserves damnation.

Interestingly, John expands on this understanding of righteousness in verse 10: "Concerning righteousness, because I go to the Father, and you no longer behold Me." Jesus points to Himself as the original standard of righteousness in the world. After His ascension, the Spirit was sent out to execute the mission of manifesting such holy standards. The Spirit often does this by prodding a pastor to preach on righteousness or a parent to rebuke a child for impoliteness that fails to please God's standards.

Admittedly, it is easy to forget or dismiss the importance of a righteous life. We become content with, "I'm not that bad" or "At least I'm better than him!" Those who have said such things have, to some degree, hardened themselves against the Spirit's conviction of righteousness. Believers instead need to agree with the Holy Spirit's assessment and then repent and believe in the Gospel. After salvation, the Spirit will promote the believer's righteous life to bear this holy standard in the world: "The fruit of the Spirit is love, joy, goodness..." (Gal 5:22–23).

Theological questions

We still need to explore how much of the Spirit's work of conviction is "irresistible," as the Calvinists like to state. John 1:9 speaks of a kind of light that touches every man, "There was the true light which, coming into the world, enlightens every man." But this illumination does not always cause a favorable response, "He came to His own, and those who were His own did not receive Him" (John 1:11). But let us not be too fast to conclude that enlightening is the same as conviction.

Although raising of the banner of righteousness is a huge step that religion can never accomplish, it is still insufficient. Remember, there are three steps, not two. Let us go on and carefully trace the third work of the Spirit's conviction by contemplating judgment.

D. The Holy Spirit's Conviction of Judgment (John 16:11)

> And concerning judgment, because the ruler of this world has been judged (John 16:11).

The third area of conviction, following sin and righteousness, is judgment. This theme of judgment is a natural continuation of the first two because judgment naturally builds upon the inadequacy pointed out in the first two areas. While some chide preachers for using hell or judgment as a means of manipulating people, we would do well to rebuke those so willing to deride the teaching of judgment that Jesus considered so essential. Our naive ideas of the process of salvation encourage our willingness to toss crucial teaching aside. Barna Group reported of Americans in 2003,

> Yet, although just 38% of the adult public have confessed their sins and accepted Christ as their savior, 99% claim they will not go to Hell after they die. In fact, a majority of Americans do not believe that Satan exists and most adults are leery about the existence of Hell.[5]

Even though many refrain from openly speaking of judgment and hell, Jesus and the Holy Spirit have made it a crucial part of the gospel message. The first two aspects of conviction push a person from their formerly satisfied moral state into the certainty of their fallenness. This third aspect of judgment ushers people straight to the point of lostness before God's holy judgment throne.

---

[5] Spiritual Progress Hard to Find in 2003 online at barna.org.

Let's think this through. Many today believe judgment is incompatible with the love of God. Surely, it is not. Jesus asserts God's mercy as well as judgment. Jesus here in John 16 did not stop with the first two aspects of conviction. The awareness of sin (aspect 1) brings a person to see his shortcomings of his personal standards. The conviction of righteousness (aspect 2) amplifies this lostness by pointing out God's holy standard, increasing the list of shortcomings. This third aspect of conviction—judgment—brings a person to ask the important question: "What must I do to be saved" (Acts 16:30)?

Judgment poignantly indicates the conviction's threat along with the penalty of eternal death so that we will seek salvation through the gospel. As Jesus wisely stated, it is only the sick that go to see the doctor (Matt. 9:12). Without conviction, the cross means nothing. Without knowledge of our sinful state, we will not seek out a Savior; therefore, the Holy Spirit wisely brings awareness of judgment so that we might seek and find Christ, life, and peace.

Although we associate hell with judgment, it is only the last aspect of the teaching of judgment. There are several parts to the whole concept of judgment. Judgment first hears our case, highlights our guilt and the failure to do what is expected, and then shows how our deficiency makes us accountable to God. It hears any defense and only then is the final judgment issued, along with the sentence of eternal death.

Other religions are, as a whole, very vague about sin and its penalty, if they're even mentioned at all. In most cases, sin is otherwise defined. In the scriptures, however, the reality of sin is made very apparent. The scriptures point out the tension between the holy God, who must judge and stamp out any rebellion to His authority, and mankind, who counters God by living in ways they feel comfortable with. The Spirit's work of declaring judgment is part of God's grace because it precedes the time of judgment and allows for repentance and escape through God's redemption on the cross.

Judgment speaks of a certain penalty issuing from the conviction. The judge might say upon observing the evidence, "You are guilty and therefore deserve judgment." Judgment is not to be thought of as the final statement of giving penalty and the carrying out of it, but the many parts leading to and including suffering the consequences of not living by God's rules. The final judgment of the sinner is not meted out at this point. No "hell" is mentioned here. The conviction of judgment is not equated to the giving out of the judgment penalty—actually sending one to the lake of fire—but to the stinging awareness of its certainty, thus giving a person time and faith to do something about it.

The Holy Spirit, as Jesus, brings people to the point of salvation as a complement to salvation's full process. The purpose of the three levels of conviction is to humble their hearts and bring them to salvation. When a person is convicted in their heart of sure judgment and yet hasn't been sentenced, there is time for the unbeliever to awaken to the coming danger and flee such judgment. This is why Jesus preached the message of hope and blessedness and emphasized the need to become poor of heart. "Blessed are the poor in spirit, for theirs is the kingdom of heaven" (Matt 5:1).

> Declaration of judgment is part of God's grace because it precedes final judgment and allows for repentance and redemption through the cross.

A Deeper Look (John 16:11)

Jesus added a careful explanation in verse 11: "And concerning judgment, because the ruler of this world has been judged." This might seem confusing at first but only because we do not have a comprehensive understanding of judgment. Let us look at the truths brought up in this verse.

Before Jesus' death and resurrection, Jesus spoke of the judgment of the ruler of the world, "Now judgment is upon this world; now the ruler of this world shall be cast out" (John 12:31). Jesus can say this because He had already intended to fulfill His part by bringing the enemy to judgment. Jesus' work finalizes the evil one's sentence and eventual execution.[6] Here's one concluding point to keep in mind: apart from God's grace, judgment is settled and something to be greatly feared by everyone. Further exasperating this threat, however, is the fact that mankind's judgment will be folded into the judgment of the evil one. Just as the salvation of God's people is linked to Jesus' resurrection and ascension ("in Christ"; Eph 2:4-7), mankind's judgment is joined to Satan's judgment (Rev 20:11-15).

> And the devil who deceived them was thrown into the lake of fire and brimstone, where the beast and the false prophet are also; and they will be tormented day and night forever and ever. And I saw a great white throne and Him who sat upon it, from whose presence earth and heaven fled away, and no place was found for them. And I saw the dead, the great and the small, standing before the throne, and books were opened; and another book was opened, which is the book of life; and the dead were judged from the things which were written in the books, according to their deeds. And the sea

---

[6] It is possible that Jesus is alluding to how the ruler of this world has already been judged and kicked out of heaven (Job 1:7).

gave up the dead which were in it, and death and Hades gave up the dead which were in them; and they were judged, every one of them according to their deeds. And death and Hades were thrown into the lake of fire. This is the second death, the lake of fire. (Rev 20:14)

Theological Reflections

There are some who might disagree with our assertion that the Spirit's conviction is a primary work while man's response a second, but it is evident that the world does not seek the Lord on its own. The Spirit of God takes the lead role in creating a new life in the unbeliever. It starts with conviction, by which the awareness of God's values exposes a person's weakness. A person might feel the presence of the Spirit when they lie, which results in that person feeling his or her guilt and experiencing a reproof of their error of dishonesty.

Jesus teaches us that the process of conviction happens as follows: The Holy Spirit approaches a person, makes him or her aware that what they are doing is wrong. Conviction is like the light that makes the shadow apparent. It is part of the overall plan of God's salvation, but it clearly is not salvation, as it only speaks awareness of how the Lord is not pleased with what a person is doing. People are often not aware of what it is that troubles them because they are not being sensitive to the Spirit's work in their lives.

In my life, the complete process of salvation took less than five minutes, though for others it may take years. Within that short time, all was made clear to me, including the awareness of my sin, God's righteous standards, and my deserved judgment. I saw myself falling toward the fiery pit below. I needed no explanation of the significance of this because many of my sins, that before I had dismissed, were now accusing me and showing me my deserved judgment! At that point, I called out to God to save me, He graciously showed me that Jesus was the Savior. Thus, I believed and my guilt—that awful burden and threat of judgment—were thrown off. I hardly knew where I was going, but I knew I had to look for an escape from judgment. Conviction leads to salvation; this is the way the Spirit graciously activates the saving process in our lives.

This conviction process is only the beginning of God's work in human lives. We can legitimately ask, "Does such work from the Spirit always lead to salvation?" The wording in the verse is not clear here, but the extensive context does seem to encourage us to conclude that God is actively operating in the lives of certain humans for His purposes. Jesus says much more on the night of His betrayal, but He does make very clear that the Spirit carries on the process of saving people and prepares them for being born again, which is equivocal with salvation and the theme of our next chapter.

Summary

The conviction Jesus speaks of is more than a simple awareness of our sin or function of our guilt, but the careful and deliberate work of the Holy Spirit in an unbeliever's life to make him or her aware of their moral shortfall before God and the demand for full judgment. Although Jesus' purpose has not been fully discussed yet, we have hinted that the whole reason for this conviction is to lead a person to salvation; thus, we now see the love of God working through the Holy Spirit just as it worked through the life of Christ. God's Word must be preached, highlighting the need for righteous living and the judgment associated with sin, and it must continue to be preached. Even here we can see the important way in which the Sprit of God works along with the Word of God to bring about new life. There are ramifications of this convicting work of the Spirit in believers' lives too, but the focus here is on the way the Spirit saves sinners. God poises Himself to save the lost by awakening them to their lostness so that they might hear and believe the Gospel.

Discussion Questions

1. Have you experienced this type of conviction in your life? Share about the increased awareness of your sin and guilt.

2. Did you believe because of a sense of loss and need for a Savior or for religious, political, or convenience sake?

3. Do you believe God is right to judge you for your personal sins?

4. Provide two areas of righteousness that you have been made aware of at some point since your new birth in Christ.

5. Can people see Christ's standard in your life—your words, gestures, actions, etc? Pick one and share how God has used you in the life of others.

6. Select one "fruit of the Spirit" (Gal 5:22–23) and examine your life in light of that. What is the standard of the Spirit? What needs to be changed to reach that point?

7. Have you carefully observed young children respond to the conviction of the Holy Spirit? Explain. What should be done if you do not see that conviction—even if they raise a hand indicating a willingness to follow Jesus?

8. What part does the conviction of judgment and hell play in salvation? Can a person come to know the Lord without this? Explain.

9. How does the revelation of how the Holy Spirit works in unbelievers relate to believers? Why did Jesus tell us this?

10. Do you think of yourself as one who works with the Holy Spirit when you mention the judgment of God or eternal judgment to others as part of His convicting work? Explain.

11. Why does the love of God compel the Spirit of God to convict people of their judgment?

#4 The Birth of the Spirit (John 3:3-8)

Life in the Spirit!
Experiencing the Fullness of Christ

"So is everyone who is born of the Spirit"
(John 3:8).

Rebirth, Regeneration, and New Life

The conviction of the Spirit is the beginning of the conversion process through which God, in time, saves a person. The process comes fully into play when the Spirit brings forth a new spiritual life by giving them a new life that is animated by His presence.

As a master teacher, Jesus carefully connects the hidden salvation work of the Spirit of God to the physical birth of a child. Today, with our modern cameras, we can peek into the womb; and so, with Jesus' words, we too can gain a special glimpse into this most mysterious and yet awesome creation work of God that is happening today in our midst! Our study on spiritual birth takes us first to Jesus' words recorded in John 3 and then to the epistles.

A. Spiritual Rebirth (John 3:3-8)

> Jesus answered and said to him, "Truly, truly, I say to you, unless one is born again, he cannot see the kingdom of God." 4 Nicodemus said to Him, "How can a man be born when he is old? He cannot enter a second time into his mother's womb and be born, can he?" 5 Jesus answered, "Truly, truly, I say to you, unless one is born of water and the Spirit, he cannot enter into the kingdom of God. 6 that which is born of the flesh is flesh, and that which is born of the Spirit is spirit. 7 Do not marvel that I said to you, 'You must be born again.' 8 The wind blows where it wishes and you hear the sound of it, but do not know where it comes from and where it is going; so is everyone who is born of the Spirit" (John 3:3–8).

Foundational Lessons

Jesus carefully establishes the foundational teachings for life and salvation through this conversation with Nicodemus, who was being drawn and responding to the Spirit's work of conviction. Although Nicodemus approached Jesus at night, he did indeed approach the Lord, and so Jesus was willing to share more with him (James 4:8). Christians typically focus on salvation from their personal point of view rather than from God's. However, in John 3:3–8, Jesus was willing to not mention the crucial role of faith or belief, even though it plays a crucial part of salvation. Faith's importance to salvation will be seen in later verses (John 3:14 and onward): "For whoever believes..." (John 3:16). John is not undermining the door to salvation; instead, he is using this conversation to stress that the way a person is saved is not through developing a set of good works but to reveal God's role in salvation. (Compare this with the Holy Spirit's conviction.)

Jesus imparts these hidden truths to help us better appreciate and realize what needs to occur before one can by faith be spiritually reborn. For Nicodemus, the many religious Jews, and all of us without the Spirit's prior work in our lives, there is no faith and no spiritual interest. Man cannot know God without God's special work of grace. Without the wind, no kite flies. Without the new hidden seed of life, there can be no rebirth. Religion in and of itself does not save. Pious religious works cannot be substituted for or equated with God's work of spiritual life. Human beings cannot on their own cause themselves to be interested in truly spiritual matters (Rom 3:11–12).

Spiritual Birth

The phrase "born again" is repeatedly used in John 3. This discussion is not unique, but its prolonged treatment is. John earlier mentions "born of God" in John 1:13: "who were born not of blood, nor of the will of the flesh, nor of the will of man, but of God." Salvation ultimately rests in God's work in us, regardless of our family heritage or faith. There is no doubt that Jesus is referring to a new spiritual work that needs to be done in the heart of mankind to draw him or her close to God. In this discussion with Nicodemus, Jesus reveals the corruption of the Jewish priestly line—which would, in the end, kill Him—and points people back to God and His redeeming grace.

The idea of a need for a new spiritual life is not totally new for it was first embedded in the Old Testament with the phrase "circumcised of heart." The phrase is used both in Deuteronomy and Jeremiah (Deut 10:16; 30:6; Jer 4:4; Ro 2:29) and alludes to physical circumcision, the sign of the covenant. Cutting away the physical foreskin is a depiction of ridding oneself of that layer of pride that serves to shield or isolate one's sinful heart from God: "Moreover the LORD your God will circumcise your heart and the heart of your descendants, to love the LORD your God with all your heart and with all your soul, in order that you may live" (Deut 30:6). Note here how God operates on their hearts in such a way that they will "love the Lord your God with all your heart." Ezekiel says the same thing, "Moreover, I will give you a new heart and put a new spirit within you; and I will remove the heart of stone from your flesh and give you a heart of flesh" (Ezek 36:26).

At times, the scriptures tell us that God gives us a new heart or will circumcise us, but then in other verses instructs us to circumcise our own hearts: "Make yourselves a new heart and a new spirit!" (Ezek 18:31). Although we are told to do these spiritual operations of "making a new heart" or belief, thus establishing the properness of them, the point is that we cannot accomplish this on our own—even when we are told to. Does not the Old Testament openly manifest the pathetic situation of our hearts (Judges 20)? Here in John 3, Jesus clearly sets before us the greater work of God in our hearts so that we will know that salvation is only by grace and not by our works or efforts, despite it being our responsibility to do so.

Jesus then speaks to how God will give us new hearts in John 1:13, and Peter says, "caused us to be born again" (1 Peter 1:3). Paul refers to being born of the flesh two times (Gal 4:23,29). In his first epistle, Peter uses the phrase "born again" two times (1 Peter 1:3,23). John, however, really picks this up as a major theme in his first letter, mentioning it six times (1 John, 2:29; 3:9; 4:7; 5:1, 4, 18).

B. Spiritual Rebirth in the Epistles

In the epistles of John, the pregnant phrase "born again" in reference to spiritual birth is used ten times, solidifying our understanding of the spiritual birth and expanding its application into the Christian life.

- Peter twice states God's significant part in choosing and empowering His people (1 Peter 1:3,23).

  > Blessed be the God and Father of our Lord Jesus Christ, who according to His great mercy has caused us to be **born again** to a living hope through the resurrection of Jesus Christ from the dead (1 Peter 1:3).

  God "caused us to be born again." God, the Creator of not only the physical world but also of the spiritual world, calls into being spiritual life through the Spirit. The Lord is the Great Cause for all things but also acts as the mother of spiritual birth.

  > For you have been **born again** not of seed which is perishable but imperishable, that is, through the living and abiding word of God (1 Peter 1:23).

  The new birth comes from the "living and abiding Word of God." This is the reason the Holy Spirit only directs us according to God's Word, the Bible. If we want to grow in the Spirit, then we must feed ourselves the scriptures. The first rule that believers must use to discern God's voice is to see whether what we hear is in accordance with the scriptures.

- Paul uses the concept of new birth to emphasize the means by which one gains the life of God (Gal 4:23,29).

  > But as at that time he who was born according to the flesh persecuted him who was **born** according to the Spirit, so it is now also (Gal 4:29).

  The first birth represents the life of works or merit, i.e., fleshly, resulting in religiosity accompanied by a false sense of security. The second birth, being born of the Spirit, comes by the promise of God's work in us. The Spirit gives faith for us to believe.

- John emphasizes the spiritual life that naturally arises from the spiritual birth (1 John 2:29; 3:9; 4:7; 5:1,4,18).

> No one who is born of God practices sin, because His seed abides in him; and he cannot sin, because he is born of God (1 John 3:9).

If we are born of God, we will share the holy nature of God, loving what is good and shunning that which is evil. The genuine believer's spiritual nature loves the things of God and hates the things of the flesh because he/she now possesses the same nature of God. The phrase "born of God" is twice used, the first time to characterize the believer and the second to explain that it is the reason he or she no longer sins.[7]

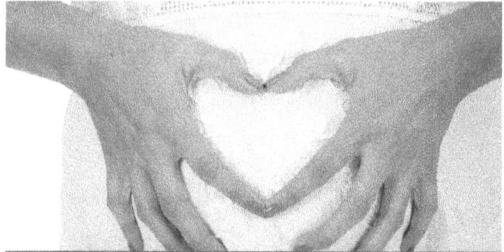

What does each spiritual birth promise?
What does God desire from each believer's life?

> Beloved, let us love one another, for love is from God; and everyone who loves is born of God and knows God (1 John 4:7).

Those regenerated by God's Spirit necessarily love one another and know God. While earlier John stressed a new holy nature, hating evil, he comes from another angle here speaking about God's nature of love and how that nature will not indulge in selfish behavior because His children share God's nature of love.

---

[7] We have discussed the phrase "practices sin" elsewhere in our 1 John web series. The English version emphasizes the persistent behavior of sin because of one's unchanged sin nature in contrast to actual falls into sin that go counter to one's inner love and desires.

Summary

The apostles build upon Jesus' words, demanding that those who claim to be spiritual live it out because they have been born again and share the holy nature of God. If one is born of God, then one will live like one's Father, the Lord. In contemporary language, "Like father, like son." Paul the apostle describes it differently, "You are a letter of Christ, cared for by us, written not with ink, but with the Spirit of the living God, not on tablets of stone, but on tablets of human hearts" (2 Cor 3:3).

Spiritual birth has many implications, three of which the apostles expound upon.

- Peter–the origin: Like a mother who gives birth, so God gives birth to our spiritual lives.

- Paul–the means: We gain the new birth not from our works but from God's promises.

- John–the results: Believers should anticipate fruit from their lives consistent with God's purpose.

C. Baptized with Fire

In order to become Jesus' disciples, a greater work from God must happen! John the Baptist refers to this when He spoke of the indwelling of the Spirit of God (i.e., Acts 2:3) and fire. We must be born again; that is, we need, through God's wisdom and creative living power, to discover new life.

> John answered and said to them all, "As for me, I baptize you with water; but One is coming who is mightier than I, and I am not fit to untie the thong of His sandals; He will baptize you with the Holy Spirit and fire (Luke 3:16; Matt 3:11; Mark 1:8).

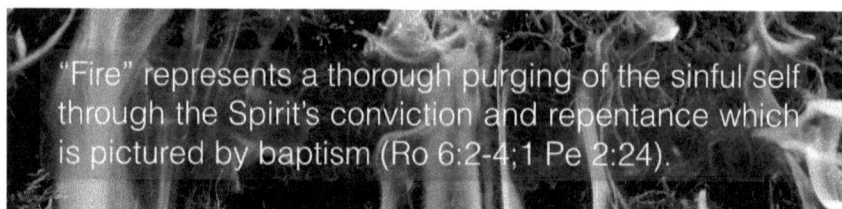

"Fire" represents a thorough purging of the sinful self through the Spirit's conviction and repentance which is pictured by baptism (Ro 6:2-4;1 Pe 2:24).

John baptized with water to call people to repentance. This was a symbol of death to their old lives so that they could live new lives. It appears that we should connect this fire to its purging aspects. Fire represents a thorough purging of the sinful self through the Spirit's conviction followed up by repentance, which is pictured by baptism (Rom 6:2–4;1 Peter 2:24).

The second aspect of baptism is depicted by the coming out of the water. This pictures the new birth, bringing new life and dependence on the Spirit's ongoing work in the believer, hence the descriptive phrase "spiritual life." Jesus' greater work will be symbolized by the presence of the Holy Spirit and fire.

> May it never be! How shall we who died to sin still live in it? Or do you not know that all of us who have been baptized into Christ Jesus have been baptized into His death? Therefore we have been buried with Him through baptism into death, in order that as Christ was raised from the dead through the glory of the Father, so we too might walk in newness of life (Rom 6:2–4).

Water baptism cannot bring saving repentance, but the Holy Spirit powerfully convicts us, reveals our wretched selves deserving of judgment, gives hope of forgiveness in the cross, and assures us of the undeserved promise of eternal life. This is God's work. If we depend only on water baptism and tradition, we will completely miss God's work for our lives. Jesus baptized "you with the Holy Spirit and fire," which signifies the birth of spiritual life.

Christians are not only forgiven but given a new heart and life, animated by God's holy will and purpose. So both salvation itself and the living out of it is totally dependent upon God's grace through the Holy Spirit. The resulting changes bring many ramifications that we will later look at, but their constant power and purpose are driven by the truths related directly to God's Spirit working in us.

The word "fire" associated with the Holy Spirit in Acts 2:3,19 was not later used in Acts because that one baptism with the "Holy Spirit and fire" at Pentecost stands as a special and unique event. Every believer, however, still needs that spiritual surgical act by the Spirit upon their lives, to bring them to repentance and ushering in new life, which acts as a promise to continue to care for the new lives of God's children.

Summary

A true believer obtains new birth from the Spirit of God and, though not often understood at the start, the Spirit of God brings increasing comfort, security, leading, and empowerment to do God's will.

D. The Wind and Life Illustration (John 3:7–8)

> Do not marvel that I said to you, 'You must be born again.' The wind blows where it wishes and you hear the sound of it, but do not know where it comes from and where it is going; so is everyone who is born of the Spirit. (John 3:7–8)

Jesus highlights the mysterious spiritual birth process with an illustration of the wind. The wind cannot be seen nor can the Spirit of God, but both bring about animation. Everyone born of the Spirit is known by the effects of the new life that quietly and subtly brings great transformation. This movement and power from the Holy Spirit are called life—new life, eternal life.

The miracle of new life happens hidden within the walls of a mother's womb. Each birth is the crown of the extended formation of a new life as it makes a grand entrance into the world. From the dark mass at the creation of the world, God, through the Spirit, brought order and life. The Spirit, likewise, broods over the birth of the spiritual newborn. Peter says, God "caused us to be born again to a living hope through the resurrection of Jesus Christ from the dead" (1 Peter 1:3).

Summary

Our good works start with His good work of a new spiritual life so that He gets all the glory as the Father of us all. We all must start as newborn babes. This command is never overused! "You must be born again" (3:7). Let me draw a few conclusions from these verses:

1. "You must...." We are ultimately responsible for our response to God. As much as we might connect Jesus' words to predetermining one's salvation, there is the plain sense that salvation, much like a possession, is something we either have or do not have.

2. "Must" implies the necessity of obtaining new life from the Spirit; it is an essential work of God in our lives. This is not merely a preference, nor is it considered important only for those in full-time ministry; it is important for all of us who want to have our names written in the book of life (Phil 4:3; Rev 20:12,15) and to find full protection from God's wrath in Christ's atoning work on the cross (Rom 3:25, 1 John 4:10).

3. "Born again" vividly encapsulates the spiritual birth process, which signals God's work in our salvation in contrast to our effort or worth (our physical birth). This does not nullify our faith (John 3:16), but Jesus clearly communicates the greater work that has been

completed behind the scenes and results in a more thankful and respectful heart. True spirituality starts with a new birth and life.

4. Jesus does not merely hint at the importance of the spiritual work of God in our souls, but repeatedly states its necessity (3,5,7). Just as a child is born helpless and not able to sustain itself, so Jesus is pointing to our complete helplessness in contributing anything toward our salvation.

5. The first birth, along with all of life's works, is inadequate. The second birth triumphs over the first. There needs to be a healthy dissatisfaction with the stain associated with our human birth if we are ever going to seek the later. Genesis testifies of man's fall from God's grace, the blackening of sin, the domineering control of the evil one over humans. These things make the first birth inadequate on a number of fronts. Jesus doesn't focus on the reason for the new birth but its necessity, leaving us to conclude there is no other way to escape our first life's dark plague upon our souls except by gaining a new birth through the gracious Spirit of God (Rom 5:11–21).

A clear understanding of the new birth is necessary to differentiate God's genuine spiritual work in the believer from religion or man's efforts. Spiritual new birth negates any significant contribution to our Christian lives of our own ability and causes us to constantly seek His help to live out His purposes through our lives.

Discussion Questions

1) Recount what happened when you were born again. (If you were not, seek God to change your heart and seek forgiveness through the cross.)

2) Contrast what you were like before you were born again with your life afterward. List some differences.

3) Our persistence in seeking God's grace in our Christian lives greatly depends on the consciousness of our dependence upon God. This dependence can be strengthened as we meditate on how He spiritually birthed us. Spend 5–10 minutes pondering this marvelous truth.

4) Go out and watch the wind for a bit and meditate on the Spirt's work in your life. What is the wind doing? Similarly, what is God now doing in your life through the Spirit?

5) How does being born again relate to being saved?

6) What happens when we treat Christianity as a human religion rather than a group of believers enlivened by the Holy Spirit? Describe how a dead person is like a dead church.

7) Why do you think some believers are very clear on the time when they came to know the Lord while others are not?

8) Why do the pictures of the fire and wind help us understand God's hidden spiritual work in your life?

#5 The Assurance of the Spirit (Romans 8:14–17)

Life in the Spirit!
Experiencing the Fullness of Christ

The new believer is likened to a little child who can easily get hurt, lost, or taken. The young believer is especially vulnerable because certain key points of discernment are not well fixed in their minds. They are easily influenced. Certainly, they belong to the Lord, but they become instant targets to the evil one if not carefully watched over. Basic Christian truths like assurance provide the basic beliefs that lead to a strong and well-balanced Christian.

> "The Spirit Himself bears witness with our spirit
> that we are children of God" (Romans 8:16).

Assurance of salvation teaches that those who believe in Jesus as their Lord and Savior belong to God's spiritual family forever. It is assuring because nothing can ever change that status. They are God's forever— even when they fall. Not all believers believe in a secure salvation, though, because, most often, they believe salvation is based on their good works. Salvation is based on our faith in Christ's saving work on the cross, but here we will instead focus on the clear biblical teaching of the Holy Spirit's part in assuring the believer. What is there to assure if salvation is not assurable? This truth is important for mature Christians to remember for they often, as a discipler, mentor, parent, Christian friend, or pastor, through the Holy Spirit must faithfully assure young believers of their sure place in God's favor.

The Holy Spirit's work often goes unseen, which gives us room to forget His integral role in building up the people of God. My conviction is that when our awareness of how He works in us and others is heightened, we can more actively and dependently work with the Lord, through the Holy Spirit, to strengthen the people of God.

The Holy Spirit assures believers of their salvation to build up their confidence in the fact that they eternally and securely belong to God's spiritual family. Belonging to God's family has many important ramifications for our ongoing spiritual lives.

A. The Need for the Spirit's Assurance (Rom 8:14)

> For all who are being led by the Spirit of God, these are sons of God (Romans 8:14).

Paul speaks about family and sonship here, "These are the sons of God." The assurance that we belong to God's family forever enables believers to find comfort, strength, and focus on our spiritual development. Being led by the Spirit of God is a mark that testifies that we are part of His family, but it also acknowledges the privileges of being part of God's family.

In verse 14, Paul claims that if we find that the Spirit of God is leading us in our Christian lives—no matter how long we have been a Christian—we can be fairly assured that we are God's children.

> *If we are led by the Spirit, then we are*
> *God's children.*

Think of a mother toting her children into the store, telling them not to touch the candy and to follow close to her side. These are her children. She is responsible for them and therefore vocally and physically guides them. Perhaps she will take one child by the hand and hold the other smaller one so that he will not wander off. "Being led" can mean many things so I will further discuss what this might look like in another chapter, but here we are simply looking for the signs that bear witness to God's work in the believer's life. Paul uses this basic aspect of the Christian life to strengthen the believer's confidence in their sonship so that no matter what they might face in their lives, God will still care for them. This truth is especially important for those who have grown up in divorced or otherwise decimated families where basic trust in relationships has eroded.

The evil one greatly fears new believers growing strong and living out a Christ-like life, so he strategically seeks to cripple each new believer. They are instant targets for Satan. The reason that many discipleship training resources and even evangelists strongly emphasize assurance is that these trainers know, both by experience and by the Word of God, that the easiest way to spiritually cripple believers is to steal away their confidence early on in their Christian lives. Once their faith is weakened, it is very difficult to reestablish that basic trust. Here are a few examples of temptations that Satan may lob at new believers to deter them:

- God doesn't love you! If He did, He wouldn't....

- God doesn't accept sinners like you. Look how you just sinned!

Thus demons strike against the believers' confidence in their salvation and attempt to convince them that these false statements are truer than God's Word.[8] However, the truth is utterly clear. I remember when I was saved how the truth, "Believe and have eternal life" delightfully sounded through my mind. So, no matter how many doubts surge upon the faith of genuine believers, they should remember that they are the Lord's and, as God's children, are being formed into His image. Verse 14 affirms this. Paul doesn't mention here how a person comes to know God (though he does in Romans 3–5) but instead chooses to strengthen the believer's confidence in Him through experience. Let me give an example.

> God does not leave His children like orphans
> but adopts and cares for them!

Joy, a believer, finds herself very downcast and asks God to somehow help her. Later that day, the Lord brought a friend by who shared some verses with her that really encouraged her. The Spirit led her and cared for her. He wouldn't do that unless she was really His child, but because God so clearly answered prayer, her faith is bolstered as she remembers the way her Father answered her prayer, even though the evil one attempted to destroy it. This conflict portrays the dynamic play between good and evil forces in a Christian's life. This is spiritual warfare.

---

[8] Though we are saved by faith, Satan often is clever enough to change our persuasion and place our confidence on our works—as if we were saved by good works.

B. The Assurances of the Spirit (Romans 8:15–16)

> For you have not received a spirit of slavery leading to fear again, but you have received a spirit of adoption as sons by which we cry out, "Abba! Father!" The Spirit Himself bears witness with our spirit that we are children of God (Romans 8:15–16).

Beginning in verse 15 with the word "for," we see Paul's careful explanation of how the Spirit assures the believers. The four instances of the word "spirit" are all the same Greek word (root word *pneuma*), but as we note by the capitalization, the translator felt one of those instances was in reference to the Holy Spirit (v. 16).

- The **spirit** of slavery produces fear that is due to our sins, guilt, death, and judgment.

- The **spirit** of adoption produces personal bonding, affection, and intimacy with God our "Daddy."

- "The **Spirit** Himself bears witness" (16) boldly affirms in our hearts and minds that we belong to Him and can trust Him. He implants a message into us, which brings about a growing confidence in the Lord's ways.

- "With our **spirit**" (16) reveals that the Holy Spirit brings this message to our inner beings. He does not randomly instill this confidence through bearing witness, but works within individual believers, building up their belief that they are indeed God's children, however impossible it might seem to them.

Our inner spirit is produced through a blend of our thoughts, moods, and feelings, which in turn affects our decisions. The "spirit of slavery" describes the impersonal mix of thoughts that identify the fears induced by our guilt, which then produces fear. The spirit of adoption produces a contrasting sense, an inner awareness of belonging to one's spiritual Daddy.

Before I was a believer, I did not sense I belonged to God, even though I believed in His existence. He was distant. I did not sing songs of worship from my heart but only with the stale compulsion of religious duty. Clearly, God's Spirit did not resonate such feelings or moods in me. I had no desire to be with or connect with God, not to mention to think of my affection for Him. But when I believed, my understanding of and desires for God completely flipped, going from estranged to intimate—even though nothing outwardly had changed. God did His special work of salvation in me and, through the Holy Spirit, convinced me, which enabled me to rejoice in knowing God through Jesus Christ.

New lifestyle
New awareness
New Affection
New life
ASSURANCE

The spirit of adoption, like the spirit of slavery, is not a special messenger but describes our inner spirit that has been influenced by different spiritual events. Salvation describes the actual process of spiritual deliverance, the act of being taken from the domain of slavery and the evil one (Col 1:13) and delivered into the safety of God's arms. But assurance of faith describes the inner faith that convinces you that you are forever God's, you have been adopted into His family. The same spiritual truths operating behind the scenes greatly affect our persons.

Verse 16 recaps what has been said, "The Spirit Himself bears witness with our spirit that we are children of God." The Spirit of God who lives

in us has freed us from the old sinful influences that ensnared our spirits, and now affirms that we are children of God. I know, beyond the shadow of a doubt, that "I belong!" There is no more room for rejection and isolation. Personally, we should sense that God is our Father and that He loves us. I do not need to conjure up feelings, but having been released into this knowledge of adoption, it liberates me to respond to Him as His child.

C. Ongoing Assurances of Belonging (Rom 8:17)

> The Spirit Himself bears witness with our spirit that we are children of God, and if children, heirs also, heirs of God and fellow heirs with Christ, if indeed we suffer with Him in order that we may also be glorified with Him. (Rom 8:17)

The Holy Spirit frees our inner persons not just with words but with powerful behind-the-scenes action, namely, basic doctrinal truths such as regeneration, justification, sanctification, and glorification. They describe the process of how God literally adopts or "makes" us His children.

Our assurance testifies that there is no conflict between our inner spirit and the great spiritual changes that took place in our lives. Our inner spirit will first notice openness and then affection, which is then followed by confidence, all of which produce ways to express or live out our new spiritual life.

There are many who think of themselves as God's children but are not. This misaligned belief is the scary mismatch of a religious profession without true regeneration of the Spirit. They hear others describe them as God's children because of their church attendance or simply because they were born, but they are spiritually illegitimate. Belonging only comes through belief in Christ through the new birth of the Holy Spirit that brings spiritual life. When this life comes, so does the Holy Spirit's work on our hearts in affirmation of our new status. When I became a believer, such a great renewal of my heart and mind caused me to give great praise to God. I knew I had been adopted—not just through the truth of God's Word but through the internal witness of the Spirit of God. And so it is with all genuine believers.

We need to be careful of relating the assurance of a believer with the doubts that plague some true believers. God structured the growth of new believers such

New Life	New Nature
New Affection	Desire godliness
New Awareness	See differently
New Lifestyle	Live uprightly

that they need personal discipleship, just as babies require personal care. When this spiritual help is missing, Satan can easily come in with his wrecking ball and destroy what confidence the new believer had about his or her salvation. Instead of confidence and faith to move ahead, they are loaded down with questions of guilt and doubts. The Spirit is present but hidden behind false guilt, untrue thoughts, and bad experiences that can cause much confusion. We should not conclude that a lack of confidence means a person is not a genuine believer. Careful conversation of one's conversion should help clarify whether the person is a genuine believer or not.

This Spirit's wind blows into our souls and starts with a new life, leading to the confirmation of being our Heavenly Father's child. Verse 17 continues to describe this thrust of dynamic change by stating how God's child not only belongs to his family but joins all His children in inheriting all that Christ has won through His victory on the cross. Christ shares with us all His riches and reassures us that even in suffering we share this grand hope (1 Peter 1:6–9). Assurance of belonging brings reassurance of eternal life where we will be glorified with Him.

D. Promises Galore! (1 Peter 1 and John 3)

The assurance of our salvation is so important that it is repeated in many places. Let me mention two.

> 3 Blessed be the God and Father of our Lord Jesus Christ, who according to His great mercy has caused us to be born again to a living hope through the resurrection of Jesus Christ from the dead, 4 to obtain an inheritance which is imperishable and undefiled and will not fade away, **reserved in heaven for you,** 5 who are protected by the power of God through faith for a salvation ready to be revealed in the last time (1 Peter 1:3–5).

Peter mentions many things that are similar to what Jesus and Paul have already said, but it is good to clarify the way in which the scriptures want to reassure our hearts that we are His and belong to Him.

First, we are told that, by God's mercy in Christ, He has "caused us to be born again to a living hope." That new life brings the promise of hope just as any plant will bear promised fruit. The fact of a new life engenders all sorts of wild true hopes. The facts of these spiritual truths assert our new position in Christ, having been born into God's family bearing forth great hope. The living hope speaks about how it radically shapes our perspective in an ongoing way. Our inheritance, "to obtain an inheritance" (1:4), shows how hope develops from our being born into God's family. Assurance, then, comes from the permanence of this salvation, which will not fade away, for those who are protected by the power of God through faith (5).

John's Perspective (John 3:16–17)

> For God so loved the world, that He gave His only begotten Son, that whoever believes in Him should not perish, but have eternal life. 17 For God did not send the Son into the world to judge the world, but that the world should be saved through Him (John 3:16–17).

We, perhaps, should conclude this section with one of the most famous verses in the scripture—John 3:16. The promises of God are so powerful because they start with His love and are targeted to bring grand transformation to our lives. God's plan is always successful (though it did not look like it at first). The power of John 3:16 is found in an open promise to those who believe, offering the great hope of eternal life. People are familiar with death and its effects. We wonder how there can be so much evil and selfishness, but these are mere signs of the deadly principle at work in the human race. True life, however, being radically different, speaks about the quality of living in God's presence and the ongoing nature of this new relationship with Him. The Holy Spirit assures our hearts most often through the Word of God. The Word of God becomes alive through the ongoing work of the Spirit of God.

Summary

God assures His children that they belong to Him. Their spiritual birth brings eternal life and therefore great confidence and assurance of God's constant care. An inheritance, protected in heaven, is assuredly ours forever. This assurance is and will be abused by those who only profess to believe and yet who are not genuinely born again; and yet, the Holy

Spirit still uses the Word of God and its promises along with inner affirmation in our souls to assure us that we are His.

Discussion Questions

1. Recount any inner assurance of being the child of God at your salvation or later on.

2. What are some important aspects of being a part of a family?

3. What is the difference for children if, when growing up, they did or did not sense they belonged in a family? Have you experienced or known someone who did not feel that they were part of God's family?

4. Describe how the Spirit of God brings assurance.

5. What questions of assurance do you or others have?

6. How does one help a person resolve his or her doubts about their salvation?

7. How does the degree of assurance affect or otherwise reflect one's spiritual growth?

Section 2: Christian Growth: Strength and Dedication

"For all who are being led by the Spirit of God, these are sons of God" (Rom 8:14).

We can almost hear the sailor yelling out, "Land ho, the Island of Christian Growth!" On this island, we explore the many reasons why Christian believers do not grow strong and dedicated but live caught in a swirl of personal issues. The Spirit of God means for each believer to be strong and to give his or her life to the Lord so that He can use them to manifest His love and truth to others.

#6 The Leading of the Spirit (Gal 5:18)

Seeking God's will remains an ongoing special interest topic for believers. The assumption is that God, through the Holy Spirit, gets involved in detailed aspects of our decision-making processes, giving us great help in leading a wise life that is filled with His blessings. It certainly makes sense that believers, the children of God, would seek their heavenly Daddy's wisdom for their lives. Additionally, the Holy Spirit has great interest in fostering the abilities of God's people so that they can make good and wise decisions. He specializes in knowing and leading His children in God's good, acceptable, and perfect will (Rom 12:2).

A. Led By the Spirit (Gal 5:18)

But if you are led by the Spirit, you are not under the Law (Gal 5:18).

The Spirit of God, as this verse suggests, faithfully leads God's children. "Led" has many meanings, including to lead, take along with, guide, and direct, but we will focus on the two main ways the Holy Spirit leads us. The first method is more apparent from this verse because it speaks of the Spirit's general guiding work in believers' lives. The second method is also found here, but is more disguised and refers to special and specific leading.

The Holy Spirit empowers and guides His people into doing God's will. The powerful presence and influence of the Holy Spirit's work in a believer's life becomes a clear indication that they are sons of God, that is, genuine children of God whether male or female. The phrase "led by the Spirit," then, demonstrates that the Holy Spirit takes an active part in the Christian life that Paul can easily point to as life changing. The inward work of the Spirit, then, brings outward changes that can be seen as a sign of His work. For example, when God's people come to know Him, the love of God fills their hearts for other people. These desires, and the needed commitment to love, arise from the Holy Spirit; therefore, it can be asserted that their love is inspired or led by Him.

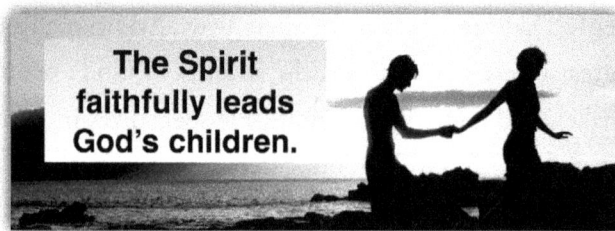

The Spirit faithfully leads God's children.

The Spirit's presence in a Christian's life, then, demonstrates that one is no longer under the Old Covenant of works but under the New Covenant and are empowered by the Spirit of God. The Christian is largely shaped not by outward Laws that constrict one's life but the inner leading of the Holy Spirit, which is always consistent with God's holy laws (Heb 8:8–11).

Paul further amplifies this verse by a similar one, "For all who are being **led** by the Spirit of God, these are sons of God" (Romans 8:14). The word "led" is often translated as "brought." It can easily be thought of as "worked in" or "helped out by." The work of the Holy Spirit, then, in His leading, plays a key role in our lives. He works first, and we follow. Followers of Jesus are not to live their Christian lives without His powerful presence—in fact, they cannot. It is for this reason that we confirm the Christian faith as a miraculous one: "by the sanctifying work of the Spirit" (see next chapter in our discussion of 1 Peter 1:2). This inward power greatly differs from the so-called confidence in the morality of the Christian religion to help us.

Perhaps a quick glimpse into counseling offices would help us better appreciate the general leading of the Holy Spirit. Modern psychoanalysis, as a whole, does not expect to know or provide a solution to man's deeper problems. Yes, they give advice, but even with that advice, they are typically just helping a person think through what the counselor thinks is good advice. If a person gets angry or anxious, they largely try to provide the right drugs to subdue extreme reactions. They do not resolve the issues of anger because they are powerless to do so. They do not know what to say nor do they have the power to heal. This is radically different from the Holy Spirit's counseling work.

The True Counselor shames these mock counselors who do not provide real healing but only provide outward constraints through drugs and weak advice. The Holy Spirit's full knowledge of the mind of God creates a huge gap in how He helps his people provide good biblical counseling. The phrase "Spirit of God" is used eleven times in the Bible, which depicts the full access the Spirit has to God the Father (Matt 3:16). There is no major disconnect between guidance and empowerment as we see in philosophy. The believer can be fully confident that in whatever the Lord leads us to do, He will provide the means to do so. If He counsels us against anger and bitterness (Eph 4:31), then He will provide grace for this. We can look to Him for whatever insight and help we need. Again, we will look at this from a personal perspective in the next chapter on sanctification, but do remember that this basis is what provides confidence to the Christian biblical counselor of God's provision of powerful words that lead to deliverance and joy in Christ.[9]

This general guidance and confidence in God's work can also be seen by the situation(s) in which He places us to live out our lives. Our confidence is that, wherever we end up, He will help us live godly lives. This can be partly seen in the discussion of knowing and claiming God's promises. For instance, the Lord led me to start the BFF ministry in November, 2000. It was founded in complete hope on God's leading to provide the vision, support, and funds. Without a sure supply of funds from supporters, we couldn't form a budget. However, for over fifteen years now, God has supplied for our needs in amazing ways. It seemed impossible to accomplish this with seven, and later eight, children, but God knew where He was leading us. I was a follower and truly dependent on Him! God heard my cry for help by providing special direction to start this ministry, and the Spirit provided the general grace to sustain it: peace, guidance, personal strength, clarity of mind, financial provision, etc. As He worked on my faith, He worked in my wife's faith too.

---

[9] Look how God's Spirit helped Jesus: "The Spirit of the Lord GOD is upon me, Because the LORD has anointed me to bring good news to the afflicted..." (Isa 61:1).

I like Hudson Taylor's approach: "God's work done in God's way shall never lack God's supply." When a person becomes a Christian, he or she can totally depend on God's grace for everything he or she needs to live out a godly life for His glory. Think of a furnace that heats up a house. It must be fueled by some power supply. In a similar but more grandiose way, the Holy Spirit fuels the Christian life. If the Christian believer is living out his or her life properly, then it is only because of the Spirit's presence. This powerful presence or leading of the Spirit is so typical that Paul exhorts believers as a whole: "If we live by the Spirit, let us also walk by the Spirit" (Gal 5:25).

B. Finding the Will of God (Exodus 13:21)

The second usage, which is more often associated with leading, is His personal guidance, as against His personal empowering. As we discuss these verses, we ought to remember that without general empowerment to live a godly life, there can only be a failure to discern and live by the Spirit in areas that we consider important. It will be impossible to know God's will on less important matters if we neglect the foundational ones. Consider how contrary it is for a young man who is consumed by bitterness or lust to seek God's direction for his future education and career steps. It is the Spirit that gives us the desire to live holy lives and to, in general, please the Lord. This mindset to do God's will is essential for seeking specific guidance.

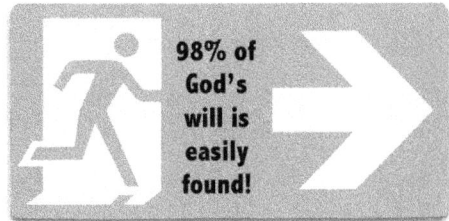

98% of God's will is easily found!

The Bible is filled with such disobedience. God's people, now or then, did not always desire to follow God's leading. The people told Jeremiah to counsel them on whether they should go to Egypt. "Whether it is pleasant or unpleasant, we will listen to the voice of the LORD our God to whom we are sending you, in order that it may go well with us when we listen to the voice of the LORD our God" (Jer 42:6). Jeremiah told them not to go to Egypt but that it would be fine to stay where they were in Israel. But they refused and brought judgment on themselves by insisting on going to Egypt and finding an unpleasant end to their lives there (Jer 42:17).

The Bible is full of specific guidance. The Lord told Jeremiah to buy a field even though the city was just about to be captured (Jer 32:7). Jesus "had to" go through Samaria (John 4:4). Jonah was to preach to the Ninevites (Jonah 1:1–2). Noah was to build the ark according to specifications God provided (Gen 6:13–22). David somehow sensed it was appropriate (i.e., God's will) to move the ark of the covenant back to Jerusalem, but, by ignoring the Word of God on how one should handle the Ark, several people were killed and the parade ended in confusion and dismay (2 Sam 6:1–10). David learned God's will the hard way, but when the Ark was borne on the shoulders of men as the Law instructed, instead of it being pulled by oxen, there was no problem following through with the longing in his heart (2 Sam 6:13).

This book is not on discerning the will of God but on how the Spirit is not just a general force surrounding each believer and is able to specifically direct every believer or the church as a whole (Rev 2–3) as needed. The vivid image of the cloud/flame that led the Israelites out of Egypt and to the Promised Land for forty years comes to mind. "And the LORD was going before them in a pillar of cloud by day to lead them on the way, and in a pillar of fire by night to give them light, that they might travel by day and by night" (Exodus 13:21).

This guiding hand of the Lord is just what we see when we look at how the Spirit of God led Jesus. "Then Jesus was led up by the Spirit into the wilderness to be tempted by the devil" (Matt 4:1). Or, "And Jesus, full of the Holy Spirit, returned from the Jordan and was led about by the Spirit in the wilderness" (Luke 4:1). The Spirit of God fully guided Jesus, in this case, to where He should go. Although this is seen as directional leading, there is also an associated promise of His empowering (the first point), that God would be there to supply all His needs. As He fasted for forty days, Jesus would be exposed to the full brunt of Satan's temptations. God the Father's care and guiding hand is all-important, not just for Jesus in the midst of His temptation, but for all believers.

Directional leading is prioritizing by nature. Among the many choices before us, the Spirit of God directs us to adopt one choice over another. During the 9/11 attacks in New York City, I read numerous testimonies of people who did not show up that day for work because things happened in their lives that either prevented or otherwise guided them. Many were saved by God from that devastating attack. The Spirit of God enables believers to take a certain course of action that pleases God and accomplishes His will. This is His empowering work. A clear knowledge of what God wants is the key to this guidance, but He also provides us extra faith and ability to help us when decisions are being made so we will not worry.

Now before going on, let me remind you that there are many things the Spirit seems quiet on, even things that I or my wife might consider very important. Those decisions might have to do with a child going to a college or making a choice between a job. There are many such decisions we face where we do not gain personal guidance from the Spirit, though

He is present. Interestingly, God does seem to intervene at various points in our lives using closed or open doors.

After getting married and continuing on in my college education, my wife and I were seeking inexpensive but livable accommodations. On the long trip to Florida, I thought (now I see it as inspired by the Holy Spirit) it would be great to buy a mobile home and sell it rather than rent, but we were young and poor. Impossible! I don't even think I asked God for this. God, however, intervened by having a man who rents homes also offer us to buy one of the mobile homes in his park. Having no money or resources, he offered to cosign the loan. By selling it off one and a half years later, we could leave the university debt free and move on to the next stage of an internship, readying ourselves for overseas mission work. Guidance and empowerment worked hand in hand.

The Spirit of God directs and guides, but we are forced to conclude that, in many cases, the Lord recognizes that we can make proper decisions without any extraordinary guidance or interference. While seeking God's general wisdom, He allowed me to choose the courses I wanted to take or whether I would bike or drive to school. Generally, we simply trust that the Lord gives us what is necessary to carry out His general work; it is sufficient. So why provide special guidance when what we have is sufficient? There are times when special guidance is necessary, and He is faithful to provide it! A father, similarly, will not repeat the daily expectations he has for his child every day because he trusts that the child has already, at some point, learned what he knows he should do; however, if the father senses that his son needs some special direction, he freely communicates with his son. This is why we constantly need to seek His wisdom and rely on the Spirit; otherwise, we will miss the special ways that He specially guides and leads us.

Another example might help cement this concept. Because the Lord has called me into this ministry of writing, I often seek His guidance. In the morning, after a prayer time and reflection on my day's events or the challenges set before me, I pause and seek God's wisdom and insight. Often, the Spirit of God will bring to my mind certain ways to think about different issues, ways I could approach writing an article, etc. This is the Spirit working. Sometimes, it seems but a random thought, but at other times, the thought becomes more developed. If I reflect further on it, the singular thought becomes a whole paragraph. In other words, He is guiding me on how to proceed. He is teaching me. These thoughts are always consistent with the Word of God and yet they provide special guidance in how I should proceed with my day. I allow such guidance to prioritize what I do—call this person or add this paragraph to a certain chapter. This does not appear to be a special spiritual gift but the Spirit's individual work to help get the Father's will done through my life.

Let's consider the gifts of the Spirit just for a minute (we will discuss them more specifically later). Let's say that a sister has the gift of wisdom (1 Cor 12:8). This gifting is proof that the Spirit has chosen to work through her abilities and placement to better serve His purposes in building up the body of Christ. It is God's Spirit who gives a believer those desires and abilities, and so by detecting these desires and abilities within ourselves, we are specially equipped to see and help with the needs of those around us. The gift, seen in those desires and abilities, then, becomes God's guidance for us.

Let us return to our discussion on personal guidance, a subset of the greater general guidance that the Spirit provides. Believers seem so fixed on knowing or seeking God's will regarding some specific decision that they seem to miss out on the more powerful directional truths that lurk underneath. By missing out on these directional truths, a believer can easily get worried and take things into his or her own hands. First, we need to remember that the Spirit actually knows what we need. Jesus says, "Therefore do not be like them; for your Father knows what you need before you ask Him"(Matt 6:8). This truth gives us faith that there is nothing that we can run into that we must panic about. God already knows and cares for those genuine needs.

Second, the Spirit communicates that knowledge to us in a timely manner so that we can respond in a timely manner. The Spirit knows what we can handle and so will only provide what we need when we need it. For example, God revealed several dreams to Joseph. They were given very early on because they would be used by the Lord to give Joseph hope when he was betrayed by his brothers and treated as a slave. Only in the distant future (Gen 37:5–10) would those dreams from his childhood be fulfilled.[10] There are always reasons for God's timing. We generally think God's leading has only to do with what is good and favorable, but, in some cases, this is not necessarily true. In Jesus' case, it meant that He would meet the devil, which was one of His most intense battles.

The Spirit, then, always leads us into conformity to God the Father's plan for our lives. The Christian should not be consumed with getting God to fulfill his personal needs but with help to know and complete his part in God's will. The Spirit, working perfectly with the Father in heaven, knows and communicates God's will to us as is necessary.

---

[10] I love how the pagan king recognizes and describes the Holy Spirit: a spirit of the holy gods: "Daniel came in before me, whose name is Belteshazzar according to the name of my god, and in whom is a spirit of the holy gods" (Daniel 4:8).

I have surmised that the reason Jesus spent time alone with the Father, sometimes even a full night, was to know His Father's will and be strengthened by it (John 6:15). One of the greatest barriers to gaining clear discernment of God's will stems from not fully dedicating our lives to do His will and yet expecting Him to lead us on rather unimportant matters—though they may seem very important to us. This is like asking for directions to someone's house, but only wanting the local streets and ignoring the need to know the larger streets that lead to the local streets. When we regularly spend time with the Lord in obedience, we can be confident that the Spirit of God will direct us so that we can know and do His will. Keep in mind, however, that this does not mean we will gain specific guidance if what we need is already there! The Lord wants us to stay close to Him daily and therefore be always alert to His general wisdom and guidance.

C. Purpose and Guidance (Isaiah 11:2–3)

The personal guidance of the Holy Spirit is a very important part of what He does. Jesus was greatly blessed because of the revelation of God's will through the Holy Spirit.

> The Spirit of the LORD will rest on Him, The spirit of wisdom and understanding, The spirit of counsel and strength, The spirit of knowledge and the fear of the LORD. And He will delight in the fear of the LORD, And He will not judge by what His eyes see, Nor make a decision by what His ears hear (Isaiah 11:2–3).

The "Spirit of the LORD" is the same as the "Spirit of God." Although one might assume that the spirit is the mere force of God, we know from the later explanation that the Spirit of God is a mighty personal force, God Himself. Jesus carried out His ministry by the Spirit's anointing. The Spirit's presence, as prophesied in Isaiah 11:2–3, serves as Jesus' constant companion ever since He descended upon Christ at His baptism. But this accompanying presence is also typical of how the Spirit of God lives, or dwells, in believers (1 Cor 6:19). In the New Testament, the Spirit lives in the believers and thus becomes familiar with the person and is able to communicate God the Father's will to them, which contrasts with the Old Testament wherein the Spirit would come and go. Again, as we look for personal guidance, we must realize that specific advice is not what we really need. To accomplish God's will, His people always need the Holy Spirit to give both faith as well as direction.

Seeking God's will is not merely a matter of finding personal guidance but a means to accomplish God's purposes. When we aren't actively seeking God's will, we end up asking the wrong question: "Which school do I want to go to?" "Should I go out on that date?" These questions are not framed correctly. We find that the Servant in the above verse had set God's will as His priority and thus tried to see the world from God's own eyes, not judging "by what His eyes see, nor make a decision by what His ears hear" (Isaiah 11:3). Every believer should first be concerned with what God wants for their lives in a broader sense: godliness, intimate relationship with Him, worship, obedience, loving others, etc. This settles the majority of questions that a person may have; the Lord is interested in the state of the heart (Prov 3:5–6). In many cases, though, a real problem develops when we count something as important but disregard or minimize that which seems irrelevant to what we want, a category under which God's will often falls. The Lord wants us to pay attention to the needs of those around us, even of the poor.

The phrase "fear of the Lord," used twice in Isaiah 11:2–3, indicates a constant vigilance and sensitivity toward the Lord's presence and will. The fear keeps us away from what is wrong because we esteem in our hearts what is right and focus on what God wants. The "fear of the Lord" is a great phrase that keeps us attentive to God's desires.

The little decisions that are left for us to decide are largely of no concern to the Lord. We can choose a red or blue vase to purchase, but we should first have our hearts settled on seeking Him, pay our tithes, and ensure that we are not spending extravagantly. The color is not usually important, and the Lord delights in our preferences.

Quenching the Spirit (1 Thes 5:19)

The verse, "Do not quench the Spirit" (1 Thes 5:19) refers to how people sometimes suppress the Spirit of God just as they throw water on a fire.[11] The point is that we can easily ignore or suppress the Spirit's leading, and unfortunately it is easy to do in our own lives. When we are prompted to make a call or don't say something when we ought—the list goes on—we argue with the Spirit's prompting and sometimes ignore or suppress His leading. When our heart is not responsive, our hearing gets worse. Our passions, feelings, or rational senses often speak louder than the Spirit of God. The issue is not whether God is clear but how we tend to focus more on outward things rather than on the Spirit of God, which is contrary to Christ's example.

Perhaps we need to add a spiritual discipline to our growing Christian routine called "listening," i.e., paying attention to the promptings of the Spirit. Start with time with the Lord in the morning, and write down the small promptings that flash through your mind. I find that if I do

11 1 Th 5:19 might be connected to the next verse, "Do not despise prophetic utterances" (5:20), but it is unlikely as they are separated by a "Do not."

this just after I have prayed and read God's Word, the Spirit often brings promptings or suggestions to my mind. What holds us back from meeting with the Lord early each day and increasing our sensitivity to what we typically might miss? We must listen more by spending more time with the Lord.

God can be fully trusted to lead as needed

People might be concerned with whether Satan is able to pose as God, asking, "How do you know the voice you are hearing is from God or Satan?" Start by making sure you have no bitterness in your heart, which is what gives the devil a foothold in your life. Many people justify their anger and acts of vengeance and even claim God wants them to straighten things out. But God clearly says in His Word, "Vengeance is mine" (Romans 12:9). If there are some issues, like anger, lust, etc., that you are dealing with, settle them first. This is why in Galatians 5:24, before it says to walk in the Spirit, it tells us, "Now those who belong to Christ Jesus have crucified the flesh with its passions and desires. If we live by the Spirit..." (Gal 5:24–25). That is remarkably clear.

Typically, when we are wholly seeking God's will and immersed in His Word and prayer, any distractions that originate from the evil one, if any, will seem utterly wicked and perverse. Third, always use God's Word as a measure against what the Spirit is prompting you to do. God would not want us to commit adultery or lie, but to be pure and speak the truth. An evil spirit might suggest an adulterous thought, but not the Holy Spirit. The Spirit of God is called the Spirit of Truth (John

14:17, 15:26, 16:13). In his letter, John simply states, "And it is the Spirit who bears witness, because the Spirit is the truth" (1 John 5:7).

The Spirit of God never counters God's Word but always speaks consistently with the truth. The Sprit of God always speaks truthfully, fully reflecting God and His Word. Thus, Satan's words are always shown to be false when contrasted to the truth, which is in effect what Jesus did during His temptation when speaking the Word of God to derail Satan's clever arguments.

D. Hindered and Propelled by the Spirit's Leading (Acts 16:6)

> And they passed through the Phrygian and Galatian region, having been forbidden by the Holy Spirit to speak the word in Asia; and when they had come to Mysia, they were trying to go into Bithynia, and the Spirit of Jesus did not permit them (Acts 16:6–7).

While our thoughts often dwell on our major life decisions and careers, God has larger goals that sometimes interfere with our preferences. Some parents want every blessing that God has for their child's life with the exception of a call into ministry. But what if that is God's purpose for their life? Why would God so powerfully place mission plans over one's comfort and care? Simply because there remains an urgency of preaching the Gospel to the ends of the world, which is incomparably more important than getting a computer for every person (even though they may be helpful) or increasing literacy or getting a better church building for those in developing countries. There is no reason we need to make the urgency of the Gospel's ministry exclusive of other interests (like literacy), but we must stay fixed on God's clear, ultimate purpose. The Holy Spirit is holy because He is fully set on prioritizing God's plan. God's mission is why Jesus did what He did when He came and lived an unjust life and died a horrible death. The Holy Spirit equips and sends His people into the mission field—despite discomfort or even the death they might face. If the Spirit sends people, should we not support them in their efforts? Do we even need to ask what the will of the Lord is?

On a slightly different note, there is a very interesting verse that speaks about how the Spirit redirected missions by holding Paul back from going to a certain place on one of his missionary journeys. "And when they had come to Mysia, they were trying to go into Bithynia, and the Spirit of Jesus did not permit them" (Acts 16:7).

What seemed right and good, to go throughout the remaining part of what is modern Turkey, was not permitted by the Spirit of God. We are not sure how Paul concluded this leading, but there is another part of the story that we should be careful not to miss. In the following verses, and perhaps part of the very means that prevented Paul from going further into Turkey, was a vision Paul had. "And a vision appeared to Paul in the night: a certain man of Macedonia was standing and appealing to him, and saying, 'Come over to Macedonia and help us.' And when he had seen the vision, immediately we sought to go into Macedonia, concluding that God had called us to preach the gospel to them" (Acts 16:9–10).

Summary

God can be fully trusted to lead us when we actively seek His will. As has been stated before, it is hard to steer a still car. First, get the car going, and then it will be easy to direct. However, it is important to be going in the right direction too! So God's people need to pursue God's primary purpose for the church and His people and be less concerned with minor decisions. We can safely generalize that about 95% of what we should do as a believer is clearly stated in the scriptures. God's will is clear. The remaining small part matters little, but if it does, then the Spirit will guide us. God's redemptive plan largely shapes this underlying foundation for our lives. Yes, buy a house, but not one that keeps your budget so tight that you cannot give to missions. If your life is so constricted, sell your possessions and get out of debt so that you can start giving to causes that the Lord has prioritized. Don't follow the bank's suggestion of getting the biggest mortgage available. The banks and institutions of this world are not thinking of God's will for you. Remember to keep one day for rest. When we seek God's plan, setting hospitality up in your home, helping the poor, sharing the gospel, then you can be confident that the Spirit will direct you as needed in other affairs.

"And the peace of God, which surpasses all comprehension, shall guard your hearts and your minds in Christ Jesus" (Phil 4:7).

Discussion Questions

1. What are some issues that you face that you would like to have extra insight on from the Lord? What specific insight do you need?

2. Is it right to seek God's will for something that the scripture clearly prohibits like divorce or a believer marrying a nonbeliever? Why?

3. Please share an experience where you clearly saw the guidance of the Holy Spirit?

4. What is one or two things that the Lord clearly wants for your life? Share how you are either doing them or not.

5. Do you contribute to missions? Explain how.

6. God says that He cares for us. Why doesn't He always give us details on what we should do?

7. Read through Jeremiah and observe the number of times God's people did not follow Jeremiah's advice; remember to include any consequences they suffered as a result.

8. What special insight do we gain from the way David learned from his mistakes in 2 Samuel 6?

#7 The Sanctification of the Spirit (1 Peter 1:1–2)

Life in the Spirit!
Experiencing the Fullness of Christ

Although we stumble, struggle, and are often totally confused about our Christian life, the mysterious process of Christian growth continues, buttressed by God's extraordinary purpose and grace. The young believer—who is often portrayed as a child—might indeed be tossed back and forth like a wave (Eph 4:14), but it is unsightly and totally unnecessary for an older believer to be so. Though the process of sanctification, in one way, has a lot to do with our day-to-day decisions, it has more to do with what God, through the Holy Spirit, intends to do in our lives. For some believers, the Christian life is much like losing your compass and not knowing which way to proceed on a foggy night, and yet you later find yourself at the right destination. My early Christian life was this way despite my sinful decisions because I did not know how to battle bitterness and lust. Similar to the signs near a construction site, the sign of sanctification announces "God is at work," communicating both incompleteness and yet purposeful activity aimed at completion. The Christian believer can safely say to him or herself that "God is growing me!"

A. By the Sanctifying Work of the Spirit (1 Peter 1:1–2)

The master transformation into God's holiness is overseen by the Father, enabled by Christ the Son, and implemented by the Spirit of God. Peter speaks quite boldly about this master plan: "Who are chosen according to the foreknowledge of God the Father, by the sanctifying work of the Spirit, that you may obey Jesus Christ..." (1 Peter 1:1–2).

God's plan to renew the life of His people is clearly seen throughout His word: "Who are chosen according to the foreknowledge of God the Father." God the Father commits to His chosen people by securing the plan through which He brings them into His presence and likeness. The plan, now, has already been worked out, and, in time, is observed in our daily lives. He is our Father, the Giver of life. God, then, implants His Spirit in us, which brings new life and a new nature, which produces right desires that stem from His own heart. "God and Father of our Lord Jesus Christ, who according to His great mercy has caused us to be born again" (1 Peter 1:3). This living water (John 4:10) and the life-changing effects of the Spirit of God empower every genuine follower of Christ (John 4:14).

While Jesus Christ's blood on the cross secures the passageway for us through the satisfaction of God's wrath against us (Romans 3:25) and though His resurrection guarantees eternal redemption (1 Peter 1:3),

the Spirit of God implements the step-by-step personal transformation. It is proper to say that we have both been saved but also will be saved (1 Peter 1:5). The phrase "by the sanctifying work of the Spirit" boldly describes the nitty gritty progress going on backstage in our Christian lives. The present and ongoing sanctification of our lives, like a multitude of miniature steps, leads to the one-time sanctified target of being made into the likeness of Christ, the Son of God (Eph 4:13), a full reflection of our Heavenly Father. Notice how the following verses consider sanctification as a completed process.

> In order that they may receive forgiveness of sins and an inheritance among those who have been sanctified by faith in Me (Acts 26:18).

> And such were some of you; but you were washed, but you were sanctified, but you were justified in the name of the Lord Jesus Christ, and in the Spirit of our God (1 Cor 6:11).

> By this will we have been sanctified through the offering of the body of Jesus Christ once for all (Heb 10:10).

So, though the children of God struggle in this world, the Holy Spirit persistently yet patiently draws them into God's presence. It is because of this that God's children can live in God's presence, pray through Jesus' Name, and host the Holy Spirit in their lives; they are themselves the temple of God (Eph 2:21-22).

The word "sanctify" in its various forms is used 60 times in the Bible and is equally distributed in the Old and New Testaments. This word has the sense of making holy, setting apart for, or consecrating (in this case, we are sanctified for our Mighty Creator). Paul speaks about this process, "For I am confident of this very thing, that He who began a good work in you will perfect it until the day of Christ Jesus" (Phil 1:6). Although Paul doesn't here use the word "sanctify," he is powerfully describing its process. So practical sanctification begins at salvation and continues on in the power of the Spirit of Christ.

Though we are very aware of the many struggles that come with making godly decisions in our lives and avoiding temptation (1 Peter 1:6), we are also part of a magnificent outworking of His plan for our godliness. The Spirit lives in our lives, and, by conviction, peace, enlightenment, etc., moves us along the continuum to holiness. The more we understanding how the Holy Spirit works in our Christian lives, the more encouraging and easier it gets. In some of my other books, I use the phrase "The Flow" to illustrate how powerful water or air currents help explain God's design of spiritual growth in our Christian lives.[12] When we learn to work along with the Lord, His power helps us more smoothly navigate between our mixed thoughts, ideas, temptations, and feelings.

So God's sanctifying work is clearly accomplished by the Holy Spirit. 1 Peter 1:1–2 does not provide much information on how the Spirit sanctifies us (he does that in 2 Peter 1:4–10), but the fact that He does leaves us no cause for boasting of our good works as they come by way of His great mercy alone. Instead, of boasting of our strength, we must strengthen our resolve to understand His ways and cooperate with His purposes.

This is exactly what Peter concludes: "That you may obey Jesus Christ." The purpose of the Holy Spirit, like the magnetic north, leads us into personal holiness, enabling us to draw closer to our holy Lord. We will not only be freed from our sin but empowered and directed to live in constant obedience to Jesus Christ.

---

[12] The Life Core is a recent book that discusses this in full.
www.foundationsforfreedom.net/Help/Store/Intros/Life_Core.html

B. The Temple of the Holy Spirit (1 Cor 3:16)

The process of sanctification is explained and presented in different ways in the scriptures. One of the powerful images that Paul uses to strengthen our concept of holiness is the temple. "Do you not know that you are a temple of God, and that the Spirit of God dwells in you?" (1 Cor 3:16). Paul unequivocally states that we, God's people, are the temple of God. [13]

This is not any common temple filled with local idols; rather, the picture of the grand holy temple of God found in Jerusalem floods our minds with many sacred images, separating holy vessels from the unholy items and people outside the temple. The specific term for temple here refers to the Holy place and the inner Holy of Holies (*naos*), which was the most set-apart place where God dwelt. We are not observers or attendees coming to the temple, but "You are a temple of God." One of the first processes the people of God must undergo is the transformation from desecrated to sacred, i.e., holy people. It is not the building but the people who are holy ("holy priesthood" 1 Peter 2:5). God's presence in His people sets them apart as His holy temple. Our bodies, thoughts, and decisions all must be in accord with what pleases our Lord. Although a believer is free from his or her sins, this hardly means they can do what they want because they now belong to the Lord and must live for His holy purposes.

Paul, in the same statement, further refines our thinking: "The Spirit of God dwells in you." Again, the people of God are not just symbolically holy by God's purpose to work in them in the future but are genuinely set apart for God through the Spirit's very presence. The Almighty God

---

[13] For a full redemptive analogy, look at Redemption Through the Scriptures: www.foundationsforfreedom.net/Help/Store/Intros/Redemption-RTS.html

actually lives in us and so his awesome holy presence shapes our character. The term "Holy Spirit" is not used here, but the term "Spirit of God," which is used 92 times in the Bible (mostly in the New Testament) is perhaps more powerful. This holy influence constantly works in our lives, convicting and shaping us.

The presence of the Holy God in our lives as the foundational growth influence on our Christian lives makes so much sense. This constant presence influences our responses, just as a guest in our home might influence us (John 1:12,14). Just think how a person in your house or at work might influence what you may say or do. In a similar way, the presence of the Spirit of God's in us greatly transforms our lives. So when the Spirit dwells in us, we should understand His higher purposes of regularly sharing His thoughts, either convicting or encouraging us, as well as helping us when we need it. He sanctifies us so that "you may obey Jesus Christ" (1 Peter 1:2). His indwelling presence powerfully communicates that we belong to Him.

God is the special guest in our lives who increasingly shapes what we do, where we go, and what we say so that we can be a better host for Him!

C. The Fantastic Duo (2 Thes 2:13)

There is much to say regarding sanctification, but our major focus is on how the Holy Spirit is related to our personal spiritual growth in Christ. Paul in 2 Thessalonians 2:13 says,

> But we should always give thanks to God for you, brethren beloved by the Lord, because God has chosen you from the beginning for salvation through sanctification by the Spirit and faith in the truth (2 Thes 2:13).

Similarly to Peter, thus confirming the importance of how God makes us holy, we will look at Paul's words. "God has chosen you from the beginning for salvation." God chose to bring a new birth to His people that is not dependent on their performance or works but upon His choice alone. Just as a baby doesn't choose the family in which he or she is born, so it is true in our Christian lives (Titus 3:5). God chose us so that we could be part of His family. This truth should cause songs of thankfulness to ring in our souls!

The phrase "for salvation through sanctification by the Spirit" identifies the purpose and means through which our Father works in us. God desires our final delivery from this sin-ensnared body. He re-emphasizes the Holy Spirit's powerful role in the lives of all believers, not just in the clergy or certain saints. God is raising the bar of expectation for all believers to be transformed by the Holy Spirit. Each believer, then should not only observe what God has done in our lives but what He now wants to do, which this verse speaks of—ongoing holy development.

But he also tells us the means by which this happens. The word "by" sets off two means through which God readies us: "Through sanctification by the **Spirit** and faith in the **truth**" reveals that though we emphasize the Holy Spirit's work in us, there really is a two-pronged stimulus forming the backbone of the sanctification process: the Spirit and the truth, i.e., the Word of God. The Spirit of God is the source of our spiritual life along with all of its appetites and purposes. The DNA of our new life in Christ is, so to speak, the Holy Spirit. His purposes become ours.

Paul also mentions the place that "faith in the truth" has in our lives. The Spirit of God brings the truth of God to our minds. He teaches and enlightens us, which interestingly includes reproofing us when it is necessary (2 Tim 3:16–17). The truth, the sword of the Spirit (Eph

6:17), is the means by which the Spirit of God transforms our lives and brings God's full work into the lives of the believers and the church.

This varied work of God through the Spirit will be expanded on in other parts of this book, but for now let's use a diagram to illustrate how the Spirit sanctifies us with the Word of God. Earlier on in Chapter 2, we noted the communication system brought on by the Spirit that enables communion with God for every believer. God is not just a distant cosmic creator but our Heavenly Father with whom we talk and make requests. Although He did choose to work in our lives by giving us a spiritual life, He also chose to give us the whole means by which we can grow in His likeness. Part of this likeness is seen in our holy character. When I became a believer, the Spirit convicted me, letting me know that bad words were no longer acceptable. Later, I read this in the Word (Eph 4:29); somehow, the Spirit further communicated this to me, and I immediately stopped swearing. He helped me break the habit much quicker by reminding me when I spoke wrongly.

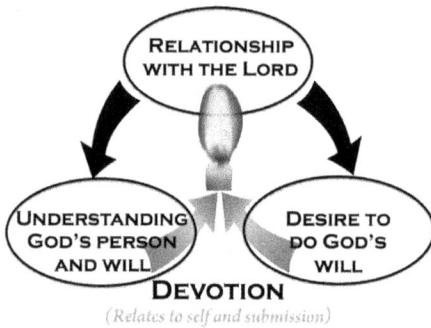

RELATIONSHIP WITH THE LORD

UNDERSTANDING GOD'S PERSON AND WILL

DESIRE TO DO GOD'S WILL

DEVOTION
(*Relates to self and submission*)

The diagram below highlights how the Spirit unites these three aspects of Christian devotion together. The Lord helps us understand God's person and will through the Word of God. He prompts us, urging us to right thinking and action through a desire to do His will and developing in us a distaste for unholy behavior. As we learn more of His Word and grow in our obedience to Him, God causes greater growth and a clearer understanding of His will like oxygen causes a fire to grow. This is the reason personal devotions (i.e., quiet time) remains the main spiritual discipline for the Christian believer. No believer can go far without spending regular time with God in His Word and in obedience.

> "To be a minister of Christ Jesus to the Gentiles, ministering as a priest the gospel of God, that my offering of the Gentiles might become acceptable, sanctified by the Holy Spirit" (Romans 15:16).

Summary

The Holy Spirit sanctifies His people by living inside them and influencing all they do. By influencing their thoughts, He makes their decisions holy. The more we increase our knowledge of God's Word, the less we will be distracted by the world. Instead of being fixed on tradition, programs, and ritual, we will daily sensitize ourselves to God's presence by meeting regularly with Him to build up our spiritual lives. The Spirit's indwelling is God's dynamic way to sanctify us, enabling God to extend His holy work deeper into our lives. Our Christian lives are precast to be powerfully, though subtly, guided by the Holy Spirit, who, in His gracious, kind, and patient way, relentlessly coaxes us to live according to the Father's calling for our lives as the children of God, thus taking on our Father's holy image.

Discussion Questions

1. What is the difference between a young and mature believer?

2. Define "sanctify."

3. Share two experiences in which the Spirit of God made you sense something was right and/or wrong.

4. Have you ever thought of the reality of being a holy temple in which God lives? What are some implications of this for you?

5. How do you daily ensure the entrance of God's Word into your life? Share how this has previously helped you.

6. Explain the flame diagram.

7. Summarize how the Holy Spirit sanctifies His people.

#8 Walking by the Spirit (Gal 5:16–24)

Life in the Spirit!
Experiencing the Fullness of Christ

Probably every believer at some point dreams of being daily guided and helped by the Spirit of God. But what does this mean practically? While the prophets of old were filled by the Spirit when He mightily came upon them, they do not well describe what the phrase "walk by the Spirit" means in the New Testament. Because of the cross, great changes that dynamically changed the way God works in and through His people occurred. The Christian life became brilliantly new—more powerful, forceful, intimate, pervasive, and common. God now works differently in His attack against sin, the world, and the devil because He works through His people, the church; this attack is described using the phrase "spiritual warfare." The Spirit lives in all of His people during this age of grace, so believers need to learn and master the basics of how to walk in the Spirit.

A. Live by the Spirit (Gal 5:24–25)

Now those who belong to Christ Jesus have crucified the flesh with its passions and desires. 25 If we live by the Spirit, let us also walk by the Spirit (Gal 5:24–25).

Every vehicle is powered by an engine, which is powered by some source. The engine takes the energy and translates it into mechanical power to move the vehicle. *Living by the Spirit* speaks of a powerful energy that is used to drive the believer's life. The whole false notion of a natural Christian is exposed by these few words. Christianity is not just another religion; rather, it reflects, if rightly understood, a great group of believers spread across time and space who together are mobilized by the Spirit of God. Instead of looking at the schisms and factions or even doctrinal differences, we are forced to see the greater work of God that calls His children to live in harmony with Him and His will. This is the kingdom of God; it is not a political or religious force, but the living God, who lives in and through His people. Drop your old notions of the Christian religion and exchange it for the truth—a people who are animated together to carry our God's holy work.

- Enlivened
- Empowered
- Illuminated

God's people do not live by their own power or on their own guidance, but by the living God through the Holy Spirit. We belong "to Christ Jesus" (24); our whole life is run by the Spirit of God. This is too awesome! To think that God moves in our lives might not be too special for some because of their tarnished ideas of who God is. They cannot look beyond their own desires where they treat God as a good luck charm to open their eyes to the glorious faithful, good, and loving God.

I want to testify that it is the most wonderful thing to be able to put down my old self along with its desires of anger, meanness, bitterness, lust, worry, jealousy, etc. But that, though it is wonderful, is only a small part of what God is doing—God has put His life in me. I get His love, power, wisdom, peace, hope, joy, etc., to fill my life! This will be discussed more below when we talk about the fruit of the Spirit. But this is the point–God, in His fullness, comes to vitalize us through the Spirit of God. We can actually choose to love those who despise us, no matter how they treat us. Though I have personal stories to affirm this, it holds true for all of God's children. This is our blessing: God's own presence in our lives.

In the Old Testament, the Spirit of God came upon certain people for special purposes, but the hope was that they would be mobilized to carry out the greater purposes God had for them. While Elijah was a good example of this, Samson was a poor one, allowing his own desires to keep him from carrying out God's greater purpose of defeating the enemy armies. There was a greater purpose, though, of forming a community of God's people and that was "that I might be their God. I am the Lord" (Lev 26:45). This verse reminds of the whole concept of redemption[14] that speaks of how the Lord has redeemed us for His own, "a people for God's own possession" (1 Peter 2:9). Because we belong to Him through Christ, He delights to fill and stir us with His holy power to do His will, lifting us far above the world's coarse and selfish ways. Ezekiel prophesies this of our age:

> Moreover, I will give you a new heart and put a new spirit within you; and I will remove the heart of stone from your flesh and give you a heart of flesh. And I will put My Spirit within you and cause

---

Please note our book, "Redemption Through the Scriptures."

125

you to walk in My statutes, and you will be careful to observe My ordinances (Ezek 36:26–27).

Living by the Spirit illustrates how our spiritual lives stem from the Spirit's constant energizing activity in what otherwise would be our common lives. This is the ultimate energy source—not the sun, which will wear out—but the glorious Son, who, through His resurrection, lives in His people who are animated by God's loving desires. God's people are not simply pawns to be created, used, and tossed, but constantly and fully affected by the Spirit's movement to guide our every moment and thought throughout eternity. To live by the Spirit means we never need to fail or fall. Of course, we will go through difficult times like our Master Jesus, but they are, like Jesus' own temptations, meant only to portray the power of God at work in our lives. Let us, then, soar by the Spirit, relying on what He can do through our lives rather than what our selfish person is able to do. God has rolled out a magic carpet for each believer to walk on, a carpet made through God's love in Christ.

By linking our spiritual birth with our Christian life, we are forced to think of God's greater purpose in our lives that have been revamped and "souped up," empowered by the Holy Spirit. Let not any believer be like Esau (Heb 12:16) who despised being God's chosen vessel to display His glorious grace in an otherwise very dark world. Live instead by the Spirit of God rather than by the cold ashes of this dying world.

B. Walk by the Spirit (Gal 5:16,25)

The two parallel phrases: "live by the Spirit" and "walk by the Spirit" are wrapped so closely together that we might mistakenly conclude they share a similar meaning. Nothing could be more wrong. Their difference seems minimal until we seriously contemplate them. "Live by the Spirit" refers to the Spirit's empowering of our lives, almost as if we are able to draw from two energy tanks, one from God and one from our empty self. "Walking by the Spirit" leads us to think of our decision in light of His instruction. It is the Spirit who influences us, and we, under His guidance, must guide our own facilities and activities. Our decisions influence the degree to which the Spirit of God can work with us.

- •Guided
- •Strengthened
- •Directed

> But I say, walk by the Spirit, and you will not carry out the desire of the flesh. For the flesh sets its desire against the Spirit, and the Spirit against the flesh; for these are in opposition to one another, so that you may not do the things that you please (Gal 5:16–17).

Paul reminds us that there is no middle road; there are only two paths, one of which we must choose. Possession of the powerful and awesome love of God is available, but we can choose to not live by His gracious guidance and instead live according to our own selfish desires. One would think that this would be near impossible—why would a believer choose something so offbeat and tragic when we can be inspired by the music of the Spirit's loving voice? When believers choose to ignore the Spirit, they are said to live in or by the power of the flesh, that is, through their selfish nature where their own desires and wishes become the chief focus. They have compromised their faith, living far below their high calling. Living by the Spirit requires faith in God's work in our lives.

The concepts of being dead to or alive to reflect our choices, whether or not we choose to be attentive to the spirit's way above the call of our own desires. A believer, for example, might want to be mean to the one who backstabs him or her, but this Christian chooses to love. Repentance describes the way we regret and turn from living for our old desires, which always bring the touch of death and ugliness. Obedience, on the other hand, is an expression of our desire and willingness to let the Spirit of God commandeer our lives.

To "walk by the Spirit" is to live under the constant guidance and strength of God through His Holy Spirit. Commands, like this, compel the recipients to give high priority to the given task and reveal its importance for a believer's life and service. By purposely living affected by the Spirit, we can avoid much of life's personal problems, though there will always be the possibility of suffering because of those around us (Phil 1:29–30). In fact, a life devoted to obedience is very simple, producing powerful welcomed outcomes. Disobedience, however, brings on confusing, ugly, defeatist, and difficult times. Christians ruin the productivity of their lives because they disobey the Spirit's guidance. Sanctification can be summarized as an increase in the number of times a believer chooses to walk by the Spirit rather than the flesh.

The phrase, "And you will not carry out the desire of the flesh" reveals the glorious means by which the Spirit keeps us from the evil stain of our flesh. We cannot live out casual Christian lives because we are, or should be, in constant spiritual warfare (how to fight is something discussed elsewhere).[15] Victory means to keep walking in the Spirit. The battle is not won by focusing on how strong you are but on keeping the evil one from redirecting your thoughts to yourself. When confused, just choose what Christ would want of you and do it by the power of

[15] *Reaching Beyond Mediocrity* shows the way to consistently live out this victorious Christian life. www.foundationsforfreedom.net/Help/Store/Intros/Reaching-Beyond.html

the Spirit. A believer's struggle always intensifies when, during temptation, they contemplate compromise.

The hostilities can be bloody. Notice how the flesh assaults us: "Now the deeds of the flesh are evident, which are: immorality, impurity, sensuality, idolatry, sorcery, enmities, strife, jealousy, outbursts of anger, disputes, dissensions, factions, envying, drunkenness, carousing, and things like these, of which I forewarn you just as I have forewarned you that those who practice such things shall not inherit the kingdom of God" (Gal 5:19–21). The list seems to go on forever! Each of them raises their fist against the Spirit's godly response. When mentoring a brother, he told me that he did not know how to date. As an unbeliever, he just did things the world's ways: talk, party, drink, sex, etc. He knew this was not the way to handle girls, but since dating was so event oriented, he just did not know how to date as a believer. The quick answer to his problem would be the opposite of what he was doing: talk without false motives, care for the other, no drunkenness, and no sex; but let us not stop there! Rather, make room for the Spirit's leading: purity, respect, care for others, and sharing the gospel. Die to the old person and refuse to follow old tendencies.

God has opened the door to "an abundant life" (John 10:10) by the way the Spirit of God guides our lives. If we suffer in our spiritual lives, it is because we have not walked by the Spirit. Spiritual warfare, then, is the battle between persistently choosing the Spirit's infinitely better way over our set of selfish desires. There are spiritual powers, good and bad, behind the scenes that either help us or seek our demise. Walking by the Spirit is a phrase that summarizes the way God empowers us to daily live godly lives through the Spirit of God when we choose to live under His guidance. The unbeliever cannot and does not want to live out a genuine Spirit-guided life (Rom 8:1–8), but the believer's greatest joy is to seek how God works in them for a supernatural life of love and care.

C. The Fruit of the Spirit (Gal 5:22–23)

But the fruit of the Spirit is love, joy, peace, patience, kindness, goodness, faithfulness, gentleness, self-control; against such things there is no law (Gal 5:22–23).

But, that's enough discussion of the dark side of the battle. The flesh only produces results consistent with the selfish nature of man. Today, as mankind turns away from God's Word, the stakes are getting higher: rape, injustice, divorce, violence, and murder. Paul the Apostle, however, doesn't end at verse 21. Instead, because of the Spirit's ongoing power in believers, he reveals the glories of the ways of God, the fruit of the Spirit. The "fruit of the Spirit" stands in stark contrast to the flesh, producing immeasurably wonderful outcomes described as fruits, which will be briefly described below.

LOVE

Love is persistently kind expressions and thoughts of others that stems from the desires of God's people to encourage and aid them, even at a cost. Love, the first-named fruit and perhaps the most commonly mentioned fruit of the Spirit, can summarize the whole of Christ-like living. Jesus Himself summarized all the commands because, by loving God and others, one cannot treat others wrongly (Mark 12:30–31). The list of the flesh uncovers the many behaviors by which those made in God's image are wrongly treated (Gal 5:19-21).

JOY

Joy is the constant flood of delight that springs up in the lives of His people and is due to the amazing acts of God's grace upon their lives. Joy is not dependent upon outward situations but instead stems from a deep confidence that all is very well with their souls. God's promises to care for them issues a deep-seated joy and delight in God's person and ways.

PEACE

Peace describes the harmonious and quiet spirit of believers who are very aware of God's great steps of pain to acquire peace between them and God. Peace does not describe the world, but it does well describe those who are engulfed by the overwhelming ways the Spirit of God carries out God's good will. Anger, hatred, and jealousy are discarded as unwanted rubbish while a superb and unbelievable sense of harmony and peace keeps their hearts in His hands (Phil. 4:7).

PATIENCE

Patience speaks of the willingness of God to work out His best ways in His time. The foundation of patience is the confidence that His people have, knowing that God's will is good and nothing will be withheld from those who genuinely seeksHim. "For the LORD God is a sun and shield; The LORD gives grace and glory; No good thing does He withhold from those who walk uprightly" (Psalm 84:11).

love/   *joy*

self-control   *peace*

gentleness   *patience*

faithfulness   *kindness*

goodness

KINDNESS

Kindness addresses the way God's people generously and tenderly treat others, regardless of the way they themselves are treated. Having discovered the power of forgiveness, kindness, like a golden crown, influences all the words, thoughts, and actions a person makes toward others because of the way they themselves are overwhelmed by God's undeserved mercy toward them in Christ.

GOODNESS

Goodness emphasizes a gracious and beneficial spirit when helping others. There are no ill-motives, or even those of gain. Much like an overflowing river, they share the very things that God has shared with them, having been touched by the goodness with which God has treated them.

FAITHFULNESS

Faithfulness rests in God's faithfulness to His people. The Lord's reliability and constancy shine deeply into their lives so that they begin to reflect that very persistence in being good, kind, and caring. Faithfulness is totally reliant on the way the Spirit consistently brings God's promises to our minds.

GENTLENESS

Gentleness and mercy are likewise outcomes of the Spirit's way when their humble spirit bows before the aggressive assaults from others. Gentleness derives its strength from constantly reckoning that God is watching over their concerns, and it admires how Jesus bore their pain on the cross, enduring all so that they could be His forever. Being so utterly accepted and desired enables them in the Spirit to forego claim to the rights that they might call their own; they recognize that it is inconsequential to their lives.

SELF-CONTROL

Self-control reminds believers of their belief that God's ways are always better than their lusts, and that they are secured through honesty and love rather than selfish and self-calculating attempts to wrestle things from others. Self-control's power regulates a person's desire to obtain his or her needs by first loving and caring for others (Matt 6:33).

As fruit, the Spirit of God naturally brings a surplus of these most desired qualities into our hearts, lives, and surroundings, which positively affects our marriages, relationships with colleagues, and others at church. The fruit is a natural outflow of the Spirit's work, not a natural spurt from our inner selves. When we want peace, live according to His prescribed ways to interact with others and to one's superiors. When you accept His work and ways, the peace of God will soon fill your heart with such qualities as the fruit of the Spirit. When the Spirit of God influences our lives, we are not told to look for money or comfort but qualities that characterize the life of Jesus Christ. We certainly should aspire to bear all of these good fruits, but they should not be thought of so much as gained but simply as the result of following the Lord. A person cannot obtain them by grabbing but by resting in God's greater purposes; only then will they see them unfold in their own life.

Summary

From the inception of our new lives, the Holy Spirit sets to working closely with us, shaping and forming our lives to be more like Christ. This truth lies behind the confidence of the discipler. The believer is granted access to the energy of the Lord through the Holy Spirit, which in turn promises grace, wisdom, and goodness to carry out all the ways of the Lord. The more the Holy Spirit affects us, the more this holy fruit characterizes our lives. The believer, then, should anticipate these works and fruit of God coming from their godly decisions, being generated from a deep faith and reliance upon Christ. The greatest joys, harmony, and peaks of kindness for God's people typically match their closest times spent with God.

Discussion Questions

1. How does the Holy Spirit energize us so that we never run out of what we need to be patient, kind, etc.?

2. List some ways that the Spirit of God affects your personal walk.

3. What is one benefit that you love about God being with you through the day?

4. Share at least one example of when you chose not to walk by the Spirit but by the flesh. What happened? How might it have been different if you walked by the Spirit?

5. How would you describe the difference between living by the Spirit and walking by the Spirit (Gal 5:25)?

6. What is one fruit of the Spirit that you would like more of? Why?

7. Describe the fruit you chose in Question 6. What advice, commands, or insights do the scriptures have that relate to securing that fruit?

8. Do you think the fruit of the Holy Spirit is linked to natural character traits or virtue? If so, how?

Life in the Spirit!

#9 The Filling of the Spirit (Eph 5:17–20)

Life in the Spirit!
Experiencing the Fullness of Christ

Various forms of the phrase "filled with the Spirit" are used in both the Old and New Testaments. The term "filled with the Spirit" might sound excessive because of the associations we have with names that sound extreme, like the "Holy Rollers," or some of their actions. We admit to excessiveness at times, but these moments should not hold us back from discovering what the filling of the Spirit means, and we should seek our Lord to fill and use our lives.

"Filled with the Spirit" is used very positively by the Apostle Paul; in fact, he even goes so far as to command us to be filled. This extraordinary influence of the Holy Spirit marks those special times God commits to revealing Himself to His people and doing His will through their lives. A biblical understanding of this phrase and its meaning will be gained as we closely look at how the term is used, first in the Old Testament, then in the New, and then more clearly defined by Paul the Apostle's usage in Ephesians 5:17–20.

A. Filled with the Spirit in Old Testament

The phrase "filled with the Spirit" is used only two times in the Old Testament, but similar wording such as: "came" or "poured out upon" are frequent (27 times). Let's first discuss the two verses that use "filled with."

"Filled with"

> And I have filled him with the Spirit of God in wisdom, in understanding, in knowledge, and in all kinds of craftsmanship (Exodus 31:3; 35:31).

> Now Joshua the son of Nun was filled with the (S)spirit of wisdom, for Moses had laid his hands on him; and the sons of Israel listened to him and did as the LORD had commanded Moses (Deut 34:9).

Signifying God's presence

The phrase "filled him with the Spirit of God" (Exodus 31:3) intimates that, at times, God in the Old Testament greatly aided a person by manifesting His presence in the person's life. In this case, it was "Bezalel, the son of Uri, the son of Hur, of the tribe of Judah" (31:2) who received special understanding, knowledge, and talent in craftsmanship through the filling of the Spirit for the purpose of building the tabernacle equipment.

Although Bezalel and Joshua were filled with the Spirit, nowhere is it mentioned that Moses was likewise anointed or filled with the Spirit. This filling, though, is inferred in at least two places: when Moses is instructed to share the burden with others, "Then I will come down and speak with you there, and I will take of the Spirit who is upon you, and will put Him upon them; and they shall bear the burden of the people with you, so that you shall not bear it all alone" (Num 11:17; Deut

34:9). Joshua received the Spirit through Moses—a beautiful picture of the anointing (Num 27:18).

> Then His people remembered the days of old, of Moses. Where is He who brought them up out of the sea with the shepherds of His flock? Where is He who put His Holy Spirit in the midst of them (Isaiah 63:11).

We do not question whether the Spirit of God was upon Moses but instead affirm it. Perhaps it did not need to be stated because of how Moses was filled with the Spirit from being in God's presence on Mt. Sinai. How interesting that the brightness of His face began to leave when he descended so that He used a veil (Exodus 34:33–34; 2 Cor 3:13–17). Moses' attitude toward the Holy Spirit is clearly seen where He wishes the Spirit of God to be upon all, "But Moses said to him, 'Are you jealous for my sake? Would that all the LORD's people were prophets, that the LORD would put His Spirit upon them!'" (Num 11:29) This alludes to what would later happen in the New Testament when God's Spirit filled all His people, empowering them for His service.

Signifying God's Gifting

The filling of the Spirit must mean that the Spirit of God so affects a person that, as in Bezel's case, God's thoughts and wisdom were his to use. Or, from God's point of view, God empowers His people in certain ways to accomplish what He wants, when and how He desires. The Spirit, then, does not merely symbolize a token from God or God's nearness but describes how God's presence influences and otherwise directs a person.

The scriptures are clear in how this filling manifested itself regarding Bezel, "In wisdom, in understanding, in knowledge, and in all kinds of craftsmanship" (Exodus 31:3; c.f. Deut 34:9). God is not limited in the ways that He can help His people; rather, the Spirit chooses how to transfer special talents to his people to get God's work done, such as in this case, the building of the tabernacle. This provides an interesting allusion to the New Testament "gifts of the Spirit," which the Lord imparted to the church through the Spirit of God. In the Old Testament, God filled the people and worked it out so they could give financially to the building of the tabernacle, but in the New Testament, the church is His tabernacle, and so God builds up the church through the spiritual gifts. God, more than often, is thinking of the finished project (Eph 3:16–19). These spiritual gifts will be later discussed, but let us conclude that God's presence is strongly associated with the carrying out of His purpose by imparting certain knowledge and gifts in His people. Part of God's presence and purpose works itself out in holy life and character, but this is not mentioned in these verses. It's not that it wasn't present, but that it was not the emphasis here.

> On the other hand I am filled with power–with the Spirit of the LORD–And with justice and courage to make known to Jacob his rebellious act, even to Israel his sin (Micah 3:8).

Micah the prophet announces how the work of God's Spirit animated him to rebuke Israel with the hope that she might hear God's Word and respond to her sin by repentance. God's power was seen in His powerful words of encouragement given to Micah so that he could properly prophesy to Israel.

Other Phrases in the Old Testament

The Old Testament is filled with other phrases that share similar characteristics in being filled with the Spirit of God, which indicate:

(1) God's presence is with them (absent after 400 BC with no prophets and judges);

(2) God's willingness to communicate and exercise His will among His people; and

(3) The Lord's general ways of accomplishing His purposes.

Let's look at a few of these phrases.

For Moses, the "Spirit who is upon you" (Num 11:17) was taken and "placed Him upon the seventy elders...the Spirit rested upon them" (Num 11:25). Joshua is called "a man in whom is the Spirit" (Num 27:18). "The Spirit of the LORD came upon him" (Othniel the judge in Judges 3:9–10); likewise, "came upon" Judge Jephthah (Judges 11:29). The Spirit of the LORD (Yahweh) is said to repeatedly come upon Samson (Judges 13:25; 14:6,19). Prophet Samuel declared to Saul, "the Spirit of the LORD will come upon you mightily, and you shall prophesy with them and be changed into another man" (1 Sam 10:6). Then, one chapter later, the very thing occurred, "Then the Spirit of God came upon Saul mightily" (1 Sam 11:6) so that King Saul could properly lead the people according to God's ways. The Spirit of the LORD departed from Saul (1 Sam 16:14) and "the Spirit of the LORD came mightily upon David from that day forward" (1 Sam 16:13).

And so, the Old Testament records the powerful work of God through the Spirit of God when He selects and works in the lives of selected individuals. "Filling with" then seems quite similar to other phrases: "came upon," "rested upon," and "is upon" (Isaiah 61:1), while the purpose, which varies depending on the particular circumstances, also signifies God's hand in men's affairs, working through other humans—a pattern we see even more clearly in the New Testament. The Spirit of

God, then, worked more selectively in the Old Testament by filling certain individuals with His Spirit, empowering the man of God to carry out His special purposes, setting a pattern for God's work in the New Testament.

Let me summarize our many Old Testament observations. Moses desired that the Spirit to be upon more of God's people (Num 11:29) and even when the Spirit did come upon the seventy elders, it was only for a temporary time (Num 11:25), resulting only in one period of prophecy for that group. In the Old Testament, the Lord was moving closer to be with His people and yet not too close. "And you shall set bounds for the people all around, saying, 'Beware that you do not go up on the mountain or touch the border of it; whoever touches the mountain shall surely be put to death'" (Exodus 19:12; 19:21–24). Joshua and the elders were allowed to ascend only partway up the mountaintop (Exodus 24:9–15), and only Moses ascended all the way. Though the people were cleansed, they were not to touch the mountain unless God's wrath came upon them. The people of God, because of their sins, needed the limitations of the priesthood and tabernacle to keep their distance from the holy God, for their sins were not forgiven in the same way as sin is forgiven under the New Testament, wherein everything literally changed for the good.

We will close this section by referring to Zechariah 4:6, "This is the word of the Lord to Zerubbabel saying, 'Not by might nor by power, but by My Spirit,' says the Lord of hosts.'" The complex picture of two olive trees constantly filling the lamp of the Lord is a testament that ensures that the lamp will always be lit. The power of God's people is not in the institutions or buildings but in the Spirit of God that continually fills them.

B. Filled with the Spirit in the New Testament

The "filling of the Spirit" is regularly mentioned in the New Testament, establishing a link between Jesus' coming, His filling, and His filling (anointing) of us. By using the phrase "filled with" we are not trying to differentiate this with the other descriptive words but rather to indicate the greatness by which the Holy Spirit wants to come upon and influence all His people.

Before the sealing of the New Covenant on the cross, the Spirit only came selectively upon certain individuals as He did in the Old Testament: John the Baptist and others associated with Jesus' holy birth, and then Jesus Himself.

Before the New Covenant

- **John the Baptist's Birth**

  For he will be great in the sight of the Lord... and he will be filled with the Holy Spirit, while yet in his mother's womb" (Luke 1:15). "...when Elizabeth heard Mary's greeting, the baby leaped in her womb; and Elizabeth was filled with the Holy Spirit" (Luke 1:41). "...Zacharias was filled with the Holy Spirit, and prophesied" (Luke 1:67).

It is not just John the Baptist who was filled with the Spirit, or Zacharias the priest, but even Elizabeth—perhaps the first women this is said of—was filled with the Spirit of God. God's presence in Elizabeth initiated a special work of the Lord. God not only brought Elizabeth's miraculous birth of a son in her old age but openly declared the same through prophets and prophetesses so people would observe God's work and hear His Word.

- **Jesus' ministry**

  And the Holy Spirit descended upon Him in bodily form like a dove, and a voice came out of heaven, "Thou art My beloved Son, in Thee I am well-pleased" (Luke 3:22; Mark 1:10; John 1:32). "And Jesus, full of the Holy Spirit, returned from the Jordan and was led about by the Spirit in the wilderness (Luke 4:1; Matt 4:1; Mark 1:12).

Much can be said about Jesus and the Holy Spirit, some of which is discussed in other parts of this book. But our purpose here is to show that Jesus was also "full of the Holy Spirit" from the day of His baptism when the Holy Spirit descended upon Him like a dove. This is a picture of the Father anointing His Son, the Messiah, for His work. And so, Jesus' work was fully empowered by the Holy Spirit because it is said of Him that He was "full of the Holy Spirit." (I believe Jesus conducted His ministry through this filling rather than through His divinity, which He declined to use as noted in Phil 2:3–11.) "And Jesus returned to Galilee in the power of the Spirit; and news about Him spread through all the surrounding district" (Luke 4:14). This conclusion is important in several ways.

First, it shows that God's people would have the same Spirit working in their lives as Jesus had. Nothing, therefore, would need to hinder God's people from accomplishing His purposes. This truth builds up our faith. Second, the church is seen as a continuance of Jesus' ministry after His resurrection. Clearly, this is seen in John 14–16 and Acts, which will be further discussed later in this book. This is the reason the transfer of the mantle, so to speak, in Matthew 28:18–20 is so powerful. God's people are responsible to fulfill God's mission for the world. Third, we are very interested in the way the Holy Spirit would anoint the people of God. Lastly, the phrase "filled with" implies the presence and certain giftings of the Holy Spirit. The significance of being holy is to remind us that they are indicative of God's holy work and purposes.

After the New Covenant

The initiation of the New Covenant brought huge changes to how the Spirit of God would work in His people; rather than working in a few select individuals, the Spirit's purpose is to fill all of God's people to accomplish God's greater redemptive will. We conclude, therefore, that the people of God are now to be regularly filled with the Spirit of God, utilizing their Spirit-imparted gifts and living out holy lives all while accomplishing the mission to spread the Gospel of Jesus Christ to the world.

In the OT the Holy Spirit could not come close to God's people due to their sinfulness so they were shielded from God in the tabernacle.

In the NT the Holy Spirit can and does come and indwell in His people due to the forgiveness of sin through faith in Jesus' death on the cross.

The extra empowering is especially noticed in the huge thrust of sending the church out to the world starting in the Book of Acts but continues down to this day. When one sees a boat with big twin big engines, one might ask why they need such a powerful boat. More than often, they will tell you, it is for deep sea fishing. We don't want to go out into the ocean without two engines, in the case that one motor dies. And so, He empowers the church by gifting His people with the Holy Spirit, clearly identifying His intention, purpose, and means of powerfully working in and through the church.

The Spirit (of God) is used 64 times in Acts, which we can nicely separate into two sections: the church's birth and the church's life. In a later chapter, we will explore in more detail Ephesians 5 and Paul's use of "filled with the Spirit of God." We are merely touching upon this topic here and do not mean to be thorough. Tougher issues will be discussed separately toward the end of the book. Though the word "Spirit" is used 223 times in the New Testament, we will focus only on Acts here.

- **The Church's Birth in Acts**

  "For John baptized with water, but you shall be baptized with the Holy Spirit not many days from now" (Acts 1:5). "But you shall receive power when the Holy Spirit has come upon you" (1:8). "And they were all filled with the Holy Spirit and began to speak with other tongues, as the Spirit was giving them utterance" (Acts 2:4)....

With only these few verses, we can already see the great impact the Holy Spirit has had upon the church, just as Jesus predicted, "And behold, I am sending forth the promise of My Father upon you; but you are to stay in the city until you are clothed with power from on high" (Luke 24:49). This promise is exactly what Jesus reasserted prior to His final ascension to heaven (Acts 1:4–5), proving that the filling of the Spirit is to be identified with the phrase "baptized with."

The events mentioned in Acts 1 and 2 indicate the great changes upon the people of God. These chapters connect both the Old Testament and Jesus' words with what was happening in the believers' lives—Old Testament promises were realized. Acts 1, therefore, consists of a reiteration of the coming of the Spirit, His work in His followers' lives, and the affect He would have on them ("be My witnesses..." 1:8). They prayerfully waited for what Jesus told them would occur at the Feast of Pentecost when all the Jews had gathered together (2:1). Where before the antagonistic leaders were threatened by Jesus alone, they then faced thousands of believers similarly filled with the Holy Spirit. What powerful scenes of God's power are depicted in the first two chapters of Acts, the birth of the church led by the Spirit!

So who was "filled with the Holy Spirit" (Acts 2:4)? We should not limit the filling to only the apostles, though they indeed were filled as is evident in Peter's talk. But with the many languages that were spoken by a great number of people present, it is evident that many of the believers who waited upon the Lord in prayer were also filled. This is inferred (though not absolutely required) by the phrase, "all together in one place" and the Spirit infilling each of those present: "And at this time Peter stood up in the midst of the brethren (a gathering of about one hundred and twenty persons was there together)" (Acts 1:15).

This is further buttressed by Peter's speech in Acts 2 where he offers the promise of the Holy Spirit to all believers, "For the promise is for you and your children" (Acts 2:39). What promise? The same promise that Jesus had mentioned before He ascended, and that which the Old Testament scriptures speak of, "Therefore having been exalted to the right hand of God, and having received from the Father the promise of the Holy Spirit, He has poured forth this which you both see and hear" (Acts 2:33). How could Peter promise the Holy Spirit unless it was for all who would believe? One cannot wrestle with this powerful assertion, which is later amply testified to in the experiences of the believers in the remaining chapters of Acts, the epistles, and in church through the centuries. So, the 120 believers who were waiting upon the Holy Spirit's coming waited, and, as a result, they experienced the Spirit's power, which immediately spread to 3,000 people (Acts 2:41).

Please note that the filling of the Holy Spirit was linked to the baptism of the Spirit as predicted by John the Baptist: "He will baptize you with the Holy Spirit and fire" (Matt 3:11; Mark 1:8; Luke 3:16). Instead of working with a few individuals like the apostles, we see the Lord filling all of His people with the Spirit. The promise was for all who believed, which not only indicates union with God through forgiveness of sins but also the Spirit's indwelling presence. God is powerfully moving on earth, then and now. What and why is He doing such a thing?

The key event was the initiation of the new covenant through Jesus' blood, which greatly impacted all believers (Acts 2:37–40). Theologically, Peter worked it all out (Acts 2:22–33), understanding that God's Spirit could draw close to His people through faith. They are hidden from God's wrath in Christ the Messiah. The limitation of a greater outworking of the Spirit before Jesus' death on the cross was no longer a factor, and so, as Peter's sermon so clearly elaborates, the promises of the Spirit and all the associated blessings belong to all of God's people without partiality (Acts 2:39), to all who will call upon the Name of Jesus.

Filled with the Spirit

Focus on the Giver, not the gifts!

- **The Church's Life**

  "Then Peter, filled with the Holy Spirit, said..." (Acts 4:8). "And when they had prayed, the place where they had gathered together was shaken, and they were all filled with the Holy Spirit, and began to speak the word of God with boldness" (Acts 4:31). "And I remembered the word of the Lord, how He used to say, 'John baptized with water, but you shall be baptized with the Holy

Spirit" (Acts 11:16). "And the disciples were continually filled with joy and with the Holy Spirit" (Acts 13:52).

God is no longer occasionally working with one or two special believers as He did in the Old Testament but now works in the whole body of believers when the Spirit of God regularly fills their lives. The resurrected Jesus Christ continues to lead the people of God much as the LORD led the Israelites through the wilderness to get to the land of Canaan. As the anointing passed from Elijah to Elisha, so at Jesus' resurrection the anointing passed from Jesus to His people.

Admittedly, there are numerous passages—not a few in Acts itself—that raise questions about the characteristics of the filling of the Spirit, but all such evidence need to be seen in light of God's greater purposes for all of His people. God is powerfully at work living through His people in the world, creating a Christlike character and equipping them with spiritual gifts so they can get on with the job at hand, i.e., to make disciples of all nations (Matt 28:26–28). This is what we see throughout the book of Acts and beyond.

The Holy Spirit's International Effort

Joel prophesied well over several millenniums ago, "That I will pour forth of My Spirit upon all mankind" (Acts 2:17). Jesus told the disciples, "You shall be My witnesses both in Jerusalem, and in all Judea and Samaria, and even to the remotest part of the earth" (Acts 1:8). Peter accordingly stated, "For the promise is for you and your children, and for all who are far off, as many as the Lord our God shall call to Himself" (Acts 2:39). The biblical evidence of God's promises to reach the ends of the world—beyond the Jewish people—became a foundational teaching for the church because it was so different from what the Jews were practicing. This is the reason Jesus chose to come with the Spirit on Pentecost when those from every nation were present! It was the Tower of Babel crisis in reverse, where people from around the world were hearing the gospel in their own language, discovering God and being reunited with Him and His purposes through the gospel.

The whole book of Acts carries out this same theme, ending with Paul in Rome on house arrest and yet still preaching away to the nations, "Preaching the kingdom of God, and teaching concerning the Lord Jesus Christ with all openness, unhindered" (Acts 28:31). How the church changed in those first short years! The outline of Acts reinforces this whole idea by tracing how the Spirit of God was constantly, and yet differently, prodding His people to preach the gospel and make disciples around the world. There were some significant roadblocks, largely from among the Jews, but the Lord fashioned one church (Eph 3:6) with one leader (Himself) by carefully establishing this truth to His people. Instead of looking for repeatable circumstances, we should see these scenes of the Holy Spirit at work in three breakthroughs (four if Pentecost is included), which provide an outline for the book of Acts. Each point serves as one way the Lord kept the church together under one head (the Jewish apostles and the God of the scriptures) while breaking into different people groups. Let's briefly look at each breakthrough.

The Acts outline below demonstrably shows that the Holy Spirit is filling individuals from all people groups to expand into the world. Speaking in tongues is evidence of such a filling, a reflection of what happened at Pentecost, but it is not the prime characteristic of it. This speaking of tongues was important at that stage because of two reasons: (1) It paralleled the miraculous speaking of tongues associated with

God's coming to fill His people in Acts 1–2—the birth of the church, and (2) speaking languages that foreigners could only understand provided clear outward evidence that the Spirit of God had accepted them and filled them with His Holy Spirit. In other words, the half-Jews or Gentiles were not to be considered second class or inferior to the Jews in the church. God would equally reside in them all and empower them to be used by God in His great mission to spread the gospel.

The book of Acts can be broken down into three significant sections:

A. Gospel in Jerusalem: Origins (1:12–7)

B. Gospel in Samaria and Judea: Transition (8–10)

C. Gospel in the Uttermost Parts: Expansion (11–28)

The first section, the birth of the church, was about God moving mightily among the Jews, even though many lived around the world. The speaking of languages played an essential role in establishing the fact that God was for all the Jews, no matter where they lived. The international seekers at Pentecost were asking how the Jews were speaking these various languages, saying, "What does this mean?" (2:12). Peter affirms, starting in verse 17, that God promised to send the Spirit upon all the peoples, men and women, young and old alike. The variety of spoken languages only confirmed the presence of the Spirit, an explanation as to how they could and did prophesy in so many languages. Joel only indicated that they would prophesy, but Peter answered their question by stating that the fact of God working in these foreigners (including Gentiles converted to Judaism) could be verified by having the prophecies in their own languages! The focus was on the filling of the Holy Spirit (Acts 2:17) not on the languages. The languages at this time only gave evidence of the Spirit's filling, a fact nobody could deny.

The same thing, though, with some variances and on smaller scales, happened twice more in the book of Acts, each time being a moment when the Holy Spirit led the church to breach a wall of cultural separation. When they reached the second wall between the gospel and the Samaritans—who were seen as dogs and compromisers of faith— there was significant resistance to be overcome. Note how the Lord broke the old stereotypes:

> While Peter was still speaking these words, the Holy Spirit fell upon all those who were listening to the message. And all the circumcised believers who had come with Peter were amazed because the gift of the Holy Spirit had been poured out upon the Gentiles also. For they were hearing them speaking with tongues and exalting God. Then Peter answered, "Surely no one can refuse the water for these to be baptized who have received the Holy Spirit just as we did, can he?" And he ordered them to be baptized in the name of Jesus Christ. Then they asked him to stay on for a few days (Acts 10:44– 48).

After sharing the gospel with them, Cornelius the Roman centurion and his Jewish friends who had gathered with him, witnessed all these things that happened. The order of events is important. They were baptized with water after the Spirit came upon them after they heard the gospel. In other words, when they believed, the Spirit of God came upon these Gentiles "who have received the Holy Spirit just as we did...." Peter and the others saw the "speaking with tongues and exalting God" to be of like character to what happened at Pentecost, clearly demonstrating the Spirit of God also coming upon the centurion and his friends. So, Peter baptized them. This all followed the vision that Peter had earlier on in chapter 10, in which the Lord directed Peter to go along to Cornelius' house. So here was a Gentile but also a man who loved the things of God. The Lord told Cornelius, "Your prayers and alms have ascended as a memorial before God" (Acts 10:2).

In conclusion, we see the same thing happen in chapter 10 as happened in chapter 2, where God framed a teaching moment that confirmed to those present that the Lord was also going to save people other than Jews, even if they were not true Jews there in the land of Galilee.

> And opening his mouth, Peter said: "I most certainly understand now that God is not one to show partiality, but in every nation the man who fears Him and does what is right, is welcome to Him. "The word which He sent to the sons of Israel, preaching peace through Jesus Christ (He is Lord of all)--you yourselves know the thing which took place throughout all Judea, starting from Galilee (Acts 10:34–37).

Even Peter had to be persuaded to see that what Jesus told them had actually occurred. The gospel would go to Galilee and be spread to the many non-Jews. This section of Acts proves that the gospel would enter "all Judea and Samaria" (Acts 1:8), which included Philip in Samaria. Persecution closely followed the breakthroughs. "Then they began laying their hands on them, and they were receiving the Holy Spirit" (Acts 8:17). The Ethiopian eunuch traveling on a road going to Gaza (Acts 8:26), Saul's conversion and preaching of the Gospel (Acts 9:29–31), and then in Joppa where Cornelius and the Roman fortress was located (Acts 9:36–40).

In some cases, the miraculous speech in other languages was associated with the filling of the Holy Spirit to help convince those, like Peter, who at that time held a more traditional Jewish mindset. When convinced, the Lord used Peter to persuade other Jewish Christian leaders (Acts

11:15): "And God, who knows the heart, bore witness to them, giving them the Holy Spirit, just as He also did to us; and He made no distinction between us and them, cleansing their hearts by faith" (Acts 15:8–9).

The only other time that speaking in tongues is associated with the filling of the Spirit in Acts also served as a significant teaching moment, this time proving that the Spirit was working in Gentiles in faraway Ephesus (Acts 19:1–7). The book of Acts proves that God's work was to reach "even to the remotest part of the earth" (Acts 1:8). Our concern is not to show that speaking in tongues is always associated with being filled with the Spirit but that, in these cases, because of what happened in Acts 2, the speaking in tongues gave evidence of the connection to their experience at Pentecost, convincing even the most recalcitrant disciples that God really meant business when it came to reaching the world's populations.

> And he said to them, "Did you receive the Holy Spirit when you believed?" And they said to him, "No, we have not even heard whether there is a Holy Spirit." And he said, "Into what then were you baptized?" And they said, "Into John's baptism." And Paul said, "John baptized with the baptism of repentance, telling the people to believe in Him who was coming after him, that is, in Jesus." And when they heard this, they were baptized in the name of the Lord Jesus. And when Paul had laid his hands upon them, the Holy Spirit came on them, and they began speaking with tongues and prophesying. And there were in all about twelve men (Acts 19:2–7).

There was confusion on whether what Apollos was doing and his teaching was connected to the gospel of Jesus Christ, for they had only heard of John the Baptist and his baptism. It is only when they heard about Jesus Christ and were baptized in His name that the same Holy

Spirit filled them (proving that they were baptized of the Spirit of God like John earlier prophesied), giving evidence of it by speaking in tongues and prophesying. The group of twelve men was not big, but the scene significantly united this tiny movement to its mother movement among the Jews associated with Jesus Christ.

The filling of the Spirit showed how the work of God was penetrating geographical and racial barriers. The word "tongues" was given only in these three places in Acts (Acts 2:3,4,11; 10:46, 19:6) to show that it was the same Holy Spirit who was associated with the resurrection of Jesus according to His promise. Our understanding of speaking in tongues should not be formulated from these isolated sections to the conclusion that all believers who are truly filled with the Spirit of God will speak in tongues. The phrase "filled with the Holy Spirit" or something similar is used many times without any mention of speaking in different languages.

Our conclusion, then, is that God, early in the life of the church, used those who spoke formerly unknown languages to prove the prophecies and the exaltation of God associated with their belief in the resurrected Lord Jesus Christ in sending the gospel outwards to the world. For the early church leaders, the speaking of prophecies in different languages was significant because of the one-time Acts 2 incident, which they had witnessed. These believers, then, though they were from places like Samaria or were Gentiles and other various nationalities, were also true believers and on equal standing with the Jews who believed in Jesus the Messiah. With the proof of this lesson, there is no need for every believer to speak in foreign languages to prove they believe or are filled with the Spirit. These lessons in Acts were given by God to teach the church to accept these new members as equal, which, thankfully, they did. There is a gift of foreign language, but that is given as the Lord sees fit, but not to all (1 Cor 12:28–30). Now let's look more carefully at how the filling of the Spirit was treated in a mature church—the church at Ephesus.

C. Filled with the Spirit (Eph 5:17–21)

After following a long trail through the book of Acts, we can turn back to one passage that Paul used to clarify some of the confusion regarding the filling of the Spirit.

> So then do not be foolish, but understand what the will of the Lord is. 18 And do not get drunk with wine, for that is dissipation, but be filled with the Spirit, 19 speaking to one another in psalms and hymns and spiritual songs, singing and making melody with your heart to the Lord; 20 always giving thanks for all things in the name of our Lord Jesus Christ to God, even the Father; 21 and be subject to one another in the fear of Christ (Eph 5:17–21).

What we first notice is that there is a command to be "filled with the Spirit" (Eph 5:18). This section interestingly answers the questions, "What does it practically mean to be filled in the Spirit?" The reason Paul points this out is probably because of the confusion over the phrase "filled with the Spirit." Obviously, there were some who might have connected it to experiences similar to those filled with alcohol. He needed to first disassociate the filling of the Holy Spirit from these kind of "experiences" along with other wrong associations; only then could he teach the believers a proper understanding of being filled with the Spirit.

Paul starts in a bar or tavern where people are getting their glasses filled with wine or alcohol. Many people drink at night, sometimes on the way home, while others after reaching home. The point is the same—

they are looking for a little escape from the pressures of the world. We don't blame them, but it should not characterize believers, who have something incomparably better.

"Not get drunk with wine" stands as an obvious contrast with being "filled with the Spirit." Paul clearly directs us first to restrain ourselves from drunkenness. Wine is a depressant and certain levels can intoxicate people and make them unruly. Not a few marriages have been destroyed by the effects that alcohol had on husbands who beat their wives. Paul is contrasting this pattern of the world with what believers have—i.e., being filled with the Spirit of God. The believers center their world around greater expectations found in their relationship with God through Jesus Christ when the Holy Spirit fills His people.

"Filled" speaks of an abounding amount, wholly influenced by the Spirit (walk, guided, empowered). "Behold, the glory of the LORD filled the house" (Ezek 43:5). When one is filled with wine, that person can be influenced to a point in which he loses perspicuity, but when a person is filled with the Spirit of God, he is given super clarity to God's will (5:17). Although Paul only mentions the Spirit, we should definitely consider this to be same Holy Spirit mentioned throughout Acts, since we know that God through Jesus the Lord now actively works in the lives of His people. Since this is a command, it is a given that any believer at any time can obey this command and enter a time of being helped and encouraged by the Spirit of God. This command derives from Jesus' promise, "And I am with you to the end" (Matt 28:28).

"Be filled with the Spirit" reminds us that no matter what our Christian heritage and possible discomfort with this phrase—and yes, it has been wrongly used at times—the importance of this command still stands. On the one hand, we are not to fear being affected by God's presence for

He is a God of order, wisdom, love, and has been working out His grand redemption plan. On the other hand, there is specific fruit of the Spirit that we can look forward to.

Paul supplies four aspects of what it means to be filled with the Spirit of God. In general, we can see ourselves with other believers celebrating God's salvation and presence in our lives. The first three all have to do with praise and adoration (Acts 2:11; 10:46), while the last assures a proper attitude when living in fellowship with other believers.

(1) "Speaking to one another in psalms and hymns and spiritual songs" (Eph 5:19) stresses not the chemically induced charge of loud music via adrenaline,[16] which stimulates the flesh, but the awesome corporate use of truth in worship. Notice that he mentions the use of words: speaking. What is focused upon is not the music, but the words enhanced by the music. Psalms are songs derived from the psaltery. Hymns are traditional praise songs used in churches, and spiritual songs are those more lively tunes that inspire us and are usually focused on certain themes.

(2) "Making melody with your heart to the Lord" (Eph 5:19) reminds us of how God wants to engage our minds with words of truth in our hearts as we express our delight in the Him. Worship, in the end, is unto the Lord where our hearts delight in Him.

(3) "Always giving thanks" compels us to focus on God's goodness and intimate work in our lives. The Spirit of God will lift your soul when we focus on God's solutions rather than our problems.

---

[16] "It turns out that loud sounds directly affect our autonomic nervous system (also called involuntary - it controls the body functions that you hope never stop, like breathing and digestion), in a way similar to many stimulant drugs. Adrenaline is released, the heart rate speeds up, the guts tighten up and move. This is the rush you get from loud music—it's real and it's beyond your conscious control. Sounds addicting doesn't it?"
www.experiencingworship.com/worship-articles/sound/2001-9-How-Loud-is.html

(4) "Be subject to one another in the fear of Christ" (Eph 5:21) hints at the necessity of good relationships with others to have a close relationship with God rather than arrogance.

Interestingly, there is no mention of the need to speak in foreign languages, even though this is one of the places where speaking "in tongues" took place (Acts 19:6). This is simply because Paul, and Jesus, I believe, are much more interested in the fruit of the filling of the Holy Spirit than the evidence of having the Holy Spirit since that transitional period of proof has already passed. Paul would have mentioned speaking in foreign languages if it was commonly associated with the filling of the Holy Spirit, but he didn't. Paul instead leads us in a different direction, which is something the entire church needs to embrace, though he does still focus on the full acceptance of the international believers in the church (Eph chapters 2-3). The filling of the Spirit is a centerpiece of the Christian experience, speaking in tongues is not; it is only one aspect of a gift that is for some and not all Christian believers. Alcohol confuses the mind, whereas the Spirit of God directs our mind upon God's glory, providing inspiring songs, praise, and thanks.

Conclusion

God has opened the door for us to experience "an abundant life" (John 10:10) through the way the Spirit of God stirs and guides our spiritual lives. Those things that some associate with the filling of the Holy Spirit (e.g., being slain, laughing, tongues, etc.) are not at all mentioned here; rather, it is worship, being stirred by His truths, delight in God, giving

thanks, and humbly serving others that proves the Spirit in our lives. Spiritual gifts and fruit are an outcome of the Spirit's filling rather than the prime characteristic of God's holy presence (Isaiah 6:4).

The Holy Spirit comes upon His people in special ways in order to carry out the Father's glorious work. God wants us to be filled with the Spirit and to reject any disguised longing for the world. If we long for the world, then we are missing the glorious will of the Father. The new covenant depicts a new age in which the Spirit of God lives out Christ's life in believers. By staying close to God in worship and maintaining close relationships with others, we can embrace the greater filling of God's Spirit in our lives.

Discussion Questions

1. What are some differences in the way the Spirit filled people in the New Testament versus the Old Testament?

2. What are some similarities?

3. Why could God work so differently and intimately with His people in the New Testament?

4. How is the world's way of gaining excitement, through drugs and alcohol, different from the Christian who is excited through the filling of the Spirit?

5. What are three characteristics of a person being filled with the Holy Spirit?

6. What really happened at Pentecost?

7. What was so significant about the use of tongues (i.e., foreign languages) in the book of Acts?

8. What does it mean for you to be filled with the Holy Spirit? Please explain.

Life in the Spirit!

#10 The Instruction of the Spirit (John 16:13)

Life in the Spirit!
Experiencing the Fullness of Christ

The Holy Spirit's teacher function includes all aspects of His teaching ministry: timely revealing truth, delivery of knowledge, and imparting of wisdom. Behind this whole discussion, of course, is the recognition that God's knowledge is essential to strong, growing Christians. Like a caring parent, the Holy Spirit conveys especially needed divine knowledge to establish strong Christian lives to serve Him because He wants them to succeed.

A. The Need for the Spirit's Revealing (John 16:13–15)

The setting for this passage in John 16 significantly took place the night before Jesus was crucified. Jesus knew that, within hours, the whole world would become dark, adopting a vicious and threatening posture, which thus stirred Him to pray for and comfort His disciples (and us!). The major theme centers on the coming of the Holy Spirit. The Spirit would, from then on, accompany the disciples just as Jesus had done up to that point.

> 13 But when He, the Spirit of truth, comes, He will guide you into all the truth; for He will not speak on His own initiative, but whatever He hears, He will speak; and He will disclose to you what is to come 14 He shall glorify Me; for He shall take of Mine, and shall disclose it to you. 15 All things that the Father has are Mine; therefore I said, that He takes of Mine, and will disclose it to you (John 16:13–15).

The Need for Truth

What a momentous time, not just for Jesus, but for His disciples and the ongoing vision of the kingdom of God. What would Jesus say? Fortunately, several chapters record His precious words (John 13–17). Chapter 17 even describes Jesus' own conversation with God the Father. The Holy Spirit is intricately connected to helping the disciples during the coming crisis and the furthering of the gospel, but perhaps most intriguing is how important the truth is to them and us, even today. We might ask, "Why is the truth so important when people are threatening our life?"

John 16:13

The Spirit of truth...will guide you
He will speak
He will disclose to you

This whole issue is brought before us in the description of the Holy Spirit as the "Spirit of truth," which associates Him with truth, almost as though it's a name: Spirit Truth. This name has several implications, including the fact that the Holy Spirit is a faithful communicator. He will only say what He has heard. This makes His own words fully reliable, equivocating His words with truth. But still, most of us do not understand how the truth becomes such a key part of our lives.

The other important aspect to keep in mind is the contrast to the serpent of old, who craftily presented words to mislead. While those words led to death, the Spirit's words are good words that lead us to life. Truth includes words of guidance, instruction, and comfort that God brings to our needy souls in good time, thus strengthening us for His work and faithful service.

The Coming

The Holy Spirit is said to be coming, as expanded on in a former chapter, "The Filling of the Spirit." The Upper Room Discourse happened several days before Jesus' resurrection, making the coming day of the Holy Spirit (16:13) to be that year's Pentecost (Acts 2:1), which was a mere 53 days later. When Jesus died, His blood (i.e., death) was used to establish the New Covenant, which initiated a whole new way of relating to God and carrying out His work.

The repetitive use of "will" in John 16:13 describes how believers will be shaped by the Spirit's ongoing teaching ministry. This is a description of the new position of the Holy Spirit, defining His constant relationship with us. For example, it says, He "will guide you into all the truth," which implies that He will instruct us on how He will strategically lead us into knowing the truth. A good example of guidance is providing updated directions for a path that we are following. The GPS, for example, at each significant junction brings further clarification. The Spirit's advice might not be so instantaneous or clearcut as expected, but it can always be relied on. We can trust Him for the timeliness and accuracy for the extra information. I remember once where a GPS app led my family to this darkened building rather than our desired hotel, which we later found was three miles away. That app was definitely not accurate or trustworthy. This is not, however, true with the Holy Spirit.

"He shall glorify Me; for He shall take of Mine, and shall disclose it to you." Notice how the Holy Spirit will pass insight from the Father to those in need. God the Father is constantly reassessing our situation to timely pass on all the knowledge we need, requiring our attentiveness (this requires spiritual disciplines on our part) so to give the Father glory. Since it is future oriented—"He will disclose to you what is to come"—knowing God never faces any surprises, which in turn provides calmness to our souls. "Disclose" is used three times, meaning "to announce." If we need any knowledge, even regarding things that have not yet happened, then He can and will declare them to us.

In the diagram on the right, the circle stands for the filling of the Spirit. God's Spirit lives onsite, ready to communicate as needed. He is not us but He does live in us. When He receives information (always truth), the Spirit timely passes it on to us (the downward arrow). This, in turn, affects our decisions, as seen in the left and right

Instruction of Believers

arrows. It also shapes our heart of praise, filled with thanksgiving to God (upward arrows). As this scenario is repeated, we see how the Lord works in and through us to His glory.

The Lord connects this pattern of guidance to Himself because, in turn, it produces further reliance, peace, obedience, attentive awareness of His words, and thanks to Him. This cycle builds up our trust and relationship with God so that we can constantly delight in His favor toward us, not because of our goodness but because of His mercy shown at the cross and in our daily lives.

I will give an example of how this works with the next point, but it is crucial to learn how God wants to regularly teach us. We, normal believers, all need His teaching and, amazingly, He teaches us. When we make this connection, our relationship with Him is all of a sudden greatly strengthened. The problem is that many believers have never made this connection. Either they think God only teaches us at crisis points or that they cannot discern His teaching in their lives—the latter occurs largely because they never look for it! Let me further expand on the later point.

How the Spirit Teaches Us

The Spirit of God fills us, but how does He communicate with us? He takes from the Father and compiles it in words to impart to us the needed knowledge and faith. This communication regularly happens. Some believers say, "God never speaks to me," but if they are genuine believers, then certainly the Father has spoken to them as His children. God the Father is not a reprobate father, ignoring the needs of His children. The real problem is that we have not discerned His voice. The Spirit typically brings words to our minds (i.e., teaches us). The evil one prompts us too, but we call that temptation.

We need to train our minds to discern His words because they can be easily missed. When God's people daily meet with their Lord, they create space in which they can pause and be alert to the words and thoughts being brought to their minds during their "quiet times." This special attention to our thoughts should later be developed to the extent that we regularly check our thoughts through the day. This helps us discern temptations, words from the evil one that cause fear, dismay, etc., leading to disobedience. When we are attentive to God, we will more easily spot the demons' words and be able to reject them as false words loaded with ill motive. The devil always wants us to assess our situation apart from God and His good purposes and in this way pass off his lies to us. But God always cares for us as a Father who tenderly leads us, using His words to encourage, warn, guide, teach, and otherwise build up our faith, resulting in obedience.

Many Christians have not heard about this form of communication that leads to deeper communion with God, even though it is clearly spoken of in the Scriptures. Abiding in His Word strengthens our faith, which in turn brings glory to God (John 15:1-6). Originally, this chapter was meant to be part of the next section, but the more I thought of it, the more I saw that this instruction is needed for all believers; similarly to how prayer forms a daily part of our spiritual disciplines. I moved this chapter to this 'island' so that it concludes this major section on the instruction of the Spirit, providing the general foundation for a strong Christian life.

One huge problem with many Christians is that they live by their feelings and are ignorant of the thoughts that come to their minds from God. They live as orphans. Sin will always muddy up our minds making it so that we cannot think straight. But even if we deal with that through the cross, most believers remain unaware of how God speaks to them. No wonder they quickly again become ensnared! Perhaps this extra strength and confidence derived from hearing from God is what drives the charismatic movement forward. They are convinced God speaks with them. They are not learning only from what Christ has done on the cross, but on how He communes with them now. They look for revelation, instruction, guidance, etc., and so receive more. Some of us fear these various ways the Lord might instruct us even though they are common in the Bible. This communion with the Father is not gift-associated—only for a few—but for all of His children. Just think of how a father early on tries to communicate with his little child, "Say, 'Daddy.'" "Here you go." "Say please." The Father uses various means to help us recognize His words and properly respond to Him.

Does This Passage Apply?

Believers can rightly question the correctness of applying the John 16 teaching to our lives because it was first spoken to the disciples in a particular situation. It is also stated that these teachings chiefly apply to the forthcoming apostles, but I think it's fair to conclude that these truths also apply to all believers, the reason being that the Holy Spirit similarly helps all of God's people. The Spirit powerfully lead the apostles through the time of the cross and into the time of Acts, but we are also led to conclude that He is functioning in similar ways with all believers even into today's age.

Jesus was teaching this not only for the disciples but to show how He would differently relate to His children under the New Covenant. With the forgiveness of sin, believers can regularly commune with the Father —i.e., "pray without ceasing." What a difference there is now that we can pray in Jesus' Name!

This conclusion is also confirmed through the many verses that show how the Lord teaches and leads His people. John said it this way to all the believers: "But you have an anointing from the Holy One, and you all know" (1 John 2:20).

> And as for you, the anointing which you received from Him abides in you, and you have no need for anyone to teach you; but as His anointing teaches you about all things, and is true and is not a lie, and just as it has taught you, you abide in Him (1 John 2:27).

Clearly, John was affirming that the anointing that was upon them was due to the Holy Spirit's presence, who is now with all the believers so to be taught by Him.

Summary

In summary, Jesus taught that the Holy Spirit would come and teach the disciples. These words undoubtedly greatly helped the disciples during this crisis time, but Jesus' words not only described how God would work in their lives during that one incident and in their general ministries but for all the believers since the Holy Spirit functions with people in the New Covenant, not just in the apostles. The whole Pentecost scene and the book of Acts clearly show God equally working in believers across the spectrum of cultures. It all makes sense. God the Father takes the knowledge that believers need to know and passes it on to them through the Holy Spirit (Romans 8:14,16). Because of the deception of the evil one, we need to possess that knowledge of truth, which provides a security feature to our faith. For this and other reasons, this becomes an added reason to carefully seek the Lord in His Word and be attentive to the Holy Spirit's instruction.

Spiritual transformation requires a reordering of one's decisions in light of new insights the Spirit brings to our attention from God's Word.

B. The Holy Spirit's Personal Presence (John 14:26)

But the Helper, the Holy Spirit, whom the Father will send in My name, He will teach you all things, and bring to your remembrance all that I said to you (John 14:26).

"The Helper, the Holy Spirit" (Greek *parakletos*; *Paraklete*) has many functions but chiefly serves as the one who comes alongside a person to comfort, guide, or help. It further defines the Spirit's various abilities and responsibilities to work with all the disciples, as their counselor, teacher, guide, and pastor. In a later chapter, we will speak of spiritual gifts or general functions of the Holy Spirit in believers, making us all fully reliant on the Spirit's instruction and empowerment. The Bible teacher, then, should be fully attentive to the Holy Spirit in order to properly do his job. The same is true with counselors. The real counselor is the Holy Spirit. This verse shows how dependent we are on Him to do His will. We are merely the vessels that He fills so that we can use His words and thoughts to lovingly carry out His will. In a personal way, I am overwhelmed by how the Holy Spirit springs new thoughts into my mind and causes a deep desire for Him and His word.

Although we usually think of the words, "The Holy Spirit, whom the Father will send in My name" to be important in helping the disciples endure the next couple of gruesome days, starting with the betrayal. Jesus was also probably thinking of the ongoing work of the Holy Spirit after the resurrection and ascension. Jesus is assuring all His followers that He will continue to personally lead them, though differently, through the Holy Spirit. Jesus says, "I will ask the Father, and He will give you another Helper, that He may be with you forever" (John 14:16; Matt 28:20). This word "another" means another of the same kind. In other words, the Holy Spirit represents Jesus Himself. As much as Jesus comforted and guided the disciples when He walked alongside them in Israel, so now the invisible Holy Spirit fills and guides all of His people across the world. Jesus was one, but the Spirit is able to simultaneously fill all of God's people. The image is spectacular, giving the disciples and all His people a glorious promise of intimacy, personal help, guidance, and assistance on our mission.

The mention of "all things" includes all things that the Lord will convey to us through the Holy Spirit that we might be fully equipped to live for Him. The Holy Spirit personally teaches and instructs us so that we can triumph in accomplishing God's purposes. Since each Christian is "anointed" (lit. *Christos*), we can all be assured that the Spirit is working in us in the same general way He did with the apostles or even Jesus. We only need to turn to the book of Acts to discover the Holy Spirit actively working in the apostles and many other believers (e.g., Stephen, Apollos).

"He will teach" reflects the two-fold teaching ministry of the Holy Spirit:

> **New truths:** "He will teach you all things" releases the limits that might otherwise hinder our confidence in the Holy Spirit's ministry to our lives. We can trust Him to teach us what we need to know even in the most difficult circumstances. If He doesn't teach us, then we need not know it—even though we might be curious. However, sometimes He teaches us while we are not very attentive so we need to lead the lifestyle that enhances good times with the Lord or we will miss His valuable guidance.

> **Old truths:** "Bring to your remembrance all that I said to you" can be used not only of Jesus' words to the disciples but the truths from the Word of God that God has formerly taught us. This shows us the great need to memorize God's Word and place it on the "back burners" of our minds so that it can be instantly recalled. Let me

share with you one instance when the Holy Spirit did this very thing!

Back in the early days of the BFF ministry, I wrote in my journal describing my responses to my Indian colleague's email. I told him "I only have enough to get there to India but not back. I believe God will raise the money. But I was not prepared for this $8,000 budget." The time was short. I already was short the money for a return flight. Because of the lack of faith of not having money for a flight, I didn't apply for a visa. At that point Pastor Stephen told me the $8,000 amount I needed for the seminar, which only added the impossibility of me holding the teaching seminars that were less than ten days away. I had no problem spending that money on those pastors who were attending these training seminars. After all, it was only about $14 per pastor for three days including meals and lodging, but the hundreds of pastors attending escalated the cost. Besides, I only could get there but had no money for the seminar itself. We had no personal savings, and the BFF ministry was living on bare-bone finances.

I became extremely worried—which is rather unlike me, but we all know that whenever a person allows worry in, it will drive him batty. I was so anxious that I could not focus on my message preparation. Instead, I walked around and around in my postage stamp–sized backyard. At a certain point, I confessed my sin and pleaded for help. God brought His immediate help through two scriptures that He brought to the forefront of my mind.

The first one was, "You give them something to eat!"(Luke 9:13; Mark 6:37). In other words, the Lord took a passage that I was very familiar with and applied it to my situation. I knew about the feeding of the five thousand. Images associated with this passage instantly flooded my mind, seeing the 5,000 men and families, all hungry and desirous to hear God's Word. As I heard Him speak (not vocally but the insertion of words in my mind), my faith grew, giving me confidence that He would care for everything even though the time was ridiculously short.

I should give them God's Word and care for their physical needs. God wants to feed them through me. This realization helped me in two ways. First, it gave me faith to believe in what God wanted. I could trust that He would help me feed them spiritually. But, behind the scenes, there was another issue: the food, which is what made it so expensive— physically feeding these pastors. I could now also trust the Lord to provide for both.

A second phrase popped into my mind after I had digested the first, "What do you have?" This question stemmed from the scriptures: "How many loaves do you have?" (Mark 6:38; Matt 15:34). This was extremely significant because it reminded me not to focus on what I needed but on what I had. I was to examine what I had and dedicate it to the Lord's use. Earlier, I was thoroughly frustrated, not knowing what to do, but now I had faith to do what I needed with the small amount of money that I then had. They, after all, only had a few fish and loaves, but I trusted that the Lord would take what I had and bring in the rest as needed. So I took what I had and sent away for a visa, late as it was. When money came in for a ticket, I got a ticket—even though I did not have money for the full budget. I used what I had when I had it.

In the end, in a short time, we received many thousands of dollars, enough to both spiritually and physically feed them. We gave our five loaves and two fish, and God multiplied it so that the final adjusted amount of $9,900 was provided. I was so humbled by all of this.

Meanwhile, God wonderfully blessed the many pastors and evangelists in India.

My main point here is to show you how God used specific scriptures and their context to direct me and build up my faith. Some might call it a promise, but I saw it as a building block of my faith wherein I could now trust in what He wanted, no matter how He decided to complete His project.

Summary

Jesus might not be physically present but through the Holy Spirit He is by our side and so we need to seriously follow Him. When the Spirit is leading, Jesus is leading!

C. The Spirit our Teacher (Luke 12:12)

I chose these following verses from Luke 12 for two reasons. First, they depict physical threats similar to the ones Jesus prepared His disciples for in the Upper Room Discourse. Crises are always difficult to handle and extra comfort and guidance is important. Second, I chose them because they clearly refer to all believers and not just the apostles.

> And I say to you, My friends, do not be afraid of those who kill the body, and after that have no more that they can do (Luke 12:4).
>
> And when they bring you before the synagogues and the rulers and the authorities, do not become anxious about how or what you should speak in your defense, or what you should say; 12 For the Holy Spirit will teach you in that very hour what you ought to say (Luke 12:11-12).

Jesus starts by calling them His friends, "My friends, do not be afraid" (Luke 12:4). He speaks directly to all believers who face dangers, not just the apostles. Jesus expected these kinds of hostile situations to arise at times. Anti-Christian terrorist activities have been increasing in intensity in recent years for many of Jesus' followers. Certainly, our lives extend much longer than here below on earth (i.e., eternal life), so our comfort is in how Jesus will restore all things in the age to come. Man can only kill the body and not the soul.

Jesus clearly communicates how He will bring special comfort to His people under persecution: "The Holy Spirit will teach you" (Luke 12:10–12). Stephen, for example, though powerfully gifted, was allowed by God to be stoned to death. "And they went on stoning Stephen as he called upon the Lord and said, 'Lord Jesus, receive my spirit!'" (Acts 7:59) The Holy Spirit knew how to bring extra wisdom and confidence to Stephen to proclaim his last sermon to his persecutors, which is still recorded in the scriptures. Stephen saw Jesus standing in heaven, carefully overseeing his stoning. The point is that believers will at times face serious situations, but the Holy Spirit will always be there to instruct, comfort, and otherwise help His people. Here are some other verses that speak of how those who heard the gospel were persecuted but found comfort in the "joy of the Holy Spirit." They not only had endurance but joy!

> You also became imitators of us and of the Lord, having received the word in much tribulation with the joy of the Holy Spirit (1 Thes 1:6).

> But we should always give thanks to God for you, brethren beloved by the Lord, because God has chosen you from the beginning for salvation through sanctification by the Spirit and faith in the truth (2 Thes 2:13).

"Teach you" similarly expresses how the Holy Spirit not only passes needed knowledge on to us but does it with the purpose of fine tuning our priorities and commitments—in this case, to be a faithful witness.

Given the extreme pressures, we can be sure that the Holy Spirit will speak. Don't allow fears and worries to drown out His comforting Word: "In that very hour what you ought to say." This does not limit the Spirit to teaching us but comforts us by assuring us that what we need to know will be passed on. We can fully trust Him.

All believers then can find comfort in the sovereign wisdom of the Holy Spirit to pass on Jesus' resurrected comfort and wisdom by timely bringing to our minds what we need to know. While Jesus was limited to one place at a time, the Holy Spirit is everywhere at once with all His disciples providing not mere information but God's perspective (truth) for situations, which issues faith.

Summary

1) The Spirit is teaching! Are you learning?
2) The Spirit is by our side (*Paraclete*)! Do you have peace?
3) The Spirit is with us in emergencies! Do you trust Him?

A mature believer is characterized by constantly leaning on the Father's knowledge, wisdom, and comfort that is brought by the Holy Spirit, who not only takes truth and teaches us but actually comforts, rebukes, and helps the believer, depending on his/her circumstances, even in difficult ministry and oppressive situations.

God is not irrelevant but wonderfully available and capable of bringing His knowledge and guidance to help us properly conduct our daily lives, whether it be comforting a grieving brother or directing a stray brother. Jesus is with us by being present and working through the Spirit's help and instruction. This lesson's foundational truth is simply that we desperately need God's Spirit to live out our daily lives and that we should seek Him for that wisdom and needed strength. "But if any of you lacks wisdom, let him ask of God, who gives to all men generously and without reproach, and it will be given to him" (James 1:5). By humbly seeking knowledge, we can catch the Holy Spirit's message, which gives us God's perspective.

Discussion Questions

1. What kinds of things does God help us know? Please give an example of how the Holy Spirit has taught you.

2. The truth of God is clearly important to living a strong Christian life. What are some ways you regularly bring His Truth into your mind so that the Holy Spirit can "remind" you?

3. How does God's promise to those who are suffering persecutions show His full control over their distressing situations?

4. What is one thing you learned about God "speaking" from the example of the mission trip to India?

5. How does Jesus reign and the Holy Spirit connect?

6. What are some ways the Spirit of God has "taught" or "disclosed" something to you or others that have helped you (or others) to rightly live or minister?

Section 3: Christian Service:
Faith and Filling

"But you shall receive power when the Holy Spirit has come upon you; and you shall be My witnesses" (Acts 1:8).

This third port enables us to hop off onto the island of Christian Service, where we explore a Christian's faith and the filling of the Holy Spirit. Believers do have many different interpretations on these matters, so we must look carefully at what the scriptures say. Join with us to explore what God wants us to believe about these matters of our faith.

#11 The Word of the Spirit (2 Peter 1:19–21)

The followers of Jesus live by "the Book," the Word of God, which is now known as the Bible. This book largely forms believers' doctrine, practice, and faith (2 Tim 3:16–17). Earlier in Chapter 2, we studied how the Spirit understands the mind of God (1 Cor 2:10) but also how He faithfully distributes this knowledge. This distribution includes the teaching, prompting, and instructing (Chapter 10) of the believer, but also important are the special ways the Spirt of God has formed and uses the Bible.

A. The Spirit Forms the Scriptures (2 Pet 1:19–21)

And so we have the prophetic word made more sure, to which you do well to pay attention as to a lamp shining in a dark place, until the day dawns and the morning star arises in your hearts. 20 But know this first of all, that no prophecy of Scripture is a matter of one's own interpretation, 21 for no prophecy was ever made by an act of human will, but men moved by the Holy Spirit spoke from God (2 Peter 1:19–21).

"The prophetic word" (v. 19) is a clear reference to the Scripture and reminds us of the important role that prophecies played in its formation (Acts 1:16). Since the New Testament was not mostly written or distributed by the time 2 Peter was written, the Old Testament is largely in view here. The principles and formation, however, describe all of the holy scriptures because they were shaped by the same Spirit of God. Because the Spirit of God strengthens, guides, and otherwise helps God's people through the Word of God, God's people closely attune themselves to His Word.

There is no doubt that many people have lost confidence in the Word of God, especially with all the false stories that have emerged concerning the origin of the scriptures and the promotion of false scriptures, such as the Gnostic books. Many people end up more excited about the books that speak about a false gospel or their conclusion that the Word of God is simply the words of men. Someone recently told me (not the first!) that all of the scriptures are an interpretation of man. Each of these false approaches diminish the power of God's Word to those on the outside. Unbelief, then, becomes a curtain of sorts, leaving the scoffers distant from God's Word. But believers, through their faith and devotion to God's Word, regularly find inspiration from God.

Note how in verse 19 Peter says, "the prophetic word made more sure." Peter is saying that the Word of God was always trustworthy, but now its poignancy is even more apparent. The Old Testament consists of many prophecies, and though it remains as part of God's Word, it was not easily proven or shown to be true because the prophecies were not yet fulfilled. Consider the many prophecies of the Messiah's birth, coming, ministry, death, and return. They were not all fulfilled at the time, just as Christ's return is still not fulfilled. We are, however, made extra sure because of the many prophecies that have already been fulfilled! Christ has come and so the prophetic word is now made surer for those who need extra confirmation. In fact, the study of apologetics has emerged in order to resolve people's questions, affirming the accuracy and trustworthiness of the scriptures.

For example, during the first Pentecost after Christ's death and resurrection, Peter announced to the assembly, "Brethren, the Scripture had to be fulfilled, which the Holy Spirit foretold by the mouth of David concerning Judas, who became a guide to those who arrested Jesus" (Acts 1:16). Peter was fully convinced that, in relation to Jesus death and even Judas betrayal, that "the Scripture had to be fulfilled."

We might wonder what prophecies made Peter so convinced of this. Genesis 37 tells us how God's chosen one, Joseph, though betrayed by his brothers, would save Israel. This prophetic word also foretold the betrayal of God's own Son by his brothers (Jewish kin).

> Judah said to his brothers, "What profit is it for us to kill our brother and cover up his blood? Come and let us sell him to the Ishmaelites and not lay our hands on him; for he is our brother, our own flesh." And his brothers listened to him. Then some Midianite traders passed by, so they pulled him up and lifted Joseph out of the pit, and sold him to the Ishmaelites for twenty shekels of silver... (Gen 37:26–28).

The prophecy in these words, however, was made more apparent by other words that were written earlier regarding Jesus' betrayal. The following verses share the pain Jesus suffered when a friend turned Him in.

Even my close friend, in whom I trusted, Who ate my bread, Has lifted up his heel against me (Psalm 41:9).

For it is not an enemy who reproaches me, Then I could bear it; Nor is it one who hates me who has exalted himself against me, Then I could hide myself from him. But it is you, a man my equal, My companion and my familiar friend (Psalm 55:12–13).

The scriptures not only predicted this betrayal but also the specifics of the deal.

And I said to them, "If it is good in your sight, give me my wages; but if not, never mind!" So they weighed out thirty shekels of silver as my wages. Then the LORD said to me, "Throw it to the potter, that magnificent price at which I was valued by them." So I took the thirty shekels of silver and threw them to the potter in the house of the LORD (Zech 11:12–13).

From the New Testament account, we see this all dramatically fulfilled with accuracy, which creates a great degree of evidence. The actual betrayal of Jesus by one of His beloved disciples is prophesied, "Then that which was spoken through Jeremiah the prophet was fulfilled, saying, and they took the thirty pieces of silver, the price of the one whose price had been set by the sons of Israel" (Matt 27:9).

But let's go back to Peter's words in Acts: "Brethren, the Scripture had to be fulfilled, which the Holy Spirit foretold by the mouth of David concerning Judas." It **had to be fulfilled**. The Holy Spirit spoke through prophets like David in this case. There were many prophecies and many individuals who the Holy Spirit worked in so that they spoke and recorded these words, making them, in effect, the Word of God. Judas' betrayal seemed rather incidental, but through the many prophecies, the Jews can see the rejection and betrayal of their Savior prophesied of in their own scriptures.

We end up with a powerful set of verses that confirm Peter's words, "more sure." We need not trouble ourselves with whether the scripture is God's Word. The scriptures deserve the same attention and obedience that Jesus showed them. However, if there is a need, there are a great many apologetic resources that affirm the scriptures to be "more sure." But be careful not to end up analyzing the scriptures for truth's sake. Once convinced, live by them![17]

The Holy Spirit's Role in Forming the Scriptures

Before going on, however, I want to explore the Holy Spirit's role in producing these prophecies and scriptures. "For no prophecy was ever made by an act of human will, but men moved by the Holy Spirit spoke from God" (v. 21). Peter goes on and provides the reason for complete trust in the Scriptures. The Holy Spirit worked through men, which clearly erases the need to debate about how the scriptures came into being. The scriptures were not made by men but by the Holy Spirit. When we discuss the formation of the canon, it is not a man arguing with another over what a person had written but is clearly an attempt to recognize what the Lord has done through His Spirit. Peter did not write 1 Peter because of his own "human will" or interpretation of events but because the Spirit of God prodded and guided him to it. The inspiration of Scripture is similar to visions. There are, however, some who say they had a vision of God when in fact they are simply making something up and telling others that God revealed it to them.

Of course, people can and do contradict Peter's words, including many professors, but they do so at their peril for God Himself has so guided

---

[17] Nine times "be fulfilled" was used in the Gospel of Matthew: 1:22; 2:15, 23; 8:17; 12:17; 13:35; 21:4; 26:54, 56.

the process of the development of His Word so that it can be fully trusted.

The Holy Spirit's Usage of God's Word

Because the Holy Spirit "moved" men to write the scriptures, we can more clearly realize why we need the Spirit of God to guide us in its understanding and usage, "no prophecy of Scripture is a matter of one's own interpretation" (v. 20). Once the liberals treat the scriptures as though they are manmade or like any other historical or fictional book, they totally ignore the Spirit's essential role of enlightenment. So, even today, certain people—including many seminary professors—will state that this or that part of the Bible is not scripture or truth. They do not believe in miracles and so have no problem arrogantly cutting out the numerous sections of the scriptures that they don't believe! Their bias taints everything they do. In this way, these supposed experts, though lacking faith, spend their whole lives misreading the scriptures to their peril. They resist the Spirit of God, and this false understanding of the scripture's origins pervade the church, leading one pastor after another into the darkness of unbelief. When people do not believe in the supernatural, they disregard the Spirit's important role in the formation of the scriptures. They end up concluding that only smart people, like them, can provide authentic interpretations. Most commentaries on the Bible are a waste of time and money because they spend time writing on totally irrelevant issues, disregarding the genuine while defending the false, thus leading their students astray.

The biblical scriptures, however, play an integral part in our walk toward Christ and in our goal of increasing our knowledge of God. Spiritual disciplines, such as daily Bible studies, memorization, and mediation, help deliver God's Word into our hearts and minds, enabling the believer to be constantly Spirit-filled. But before this happens, we need to have faith and confidence in God's Word.

B. The Spirit of Christ (1 Peter 1:10–12)

As to this salvation, the prophets who prophesied of the grace that would come to you made careful search and inquiry, 11 seeking to know what person or time the Spirit of Christ within them was indicating as He predicted the sufferings of Christ and the glories to follow. 12 It was revealed to them that they were not serving themselves, but you, in these things which now have been announced to you through those who preached the gospel to you by the Holy Spirit sent from heaven--things into which angels long to look (1 Peter 1:10–12).

What Peter says in his first letter is consistent with what he later says in 2 Peter. The prophets of old were powerfully directed by the Spirit of Christ (also see Rev 19:10).

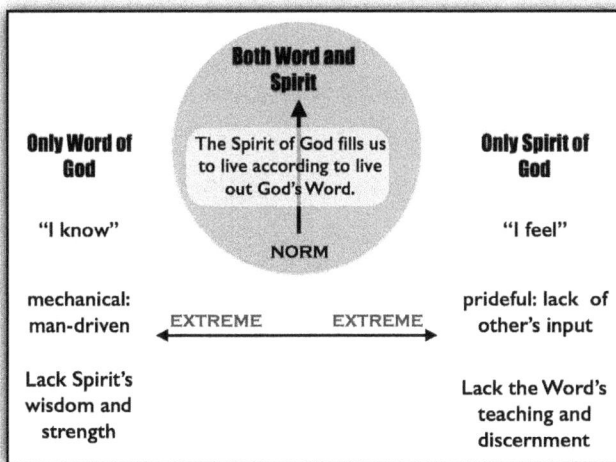

The Holy Spirit wonderfully identified with the Spirit of Christ, both before Christ's incarnation, during His earthly ministry and after His resurrection as well. Redemptive events were specifically written by the

Spirit into the fabric of time before they were stamped on the earth. The Spirit did not only inspire the prophets to say certain words from the Lord (i.e., composing scripture) but to know, understand, and love the scriptures and its message.

They knew, with reference to these Messianic prophecies, that, "They were not serving themselves, but you" (v. 21). The "you" refers to the subsequent believers after Christ's work on the cross was fulfilled. So the Spirit not only oversaw what was written (i.e., the Scriptures) but also what was understood and proclaimed as the Gospel—"Preached the gospel to you by the Holy Spirit." This same Spirit of Christ, i.e., the Holy Spirit, works in New Testament believers too, no longer making new scriptures but revealing them to us.

The gospel similarly ought to be proclaimed by the preachers, "But the Word of the Lord abides forever. And this is the word which was preached to you" (1 Peter 1:25). This is very different from what the church has been doing by ordaining ministers, indeed false prophets, who exclude the Spirit of God from their understanding. God through the Spirit worked in man to produce the scriptures, and the Spirit similarly spreads His Word by working in preachers, teachers, and evangelists who faithfully declare the gospel to those from all the nations (Matt 28:18–20).

A Joint Work

The evil one will use whatever means he can to undermine and distort the scriptures and the gospel message. It has been a constant historical challenge for the church to keep a balance between what the Spirit intuitively brings to our minds and the written Word of God. People and societies tend to bounce back from the one extreme of subjective learning from the Spirit to objective learning of the scriptures. Each extreme leads to errors that are due to ignoring other aspects of the truth.

For instance, I was brought up in a New England liberal church in the 1960s. While the congregation publicly affirmed the Apostle's Creed each week, the church had declined in their faith to where there very few that really knew the Lord. The church outwardly accepted the Bible, sang the hymns, baptized people in the name of Jesus, but esteemed their own thoughts and understandings to be more valuable and useful than the antiquated scriptures. So they, and many churches like them, drifted into the spirit of unitarianism, accepting prayers from other religious people to be equal with theirs and tolerating immoral behavior that the scripture forbids.

On the other hand, there are others, the subjective group, who talk a lot about what God has "told them." They get so carried away with hearing what God is speaking to each individual that they neglect evaluation of the prophetic message with the written Word—"But examine everything carefully; hold fast to that which is good" (1 Thes 5:21). If the objective and subjective aspects are not tightly bound, they might, like many say today, accept an adulterous affair because it is supposedly rooted in love. I have heard all sorts of things, including a supposed brother telling me that God told him to have an affair with a sister.

These extreme movements have caused great harm to the church through the ages, but at the root of them lies the question of God's absolute truth in the Word of God. The evil one deviously manipulates false teachers to provide solutions apart from God's Word, thus undermining the authority of God's Word. Note how Paul was always willing to keep propriety—order in worship service—over the usage of one's spiritual gift, "The spirits of prophets are subject to prophets" (1

Cor 14:32). Because of this, the Word must take priority over one's feelings.

The Holy Spirit is the same as the Spirit of Christ, who not only reveals the work of Christ in the Old Testament but also reveals Christ through the Scriptures in the New Testament. The relationship between the scriptures is somewhat mystical but also sensible, mysteriously joining the work of the Spirit in the actions of the believer. The Spirit not only creates scripture but also reveals the truth from the scripture. He holds the key to interpreting and applying the scriptures to our lives.

> All Scripture is inspired by God and profitable for teaching, for reproof, for correction, for training in righteousness; that the man of God may be adequate, equipped for every good work (2 Tim 3:16–17).

C. The Counterfeit Teaching Spirit (2 Peter 2:1; 1 John 4:1–3)

Satan regularly counters God's Word, as he did in the Garden, by slipping doubt into the readers' minds and fooling them with craftily designed sinister advice, just as he did to Eve (Gen 3:1–5) and Jesus (Matt 4:1–11). The only way we can discern the truthfulness of what we are hearing is by comparing what we hear against the Word of God.

Satan has not given up his part and uses every possible means to redirect people away from God, including causing them to question the authority and direction of God's Word. By casting doubt on God's Word, people ultimately question God Himself and find it impossible to trust Him who is genuinely loving and caring. The scripture says much about the dangerous influence that the evil one will have with his false words at the end times.

But false prophets also arose among the people, just as there will also be false teachers among you, who will secretly introduce destructive heresies, even denying the Master who bought them, bringing swift destruction upon themselves (2 Peter 2:1).

In contrast to prophets who were moved by the Spirit of God, we now have false prophets who are induced by the evil one to deliver false messages. There are false prophets and false teachers, but their end goal is the same: secretly introducing destructive heresies in clear contrast to the truthful gospel. John goes further by linking the evil spirits with their source.

Beloved, do not believe every spirit, but test the spirits to see whether they are from God; because many false prophets have gone out into the world. 4:2 By this you know the Spirit of God: every spirit that confesses that Jesus Christ has come in the flesh is from God; 4:3 and every spirit that does not confess Jesus is not from God; and this is the spirit of the antichrist, of which you have heard that it is coming, and now it is already in the world (1 John 4:1–3).

God's ways are counterfeited by the evil one. Instead of the Holy Spirit, there is a false or unclean spirit (Luke 9:42; Acts 5:16; Rev 18:2).

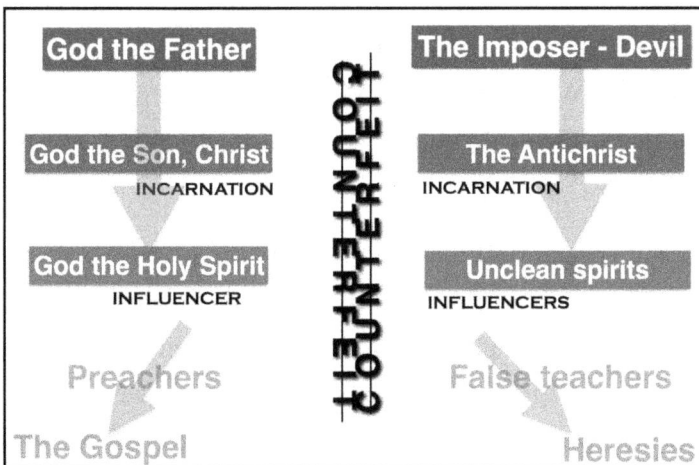

Instead of the spirit coming from and directed by God the Creator, this demon is guided by a greater demon, or Satan himself. It is for this reason that John said to "test the spirits" on whether they are from God (1 John 4:1). The Spirit from God (i.e., Spirit of God) clearly articulates the Gospel, restating the fact of God coming in the flesh, Jesus Christ. There is an opposing force that is not from God, the spirit of the Antichrist, who at some point will take form in the flesh and be called the antichrist. This spirit seeks to counter Christ's message with a false gospel so that people will follow the antichrist. Behind all the great debates today, whether it be on evolution, pro-life issues, gender selection, Christ's lack of godhood, they all find their source in the evil one who seeks to control the message (Eph 6:12).

D. The Teaching Spirit (Col 3:16)

> Let the word of Christ richly dwell within you, with all wisdom teaching and admonishing one another with psalms and hymns and spiritual songs, singing with thankfulness in your hearts to God (Col 3:16).

Today, the Spirit of God still prods His people to speak, believe, and hope in the Scriptures with the purpose of making the truth known and thus setting God's people free to know Him. Understanding the means by which the "Word of Christ" richly dwells in believers is key to inducing the Spirit to fill and use them as well as to discerning false teaching.

Christians are responsible to build themselves up in the Word of God so that the Spirit of God can fully fill and direct them. Imagine for a moment a tool that we put a lot of time into designing and developing. The investment of time and money is there because we anticipate that the tool can help us more efficiently carry out our goals. Once the tool is created, we can use it. The Word of God is much like this tool, which is present among God's people to build them up.

Summary

The Spirit of God had a major role in creating the Bible and today naturally uses it to build us up. The believer does not want an empty mind but one filled with the scriptures so that the Spirit of Christ might fully live through them.

Discussion Questions

1. Do you believe the Bible is God's authoritative voice directing our lives? Why or why not?

2. What is the difference between a false or genuine prophet/teacher?

3. Explain how the subjective understanding interacts with one's sensitivity to the Spirit.

4. How does one address the tension between those who are subjective in their approach to the scriptures compared to those who are objective?

5. In what ways do you foster God's Word to "richly dwell" in you? What benefit have you found from this?

6. Share how the Holy Spirit has influenced you in one or more ways? How do you know it was the Spirit of God influencing you?

#12 The Sending of the Spirit (Acts 13:1–4)

Life in the Spirit!
Experiencing the Fullness of Christ

The Spirit of God has unleashed a powerful movement across this world, leading millions of believers over the ages to take part in His grand redemptive plan, set in motion before time began. The Spirit is zealously motivating, guiding, and empowering God's people around the world to make disciples (Matt 28:19–20). The Spirit of God is interested in comforting the downtrodden, but there is a global mission that He is personally executing to fulfill that goal: raise up ministers of the Gospel and send them throughout the world to spread the gospel (Eph 4:11–13). Brazil recently passed Korea in the percentage of missionaries sent out. Yet, the Mongolians may have set an even higher example by forming models of a mission-sending church even though the church in that country has a brief history.

A. The Mission of the Spirit (Isaiah 61:1–2)

The Spirit of the Lord GOD is upon me, Because the LORD has anointed me To bring good news to the afflicted; He has sent me to bind up the brokenhearted, To proclaim liberty to captives, And freedom to prisoners;   2 To proclaim the favorable year of the LORD, And the day of vengeance of our God; To comfort all who mourn (Isaiah 61:1–2).

Missions began with God's eternal redemptive plan to love the world (John 3:16), but it is fascinating to observe how our Lord manifests His love in the lives of real people. It is good and right that we focus on God's love as seen in Christ's sacrifice on the cross, but Isaiah the prophet gives us another piece of the puzzle; it is here that we more clearly see the Spirit's direction. When the Servant, the Messiah, goes forth carrying the good news, He goes in the full anointing of the LORD. God has commissioned Him on this journey. We will more thoroughly discuss how the Spirit coordinates with the other persons of the Trinity in the last chapter, but here this picture powerfully shows the main thrust of the Spirit's work.

The mysterious work of the Spirit intertwines Himself with God's people to accomplish the remaining work of God's grand redemptive plan. The Spirit is not randomly healing or showing Himself great, but He does keep an eye fixed on the Father's purpose (John 5:19). This is what we find at the temptation when the Spirit led Jesus into the wilderness to defeat Satan (Matt 4:1–11) and later, when He carried the cross for His people's sins. These were specific acts, among many others, that had to be accomplished (John 19:30). All of these point to the crucial role that the Spirit plays in bringing the Gospel to the ends of the globe. Just as the Spirit filled, stirred, and empowered Christ, the Holy Spirit similarly continues to operate in His people across language divides, bringing bright hope and expectation to His people as they carry out our Lord's mission.

B. The Spirit Sends Out Workers (Acts 13:1–4)

> Now there were at Antioch, in the church that was there, prophets and teachers: Barnabas, and Simeon who was called Niger, and Lucius of Cyrene, and Manaen who had been brought up with Herod the tetrarch, and Saul. 2 And while they were ministering to the Lord and fasting, the Holy Spirit said, "Set apart for Me Barnabas and Saul for the work to which I have called them." 3 Then, when they had fasted and prayed and laid their hands on them, they sent them away. 4 So, being sent out by the Holy Spirit, they went down to Seleucia and from there they sailed to Cyprus (Acts 13:1–4).

Acts 13 serves as a pivotal passage in Acts, and indeed in the whole New Testament, depicting how the Holy Spirit would continue His work after the one-time Pentecost event. Acts 13 clearly shows how He works through the local church to send forth His experienced and faithful servants to the ends of the world. We must, therefore, conclude that any local church can be measured by its mission effort. The Spirit's words are irrefutable in their clarity. The Spirit calls Barnabas and Saul (Paul) and sends them out on a mission trip, "Being sent out by the Holy Spirit" (v. 4).

The phrase "in the church" (13:1) helps us get some perspective on the significance of the Spirit's work through the local church, which seems to create a shift from focusing on individuals (e.g., Jonah) to teams. Rightly observed, the Spirit raises up and chooses the best leaders and sends them out, not those key businessmen but those gifted (by the Spirit) to proclaim the Gospel. The phrase "I have called them" (v. 2) depicts the Spirit's integral part in calling or designating believers for special mission tasks, long or short term.

Also of importance is the Spirit's means of further communicating His purposes "while they were ministering to the Lord and fasting" (v. 2). A strong mission program is always linked to the strong teaching of God's Word. A local church, though small and seemingly irrelevant, is significant in God's hand. It is great to see, even when they do not send out their own workers, how they can help support the lives of others that commit themselves to God's purposes.

The description of the missionary team being sent off forms a powerful image to us. I remember when our pastor, family, and church members sent us off the first time to the distant mission field in Taiwan. (At that time in 1981, they could still accompany us right to the boarding gate.) In Acts 13, the local leaders embraced the calling of Paul and Barnabas, and after fasting and prayer, they "laid their hands on them, they sent them away" (Acts 13:3). The calling was overseen by the direction of the Holy Spirit—"So, being sent out by the Holy Spirit" (v. 4). The mission program remains to be a whole process involving the church, individuals, their families, and the unknown supporters, all of whom are orchestrated by the Spirit of God.

God's people do not need to be concerned with whether the Holy Spirit has lost power or is too busy in other places. He is always actively promoting the grand work of God. More importantly, we must remind ourselves that the Lord of the Harvest is looking for those who are seeking His will, wherein He will speak, appoint, equip, and send forth. A local church's response to missions is a powerful gauge on how sensitive they are to the Holy Spirit. Let's pause for a moment and listen whether the Spirit of God speaks to any of us.

C. The Spirit Equips People to Share the Gospel (1 Peter 1:10–12)

> It was revealed to them (Old Testament prophets) that they were not serving themselves, but you, in these things which now have been announced to you through those who preached the gospel to you by the Holy Spirit sent from heaven—things into which angels long to look (1 Peter 1:12).

"They were not serving themselves" reveals what a right heart looks like in a prophet. Why are we so absorbed with ourselves? It is interesting to discover how God has equipped us. Completing our spiritual gift surveys are great, but some believers can't see beyond their own nose. The reason the Spirit equips us is to fulfill His ultimate mission purposes. As in Jesus' time, the Spirit anoints the Servant because Jesus is willing to proclaim the Gospel—"The Spirit of the Lord GOD is upon me, because the LORD has anointed me to bring good news to the afflicted; He has sent me to bind up the brokenhearted, to proclaim liberty to captives, And freedom to prisoners" (Isaiah 61:1). Did you see the connection between anointing and bringing good news (i.e., gospel) and proclaiming it? Don't miss it. The Spirit does the same thing today. This is what Jesus now does on earth through His church!

"The gospel" releases the tremendous power of God's love and forgiveness by announcing the death and resurrection of Jesus Christ and offering eternal life to sinful man. They preached the gospel "by the Holy Spirit." There is a special grace from God through the Spirit that enables His people to preach the gospel truth.

> But you shall receive power when the Holy Spirit has come upon you; and you shall be My witnesses both in Jerusalem, and in all Judea and Samaria, and even to the remotest part of the earth (Acts 1:8).

The phrase "You shall receive power when the Holy Spirit" announces that the same anointing of Jesus is now upon the saints, whereas the phrase, "You shall be My witnesses" clarifies the mission for which the Holy Spirit comes upon all His people. The word "witnesses" describes our opportunity to tell others of Jesus.

It is helpful and good to note the expanding jurisdiction that His people were given so as to actively share the gospel: "In Jerusalem, and in all Judea and Samaria, and even to the remotest part of the earth." This includes the whole world! The present status of the global church is the clear testimony of the Spirit's power despite the many challenges attempting to hold back the gospel (Romans 15:19).

> For our gospel did not come to you in word only, but also in power and in the Holy Spirit and with full conviction; just as you know what kind of men we proved to be among you for your sake (1 Thes 1:5).

Lastly, we see how the Holy Spirit not only helps the Lord's proclaimers to herald forth the gospel to the world but also gives them His power and full conviction. This helps us observe how the special gifts and spiritual workings of the Spirit accompany His mission work to establish the gospel rather than make the already comfortable church more at ease. As I travel around the world, the place where most miracles are taking place is logically on the frontiers of missions, places where the gospel has not yet taken root. The Holy Spirit is much more interested in using special signs and miracles to establish His glory on the front lines (Mark 16:20) than to make the average church more comfortable.

Summary

Our churches, leaders, and selves must be in regular worship and prayer mode to be able to (1) identify what the Spirit of God wants and (2) be able to respond as necessary. There is an urgency to this work and so we should expect to see the Spirit leading and empowering His people. I was at university studying engineering when the Lord first called me to the ministry. We need to be careful not to hold up God's work by getting in debt (e.g., spending over our budget for seminary training). Although we might not understand the specific ways the Spirit works, we should see the power of the Holy Spirit enabling His people to fulfill their part in the grand redemptive plan. After all, is not the fulfillment of this mission, one of the great signs of Christ's return?

> *"And this gospel of the kingdom shall be*
> *preached in the whole world for a witness*
> *to all the nations, and then the end shall*
> *come" (Matt 24:14).*

The purpose for our lives and the church must not be to selfishly "grow" aloof from its existential purpose to send out new workers into the harvest, "Behold, I say to you, lift up your eyes, and look on the fields, that they are white for harvest" (John 4:35). Every church should focus on cooperating in the mission God has for the world. I know there are many dying churches with reduced budgets, but the only way to awaken a church is to look outward and see that even that poor church is a mighty instrument of God in the Spirit's hand. When we understand God's acceptance of us and embrace God's Great Commission for our lives, an increasingly growing work of the Spirit starts in our lives just as it has for many centuries, from the time of the Pentecost following Jesus' death and resurrection.

Discussion Questions

1. What is the significance of what the Lord did in Acts 13:1–4?

2. Examine Acts 13:1–4 and share the different activities that the Holy Spirit was involved in.

3. How is God's mission program implemented by God's Spirit?

4. How important is missions for a local church? What makes a good mission program?

5. How is the way the Holy Spirit came upon Jesus similar or dissimilar to how He works on the people of God?

6. Who prompts you to share the Gospel with others? Share how you sense the Spirit personally guiding you to do this.

7. Do you sometimes fear sharing the Gospel? Why? How could you look to the Holy Spirit to help you?

8. Name one missionary from the old days. How did we see the Holy Spirit help them?

#13 The Gifts of the Spirit-1/2 (1 Cor 12:4–6)

Life in the Spirit!
Experiencing the Fullness of Christ

The fervor of discussion on the gifts of the Holy Spirit has increased over the last few decades, including the debate on whether certain gifts are for this age or only for the early church. One's perspective on the Holy Spirit shapes how one approaches key biblical passages on spiritual gifts as well as how one anticipates how God might work in one's spiritual life. Healthy debates on spiritual gifts and other topics are fine except when they degrade into critical spirits, inducing suspicion rather than cooperation—a largely unspiritual tactic. This division has largely limited the ability of the church to work together to carry out God's glorious purposes through her. May God's Word guide our generation beyond this dissension by living faithfully to God's redemptive plan.

The Christian church, largely because of such inner disagreements, have, for the last few centuries, positioned themselves against the opposing side rather than jointly working together to fight the enemy who seeks to destroy. Each side has worthy points but none are sufficient enough to compel us to break apart the body of Christ. We should immediately move forward by standing firm together against the enemy and bring the gospel to the ends of the world. In fact, we should plainly acknowledge our inability to actually fulfill our mission as long as we are devoid of one segment of the body of Christ. There is a greater power in unity than we realize, and the enemy works hard to have us dismiss that fact. We believe God's Word can help us rightly approach the use of spiritual gifts in this age, so let us join hands in fighting our common enemy.

A. The Gifts of the Holy Spirit for our Age (1 Cor 12:1,4–6)

> Now concerning spiritual gifts, brethren, I do not want you to be unaware. 4 Now there are varieties of gifts, but the same Spirit. 5 And there are varieties of ministries, and the same Lord. 6 And there are varieties of effects, but the same God who works all things in all persons (1 Cor 12:1,4–6).

Cessationism	vs	Continuationism
Miracles, prophecy and tongues has ceased		Miracles, prophecy and tongues continues on
Such gifts establish apostle's authority		Such gifts have several purposes (common good)
Don't see gifts after the apostles' time		Those other than apostles had such gifts
Foundation laid makes gifts irrelevant		Christ's fullness is distributed through gifts

"Spiritual gifts" (v.1) are the special imparting of skill, wisdom, speech, miraculous power, etc., by God through the Holy Spirit to build up His people and reveal Himself to unbelievers. In fact, by being labeled "spiritual" (literally "spiritual things"), all spiritual gifts are by nature miraculous and the insinuation that some are not divinely empowered is misleading.

The actual phrase "spiritual gifts," although used very commonly within the church, is interestingly not used in the original Greek because its adjoining word "gifts" is absent and only inferred from the context. The use of "spiritual gifts," here, literally "spiritual things," is similar to the use in 1 Cor 14:1,12 and receives its definitive noun "gifts" from a neighboring verse (12:4) where it is used. Although the term "spiritual gifts" is not used as such in the scriptures, the translators legitimately prefer the term spiritual gifts over spiritual things. Romans 12 also uses the word "gifts" to describe this grace of God given to His people (v. 6) —though the term "spiritual" is not used to describe them (Romans 12:6–8). Having said this, it does not appear this translation or usage affects the translation of spiritual gifts or the thought that the Holy Spirit has imparted spiritual gifts to His people.

The word "gift" is used in 1 Corinthians 12:4—"Gifts, but the same Spirit"—comes from the Greek word *charisma*, which serves as the root word for charisma and charismatic, meaning grace or divine gift. This gifting offers a proof of favor—"Look how He cares for us." But it also assures us of the consistent power of God at work in the lives of the believers through the Holy Spirit. The gift implies the Spirit's ongoing work in and through our lives. He has involved us in God's plan. Lastly, "gift" or grace reminds us of our undeserving status, which should definitely humble us and keep us from all pride. (How quick we are to forget, especially when we compare ourselves with others!)

When Paul says, "I do not want you to be unaware," he is reflecting upon the basic problem of a believer's knowledge of these spiritual gifts. Christians miss out on some certain truths about spiritual gifts, which lead to misunderstanding. This was a special problem for the church at Corinth. The diagram below highlights both the developing nature of spiritual gifts as believers spiritually mature as well as some misunderstandings that lead to a wrong assessment or utilization of one's spiritual gifts.

- Stage #1 for new believers: Every believer receives a spiritual gift but doesn't understand their presence or potential because they are, rightly so, focused on living out their new life. A baby is not expected to dream of adulthood!

Obtain spiritual gifts	Discovery of spiritual gifts	Development of spiritual gifts
The new believer	The young believer	The mature believer
Little child	Young man	Fathers
Unaware of spiritual gifts	Discovery of spiritual gifts	Faithful use of spiritual gifts
Focused on newfound faith	Sometimes pridefully thinks of gifts	Caring for others is mark of maturity
All possess a gift	A gift, not to be puffed up	Opportunity to uniquely serve

- Stage #2 for young believers: Each believer grows through the stages of immaturity where because of the lack of a good grasp on God's Word and temptation, pride subtly enters in by overemphasizing his or her confidence in theology, communion with God, or possession of gifts.

- Stage #3 for mature believers: Growing never stops for these believers. Upon maturity, a believer (i.e., father per 1 John 2:12–14) values every other believer's gifts and humbly encourages each to faithfully use his or her own gifts. A good father will want all his children to succeed, each having his or her own unique place in God's will.

God's Greater Purposes

"The same Lord" (v.5) and "the same God" affirms that God is completely in charge of the distribution and variety of spiritual gifts, and interestingly deems it wise to work through His people to accomplish His divine work. This emphasis on 'one God' (also Eph 4:4–6) importantly coordinates all of the Spirit's distribution of spiritual gifts through the one Father. God is One and therefore deploys Christ's gifts in such a way to exercise His one redemptive plan. Because of this, our divisive differences and exercise of pride over spiritual gifts counteract God's purposes.

Immature concepts of spiritual gifts happen when believers gain their main identity from their service or productivity from spiritual or natural gifts. Instead, it is "God who works all things in all persons" (v. 6). Our personal value should not be defined by comparing our work or productiveness over another's but by God's acceptance of us in Christ. Spiritual gifts rightly are connected to our works as they provide us differing opportunities of service toward God and others, but they do not establish a person's value. They shape God's will and calling for their lives, the context in which they show their faithfulness to God.

There is a common confusion between our being and our work. Whenever we make our works (or our being for that matter) foundational to our acceptance to God, we forget that the foundation of our salvation is due to grace through faith (Eph 2:8–9). We gain our righteous standing through faith in Christ and not through our person or works (Romans 3:21–26).

Spiritual gifts, then, properly work by maintaining a close relationship with the Giver of the gifts. We dare not separate the gifts from the Giver for they are given only for His purposes and empowered through His kindness. Nor can we develop our gifts unless we spend time close to God. It is typically in the quiet hours that we see Him extraordinarily work in our lives.

God Works Through All of Us

"Each one" (v. 7) and "all things in all persons" (v. 6) both reveal how God miraculously works in every genuine believer through embedding His spiritual gifts in him or her "for the common good" (v. 7). "But to each one of us grace was given according to the measure of Christ's gift" (Eph 4:7). No saint was left out of this special imparting of spiritual gifts, though sin sometimes disguises it. God has magnificently equipped and called all genuine believers, enabling them to make their key contribution to God's overall plan. And so, we need the contribution of every believer to make a thorough breakthrough on every spiritual front. The image of the small prayer band thousands of miles away supporting the ongoing efforts of the frontier missionary come to my mind, enforcing the importance of every saint's participation. God wants all of us to succeed and if we are to succeed as He has ordained, then we need to generate an enthusiasm for the discovery and proper usage of spiritual gifts.

There are many spiritual gifts as stated in verse 4, "Now there are varieties of gifts." They will largely be dealt with in the following chapter, but here let these words again testify to the presence and effects of the Holy Spirit that He bestows upon the saints through the gifts. He is the author of all these gifts. They can be faked to a degree and used with wrong motives, but none are to be despised or frowned upon because the gifts hint of God's greater good purposes and further define God's grand purposes in each believer's life. (Who doesn't like the idea of receiving gifts?)

These spiritual gifts are sometimes hidden away in the busyness of life, waiting to be discovered and used. Instead of being ignorant or afraid of how God might work in their lives, genuine believers ought to look forward to how God has equipped them to serve others. This discovery, in turn, widens the vision of how God can use them in their local assemblies. Christians need to be aware of how the Holy Sprit has specially outfitted them so that they can, through these designated means, accomplish the specific purposes God has for their lives. Every genuine believer has a spiritual gift, which is given and empowered by the Holy Spirit for God's greater purposes of strengthening His body and giving witness to unbelievers.

B. Cessationism Versus Continuationism (1 Cor 12:7)

But to each one is given the manifestation of the Spirit for the common good (1 Cor 12:7).

There are other references to spiritual gifts (Romans 12, Eph 4, 1 Peter 4), but we have centered our discussion around 1 Corinthians because of the term Holy Spirit, "the manifestation of the Spirit" (v.7) is clearly used. The other references are helpful and will be discussed more in the following chapter, but we are establishing the foundation here, providing a clear understanding that spiritual gifts are given by God for His holy purposes. They are not natural talents but are dependent upon the power of God. Not only this, the ongoing work is wholly dependent upon constant communion with the Holy Spirit. Although the other passages on spiritual gifts do not refer to the Holy Spirit, the gifts described here are manifestations or signs of the Holy Spirit. It makes sense that those who are born of the Spirit also manifest the Spirit through His fruit (Gal 5:22–23) and gifts. They complement rather than stand in opposition to each other.

Equally important for this discussion on cessationism and continuationism is the purpose for these spiritual gifts. The phrase, "for the common good" (v.7) clarifies that these spiritual gifts are given with a larger purpose in mind. They do not exist primarily for one's self. God's people are Jesus' body carrying out the Father's will. God's love is made manifest by helping others (Eph 4:7). These manifestations of the Spirit are not chiefly to be thought of as signs to establish God's work, though, as we have seen in the book of Acts (chapter 9), they sometimes serve such purposes. We will more fully enter this discussion here, fully recognizing that some have already written quite extensively on this topic.

Having become a Christian early in the late 60s, I was aware of the early inroads of the charismatic movement in the church. I regularly went to a coffeehouse that was powerfully influenced by the Holy Spirit and which started in the basement of the liberal church I belonged. What started as a mere interest in coffee and chat became a significant base for spreading the gospel as the Lord transformed the leaders and its mission into being a Christian coffeehouse, "The Ship's Lantern." Because of the number of people being brought to the Lord from different backgrounds, we saw some who loved the Lord and His Word but emphasized gifts that most of us were not at first familiar with (our church didn't even believe that the Bible was God's Word!).

Now, fifty years later, the differences among Christians has not been fully resolved and as a result has produced two strongly definitive groups: cessationism and continuationism. These two terms describe either the absence or presence of revelatory and miraculous spiritual gifts since the apostolic age. I became thankful for revelatory gifts early on in my Christian life because it meant that some people from the then, staunch Roman Catholic church started reading the Bible and believed on the Lord. Later on, in my theological studies, I was introduced to the term cessationism. Only very recently did I learn the opposing term "continuationism."

The chart below summarizes the differences of each position. In essence, the cessationists believe all the gifts were given only for the early apostolic age to provide extra authority and signs for the apostles. Once the Word of God was defined[18] and accepted as the canon, these gifts are then said to have faded out. At the same time, certain revelatory and miraculous gifts, such as speaking in foreign languages, were discontinued.

---

[18] The first historical reference listing the exact 27 writings in the orthodox New Testament is in the Easter Letter of Athanasius in 367 AD."
www.churchhistory101.com/docs/New-Testament-Canon.pdf

Cessationism	vs	Continuationism
Miracles, prophecy and tongues has ceased		Miracles, prophecy and tongues continues on
Such gifts only establish apostle's authority		Such gifts have several purposes (common good)
Don't see gifts after the apostles' time		Those other than apostles had such gifts
Foundation laid makes gifts irrelevant		Christ's fullness is distributed through gifts

The continuationists, however, assert that no one has the authority to claim that certain gifts are not operational today (or for the last 1,700 years). The scriptures clearly mention them with no time limitation. Some changes have happened, of course, but as a whole, the Spirit is working in the same way through spiritual gifts. Although much can be said, let me focus on a few summary points and then importantly state our conclusion.

The two sides are unequal

It is unfair and incorrect to consider each position equal. Paul praises the gifts of the Corinthians, including the revelatory and miraculous gifts (1:4–7), putting the burden of proof on cessationalists whose arguments are unconvincing: "That in everything you were enriched in Him, in all speech and all knowledge, even as the testimony concerning Christ was confirmed in you, so that you are not lacking in any gift, awaiting eagerly the revelation of our Lord Jesus Christ" (1 Cor 1:5–7). The cessationists are the ones claiming an end to the existence of some spiritual gifts and a general reworking of the way the Holy Spirit works in the saints. They are, therefore, obligated to defend their position. They have attempted to do this, but their arguments are poor, largely based on a few vague scriptures rather than passages that clearly articulate the point. For example, they use 1 Corinthians 13:9–10 (and interestingly the other side does too) to defend their position, but this passage is hardly able to defend a whole new era of the Spirit's function for that which is "perfect" remains debatable. To assert the "perfect" refers to the scriptures being canonized is rather sketchy as much of the canonization process was an irregular process.

Greater purposes

Certain spiritual gifts are said to have been terminated long ago because of the changes that occurred in the young church, that is, there was no longer any need of the revelatory, prophetic, and miraculous gifts. The cessationalists argue that those gifts were only necessary to: (1) to establish the authority of the apostles (Eph 2:20), hence the miracles, and (2) to guide the saints who did not have the scriptures at hand. While this explanation seems clear to some, it does not provide a satisfactory one. For example, if the spiritual gifts are only there to affirm the authority of the apostles, as cessationalists affirm, then why does 1 Cor 12:7 identify the purpose for spiritual gifts as: "the manifestation of the Spirit for the common good"? The same problem plagues the second defense in regard to no longer having the need to establish God's Word in foreign places. Is it so clear that all the saints have had the scriptures in their language? I travel broadly, even to the regions in which the gospel is first being presented. The miracles present are very important to establishing the gospel in those areas. Even today, there are many saints who do not have the scriptures in their own language, and even if they did, they could not read it. Is this really a case of not having a need for other gifts? The argument is pitifully weak.

Others possess such gifts

The argument that certain revelatory or miraculous gifts were given only to establish the apostle's authority is further weakened by the fact that others also performed miracles. Stephen, for example, though not being an apostle, exercised powerful gifts of the Spirit: "full of grace and power, was performing great wonders and signs among the people" (Acts 6:8). This situation was clearly not given to establish an apostle for Stephen for he was not an apostle but a deacon (Acts 6:2,5).

This argument also necessitates that there would be no exceptions to the new guidelines of the Spirit after the apostolic age, but there are some greatly respected Christian leaders who exhibited such gifts. Spurgeon, at times, had special knowledge of a person in a huge congregation regarding some sin they had committed[19] or others like John Knox[20], who evidently had the gift of prophecy. The problem with cessationists is that they no longer see any need for these gifts and therefore denounce them. This is a very bold claim that can lead them to dictate how the Spirit of God should or should not empower others. Would it not be better to moderate their stance by recognizing that some of these gifts are not so prominent, evident, or needed in certain situations? I think so. No one is stating that all that is said and done is by the Holy Spirit. There are horrible and deceptive acts performed in the name of the Spirit, much of which is done for obvious material gain, but we need to be discerning rather than reject the whole thing outright.

A stumbling block

We are not here to support or defend either position, but one of our key passages provides, in my eyes, a huge challenge to the cessationists. Paul

[19] www.cblibrary.org/biography/spurgeon/spurg_v1/spau1_ch35.htm
[20] www.churchofthekingmcallen.org/pastors-blog/prophecies-of-john-knox/

intertwines the revelatory/miraculous gifts with other gifts accepted by all in 1 Cor 12:27–30.

> 27 Now you are Christ's body, and individually members of it. 28 And God has appointed in the church, first apostles, second prophets, third teachers, then miracles, then gifts of healings, helps, administrations, various kinds of tongues (1 Cor 12:17–28).

Does Paul take this chance to minimize the spiritual gifts that the Corinthian church was misusing? No. He does not at all hint or otherwise support the view of cessationists by grouping the gifts to be later eliminated, but instead clearly intertwines them with gifts that are accepted to continue down to this day such as the gift of helps and administration.

Inferior reasoning

Granted, some spiritual gifts do not seem so prominent today, at least in some circles. If the prophet is not the preacher, for example, then it is really hard to see how the prophet fits into many churches today. But even so, one cannot change the scriptures by one's own experiences, not to mention the fact that there are churches that can easily point to several prophets in their congregations! It is improper for cessationists to present mock cases that do not hold up to simple examination. Another example is the way they proudly offer any miracle worker to stand up and start giving evidence of God's power by doing miracles. But we all, at least those who take God's Word seriously, understand that spiritual gifts simply do not work like that. Even Jesus saw no faith in some areas: "And He did not do many miracles there because of their unbelief" (Matt 13:58). Is it really proper to ask those who have the gift of healing or miracles to prove it? Definitely not. Even the Apostle Paul did not find healing for his physical problem (2 Cor 12:8–9) and ached for Epaphroditus' near fatal condition (Phil 2:26–27).

A Positive Presentation

Before stating a few concluding points, let me state that I do appreciate both views, but I weep for the tolerated divisiveness. Excessiveness hurts the church but so does our willingness to dismiss whole segments of Christ's body as being unimportant or unnecessary. We have allowed Satan to bring havoc into the church because we are unwilling to focus on the main doctrines of unity. I am not proposing that we shrug off our discernment like Unitarians and reject the preciousness of the Gospel. Not at all.

But even so, by not focusing on unity and granting ourselves special permission to change the scriptures and disregard parts of the church for which Christ died, we ourselves assist the enemy in his devious work! Let me make three main points in my conclusion of this chapter, as I hope to make headway on a new approach.

1) Cessationism tends to be divisive at its core rather than attempting to accomplish God's greater purposes. Continuationists respond by expending their energies on opposing Cessationists. As a church, we have far too often allowed our conclusions on these issues to separate us from our brethren. If our conclusions on these minor issues divide us, then we are essentially denying the major doctrines of one Spirit and one body—which we all know is wrong. We are one body and therefore together need to find a resolution to the problem. Instead of living together as a married couple, we tolerate living separated from each other. This is beneath our calling and the needs of the church, and the world demands that we find a

genuine solution. We cannot afford to go on without each other for God's mission can only be completed if we act as one.

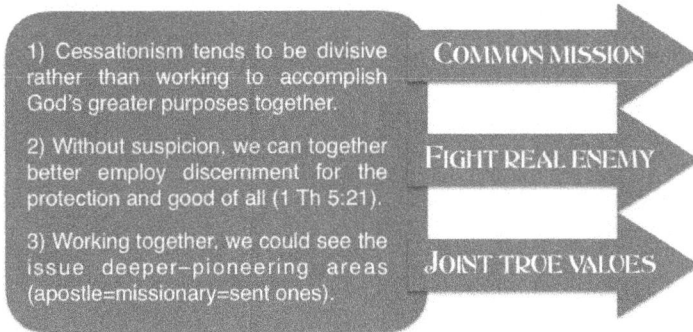

1) Cessationism tends to be divisive rather than working to accomplish God's greater purposes together. — COMMON MISSION

2) Without suspicion, we can together better employ discernment for the protection and good of all (1 Th 5:21). — FIGHT REAL ENEMY

3) Working together, we could see the issue deeper–pioneering areas (apostle=missionary=sent ones). — JOINT TRUE VALUES

2) Once we grasp the supreme importance of the one body (unified brethren), even those with differing approaches and conclusions can discard one's suspicions, which poison our relationships and grant us special privileges of poorly using scripture to support our presuppositions. Suspicion, by nature, breeds misunderstanding, even when there is no basis for it. By putting aside suspicion, we can together better employ discernment for the protection and good of all, eliminating much excessiveness. My guess is that portions of the church are unwilling to censor some practices along with their false prophets who are milking the congregations. If we stand as one, we could instead agree on some standards, such as those Billy Graham had written for evangelists.[21] Together, we could set standards or at least speak about what harm is being done by certain preaching or actions just as 1 Thes 5:20–22 instructs, "Do not despise prophetic utterances. But examine everything carefully; hold fast to that which is good; abstain from every form of evil." We are too busy defending our

---

[21] Biblical Standards for Evangelists by Billy Graham.

positions to give joint oversight with the brethren to obey the Word of God.

3) If we worked together, perhaps the issues would be cast in a deeper context, allowing for a more mature understanding. For instance, some insist that these miraculous or revelational gifts are only to be associated with the apostles and the very early foundation of the church, but perhaps it is better to associate these gifts not so much with the twelve apostles but with what they were doing: introducing the Gospel in pioneer areas, allowing the term "apostle" to be more generally translated as "missionary" or "sent ones." It is in these areas where these gifts are more regularly seen and needed.

A gracious heart would enable us to listen more attentively to many amazing stories rather than basking in our skepticism. For example, I once heard of a desperate missionary who had to bury his wife at this hostile village along the Amazon delta. The Irish missionary had to bury her there and so conducted the service in English by himself. The natives, however, heard the service. The villagers later testified, some of them becoming Christians, for they heard this man speak the service in perfect Portuguese even though later they criticized him for using very poor Portuguese. God marvelously worked at this time to bring the Gospel to that village. This historical church event helps us identify why some gifts are more prominent in some regions over others, a conclusion that I have come to as I travel in pioneering gospel areas.

Another mature understanding might have to do with the way we perceive the Spirit's work through spiritual gifts. Cessationists are wary of allowing the Spirit to "speak" to someone because it might conflict with the Scripture's authority. This concern, as I see it, derives from the way evangelicals combatted early Liberals who denied the authority of the Scriptures rather than the common believer who wants to properly exercise his or her spiritual gift. Without the filter of suspicion, we could better understand how the Spirit helps the teacher, the prophet, the administrator, the helper, etc. By emphasizing the Spirit's manner of employing and empowering His people in use of their spiritual gifts, we could leap ahead, focusing on what the Spirit is doing and improve the way we use our spiritual gifts.

Conclusion

It is unfortunate that so many Christians still believe spiritual gifts, especially the so-called revelatory, miraculous spiritual gifts, are no longer used by God to advance His Gospel and church. These unsound arguments have crippled some believers, antagonized charismatics, and, most dangerously, impeded the fast advance of the pioneering Gospel. Cessationism has unnecessarily created a division between various segments of the Christian church, making miracles, prophecy, and tongues irrelevant and so shunning different believers, causing division. While continuationism insists on maintaining the value of these gifts, as Paul states in 1 Cor 12:28–31, they often do not jointly discern and weed out excessiveness (which is a greater problem in my eyes). God's people ought to focus on God's empowering hand upon His people to carry out His divine and greater purposes to bring the gospel to the ends of the earth rather than asserting that God cannot do what He is doing. If God has used such means in the past, then He is quite likely to use them in other similar situations. I understand the reservations we have and our concerns to maintain our faithfulness to our Lord, doctrine, and ministries, but to be sure we all confess that our oneness in Christ demands a reprioritization of our responses.

Discussion Questions

1. How can we keep ourselves from getting prideful over our spiritual gifts?

2. How should we approach spiritual gifts so that we are working with believers rather than in competition with them?

3. Are all the gifts of the Holy Spirit for this age or were they only for the early church? Explain.

4. Define both Cessationism and Continuationism. Which do you hold to and why?

5. How should we understand and treat others who look at spiritual gifts differently from us?

6. Do you believe in the importance of the unity of the church of God (Eph 4:1–3)? How can that work out when we have some with different conclusions on how we should strive to maintain pure devotion to the Lord?

Life in the Spirit!

#14 The Gifts of the Spirit -2/2 (1 Cor 12:8–11)

Life in the Spirit!
Experiencing the Fullness of Christ

Spiritual gifts are God's diverse means to uniquely pour out His grace to each genuine believer in Christ, empowering them so that they have special opportunities to extend God's grace to others. Paul and others are not only concerned that we identify our spiritual gifts but responsibly and humbly anticipate God's Spirit to powerfully accomplish His spiritual work in our lives. (Remember that my definition of spiritual gift includes the Spirit's miraculous working through *every* spiritual gift not only through *some* gifts.)

One might wonder why believers have such different viewpoints of the scriptures on the many spiritual gifts. We must be careful to separate the extreme views from a consistent biblical approach. Admittedly, the enemy has used minimalist views to cause dissension and pride to cripple large segments of the church. Let us learn to navigate our lives and theologies between these extremes under the umbrella of love: "the greatest of these is love" (1 Cor 13:13). And yes, our views might differ, note how some of our main assumptions were addressed in the preceding chapter, but let us be as brothers, united in one Spirit, together outfitted for God's redemptive plan and genuinely seeking His truth in the scriptures. Extremes typically are noted by the way they exclude certain biblical truths to promote one teaching or practice, rather than grasping how all relevant truths function as a whole.

A. God's Distribution of Gifts (1 Cor 12:7–8)

> But to each one is given the manifestation of the Spirit for the common good. 8 For to one is given the word of wisdom through the Spirit, and to another the word of knowledge according to the same Spirit.

The Holy Spirit's distribution of spiritual gifts is His holy work. The Holy Spirit is the basic, foundational gift, uniting us to His presence and anointing us with His grace. The Spirit's presence is made known in several ways, such as through our holy living, love, etc., but Paul emphasizes the spiritual gift here. Note how verse 7—"For to each one is given"—clearly points out that each believer receives both the Holy Spirit and at least one manifestation of the Spirit through a gift. Verse 8 with a similar phrase—"For to one is given"—reminds us that God sovereignly distributes these gifts along His purposes. These gifts do not create our spiritual life but largely define our unique areas of contribution to building up the body of Christ, some of them at times, more evangelistic in nature, drawing people into the kingdom of God.

Although we cannot distribute such gifts, we can easily misuse what God has given to us for our own selfish purposes. Leaders need to encourage each believer to remain close to God and exercise his or her spiritual gift. Nor should we allow people to conclude that each person has or should receive the same gifts as another. Rightly understood, our spiritual gifts can be considered a mini-calling as they, in part, define our works. A gift from the Spirit implies the Spirit's commitment to regularly and uniquely work in each believer and to co-work with the Father in accomplishing His will.

A long list of these spiritual gifts starts in verse 8 and shows the diverse ways God can and does work in believers. The gifts are given, rather than snatched: "To one is given...and to another..." (v.7–8). We are, I believe, to understand this list in light of the Old Testament's special gifts of the Spirit when He came upon a few, or even during Jesus' own life and ministry. The Spirit has not changed, but His ability to anoint all believers has, and so all believers have such gifts of grace. This list identifying various gifts probably came about because Paul was making some observations of people using their gifts in the church. He saw how the Spirit helped people specially care for others, supply knowledge, etc. It is not meant to be a complete list[22] but one that manifests the work of God in their midst, "That in everything you were enriched in Him, in all speech and all knowledge..." (1 Cor 1:5–6).

"Each one" (v.7), i.e., believer, receives both the Holy Spirit and at least one manifestation of the Spirit through a gift. This gifting is one way the Father carries out Jesus' ministry through the way we serve others. Please note that the context for this is the local church. Some have dismissed the local church as being irrelevant to their spiritual lives. Many believers worship in their homes by themselves.[23] Modernism has polluted the people of God, causing them to commit their dollars and excitement to a popular Christian band rather than to a small struggling church. Spiritual growth, however, without a serious commitment to a

---

22 Yes, that can be debated too and with less problem of creating divisiveness.
23 We wonder what they really worship!

local church, is hard to come by, if not impossible. The critic who looks on from afar will die apart from the many blessings that come from the commitment to a local church. We are hardly trying to gloss over the church's weaknesses, but at least we have the Spirit's promise to work through us and others so as to wonderfully use us. We ought to connect God's purposes with how He sovereignly distributes these gifts rather than to be jealous or criticize. Jump in where you are and use your love and gifts to build up the people of God. These gifts do not create our spiritual life but largely define our unique areas of service.

On an encouraging note, a gifting implies that the Spirit is committed to regularly and uniquely working in each believer not just for salvation but for co-working with us to do God's will. A believer is often not aware of his or her spiritual gifts when first born again. This awareness is partly related to physical age, spiritual maturity, and the hearing of God's Word. Spiritual gifts are given upon belief so it is not that one does not have a spiritual gift, for all believers have at least one spiritual gift, but that they are often not aware of it. The same is true in our physical lives where many talents are not obvious until maturity comes. Usually, one's spiritual gift comes to full blossom when one matures and consistently devotes one's life to the Spirit's leading.

B. God's Distributed Gifts (1 Cor 12:8–11)

For to one is given the word of wisdom through the Spirit, and to another the word of knowledge according to the same Spirit; 9 to another faith by the same Spirit, and to another gifts of healing by the one Spirit, 10 and to another the effecting of miracles, and to another prophecy, and to another the distinguishing of spirits, to another various kinds of tongues, and to another the interpretation of tongues. 11 But one and the same Spirit works all these things,

227

distributing to each one individually just as He wills (1 Cor 12:8–11).

In this section we will briefly introduce each of the gifts from 1 Corinthians 12, providing a definition and purpose for each listed gift.

- "Word of wisdom"(v.8) is, as in the Old Testament, the way the Spirit of God passes special insight and wisdom to certain believers so that they can personally make and communicate wise decisions and the importance of those decisions. Daniel had the gift of wisdom to interpret dreams and the handwriting on the wall. Solomon was granted wisdom to make clever decisions. Often, we discover people with this gift when things seem terribly unclear and yet someone makes a suggestion that just works. Churches that have good leadership teams are really benefitted by such individuals; however, if people are competitive, others might think of it as a political ploy to gain an advantage.

- "The word of knowledge" (v.8) is the gifting of knowledge or insight to His believers so that they can optimally serve and care for others. In other words, without the Spirit working in a believer inputting this knowledge, the church or Christian would go on without its benefit. Spurgeon, as stated in the previous chapter, could know, at times, something about a person and use it in a sermon. The Spirit takes that knowledge and inserts it into the awareness of the one with the gift. This believer should not only learn how to discern the thoughts coming to his/her mind but how to carefully and timely communicate them as the Lord leads.

- "To another faith" (v.9) describes how the Spirit provides confidence to some believers for especially challenging situations, enabling them to trust God and obey Him, thus encouraging others through their faithfulness. All believers have faith in the Lord, but for especially difficult, frontier-like situations or strong spiritual warfare, special faith is needed. Sometimes, it is seen in the extreme peace in God's people even though the situations are extremely undesirable or hostile. This is not just boldness but a deep belief that God will take care of the difficult situation. Yes, we all have faith, but the faith of individuals like George Mueller and Hudson Taylor stirs us to further trust God in our simple situations.

- "To another gifts of healing" (v.9): The gifts of healing bring God's peace and healing to a person's troubled spirit and body. The word "gifts" is plural and meant to indicate that there are numerous kinds of healing. One person might be able to pray for a woman to bear children while another deals with emotional troubles. This, and all spiritual gifts, are supernatural endowments by the Spirit to help minister God's grace to His people. Without God, they would go uncared for. God's people form a team to bring God's complete grace.

- "To another the effecting of miracles" (v.10): There are many kinds of miracles that arise in varying circumstances; some people may face technical impossibilities while others face impossible situations, such as the lost of an ax head when loaned to a neighbor. Elijah, through the Spirit, caused that submerged ax head to float (2 Kings 6:5–7). This gift is also transacted by the Spirit, and though the phrase "by the Spirit" is not specifically mentioned, it is excluded only to avoid repetition. The Spirit clearly accomplishes the miracle. The Healer is amazingly willing to work through the Spirit-gifted individual, empowering believers so that the glory and praise might go to God for the miracles and wonders that occur.

- "To another prophecy" (v.10) is by far the most debated gift listed, enabling certain believers to speak words given from God to confront His people with the truths people need to hear. This can include a preacher's message "from the Lord" or a timely flash revelational insights (1 Cor 14:30–33). Believers always need to be careful of false prophesies (1 Thes 5:19–21). While some are happy to equate this with the preacher who brings God's Word to the people, others think of it more as an exhortation situation apart from preaching, while others only think of declaring future events. Though a person might have a prophetic word, it is always to be judged by God's Word (1 Cor 14:37–38). If the prophet does not heed God's Word, then he or she is not to be recognized. For clarification, let me use a recent illustration that happened at the end of a special joint prayer meeting. As I closed in prayer, an image came to my mind of a smashed perfume bottle, which releases its fragrance into the air. In response, I incorporated the vision (this is how I understood it) in my prayer. God used the picture to guide my prayers and build up my faith and in so doing to encourage His people there who were facing terrible home situations to believe God could work through them in a wonderful way.

- The gift "the distinguishing of spirits" (v.10) speaks of believers who can discern from what spirit a person is saying or carrying various actions, that is, whether it is sourced from God or an evil spirit. I remember several times a person announcing the source of someone's words and action, bringing clarity on how we should proceed in our counseling or treatment of that person. Everyone kind of knew something was wrong, but instant clarity came once a certain believer spoke. Teachers who have this gift often have special insight into how various worldly philosophies impact God's people in the world, which then helps believers be more aware and stand stronger in their faith.

- The phrase "To another various kinds of tongues" (v.10) shows that God gives the gift of tongues to some people, such as He did in the book of Acts (more accurately: language from the Greek, *glossa*). The word "tongues" was first made common in the King James Bible (KJB) during the 1600s where it had the meaning of a spoken language as well as the physical organ "the tongue." Unfortunately, the word "tongues" is still used in modern translations to perpetuate confusion. The word "tongues" should instead be translated as "language(s)" to avoid further confusion. The term is first introduced in the book of Acts where God's people were heard speaking in various foreign languages. This was said in confirmation of an Old Testament prophecy, signifying that God's people were now filled with His Spirit but also that God was reversing the thrust of the confusion of languages given at the Tower of Babel (Gen 11:1–9) to now reach out to the world with the gospel. The Spirit of God was now working in all the world. "Speaking in languages" (tongues) is the special ability to spontaneously speak aloud a coherent message from God in a language unknown to the speaker, which reveals the Spirit's special work in communicating some truth. The power of the "language" gift is not only seen in its foreignness but in its message, much like prophesy. And so, its usage in a worship service requires interpretation (1 Cor 14:5), likening it to an exclamation of God's works leading all to praise God.

- "The interpretation of tongues" (v. 10) is closely aligned with the gift of speaking in foreign languages. The need and possibility of interpretation affirms that the gift of "tongues" is really a language possessing a grammar and meaning from its words. The interpretation does not give it meaning but simply understands its meaning and communicates it in a language people can comprehend.

C. Other Spiritual Gifts (Romans 12, 1 Peter 4)

The two lists of spiritual gifts in Romans 12:3–8 and 1 Peter 4:10–11 complement Paul's descriptive list in 1 Corinthians 12. Interestingly, we do not see here the repetition of the Spirit's integral part in giving and empowering the believers with the spiritual gifts given as in 1 Corinthians 12. The word "Spirit" is not used. These other readers evidently kept the Spirit in view more than the Corinthian believers, and so Paul could instead focus on developing the member aspect rather than the Spirit-initiated aspect to produce harmony.

> 4 For just as we have many members in one body and all the members do not have the same function, 5 so we, who are many, are one body in Christ, and individually members one of another. 6 And since we have gifts that differ according to the grace given to us, let each exercise them accordingly: if prophecy, according to the proportion of his faith; 7 if service, in his serving; or he who teaches, in his teaching; 8 or he who exhorts, in his exhortation; he who gives, with liberality; he who leads, with diligence; he who shows mercy, with cheerfulness (Romans 12:3–8).

"Many members in one body and all the members" (v.4) uses the interacting functions of the physical body to describe how each person's mutual service is important to the health of the whole. This image powerfully conveys how the believers are to coordinate rather than compete in their usage of spiritual gifts. The underlying truths here are enough to solve all the problems that have arisen regarding different interpretations of these gifts. We are one body and therefore work together for the common purpose of serving the Lord.

"Gifts that differ according to the grace given to us" (v.6) is a phrase that proves all spiritual gifts have grace at their origin. Even the word "gift" here contains the root word grace (Greek: *charismata*). This grace is perhaps nowhere more powerfully seen than in Christ's great presence through His Spirit dwelling in His people, but it is also manifested through the gifts He gives. We have all gained much more than we deserve. According to His Master plan, we have been equipped with different gifts, i.e., graces. Not everyone has the same gift(s). All are a mark of spirituality if rightly used by the Spirit for His glory.

There are many gifts mentioned here in Romans 12: prophecy, service, teaching, exhortation, giving, leading, diligence, and mercy (vv.6–8). Some are the same as those in his list in 1 Corinthians 12, while others differ. Because our focus is on the Holy Spirit, we will not define each of the remaining gifts mentioned.

> 8 Above all, keep fervent in your love for one another, because love covers a multitude of sins. 9 Be hospitable to one another without complaint. 10 As each one has received a special gift, employ it in serving one another, as good stewards of the manifold grace of God. 11 Whoever speaks, let him speak, as it were, the utterances of God; whoever serves, let him do so as by the strength which God supplies; so that in all things God may be glorified through Jesus Christ, to whom belongs the glory and dominion forever and ever. Amen. (1 Peter 4:10–11)

Peter has his own emphasis. He doesn't list gifts as the other two Pauline lists but categorizes them all into two groups—but only after he, like Paul in 1 Corinthians 13, emphasizes love. "Above all, keep fervent in your love for one another" (v.8) reminds us that spiritual gifts are never to be used for selfish purposes. Whenever we find jealousy, pride, "better than" attitudes, Satan is trying to derail our gifts.

"Be hospitable to one another without complaint" (v.9) is probably not a particular spiritual gift but an expectation, like love, or an extension of love, that is thrust on all believers. Note the special caution to be hospitable without complaining, "How come I have to.... while they...?" Each of us are to be busy using our lives and gifts to serve others (demonstrating God's love through our lives). Being a committed member provides the context where one's gifts can grow, be recognized, confirmed, and utilized. Again, there are general manifestations of the Spirit of Christ as spoken of in verse 9 but also particular ones, which Peter addresses starting in verse 10.

So verse 10 addresses how one is to use their spiritual gifts while the listing, albeit quite brief, starts in verse 11. Again, because Peter does not emphasize the Spirit's part, we will be brief in our discussion here.

Peter provides two categories: speaking and serving (v.11). They are a comprehensive way of describing all gifts by virtue of how many gifts use the mouth (speech) while many others use various parts of our bodies to serve.

Summary
The discovery of and use of our spiritual gifts remains to be a great way to bring God's grace into our midst, "as good stewards of the manifold grace of God" (v.11). We need to value everyone's gift and receive what kindness and grace issues from God through the lives of others whether through general manifestations of God's love or specific ones through spiritual gifts. Whatever grace God has sent, let us receive it!

D. The Equipping of Spiritual Gifts (Eph 4:7–13)

> But to each one of us grace was given according to the measure of
> Christ's gift. 8 Therefore it says, "When He ascended on high, He
> led captive a host of captives, and He gave gifts to men..." 11 And
> He gave some as apostles, and some as prophets, and some as
> evangelists, and some as pastors and teachers, 12 for the equipping
> of the saints for the work of service, to the building up of the body
> of Christ; 13 until we all attain to the unity of the faith, and of the
> knowledge of the Son of God, to a mature man, to the measure of
> the stature which belongs to the fulness of Christ (Eph 4:7–13).

Ephesians 4:7–13 identifies the "equipping" gifts, which are often
associated with positions or responsibilities in the church that are
foundational in establishing God's people in the Word of God. All four
(or five) emphasize the proclamation of the Word of God. "He gave
some as apostles, and some as prophets, and some as evangelists, and
some as pastors and teachers" (v.11), each describing how God specially
outfits and calls some believers to be "equippers."

In each case, they use the Word of God to build up the people of God so
that the people of God will be fully equipped to do their acts of service.
"For the equipping of the saints" (v.12) distinguishes these gifts/calls as
designed to equip saints: "For the work of service, to the building up of
the body of Christ" (v.12). In summary, equipping gifts have a special
purpose of building up the body of Christ unto full maturity (c.f. v.13).

All spiritual gifts are a "measure of Christ's gift" (v.7), revealing the
relationship between God's gift to the Son and the many gifts that His
people receive. Spiritual gifts, then, are a part of the anointing of the
Holy Spirit's gift/grace through which we can express Christ's grace on
earth. We are His body—really!

Summary

These particular gifts are often associated with full-time service because they become so dominant in a person's life that it becomes a demanding call, desire, and purpose. The ministry is not associated with high pay, but the Lord works through these committed servants to enable all of His people to be properly equipped to serve (Psalm 110:3).

E. Clarification on the Gift of Tongues (1 Cor 12:27–31)

The end section of 1 Corinthians 12 provides special insight into tongues.

> Now you are Christ's body, and individually members of it. 28 And God has appointed in the church, first apostles, second prophets, third teachers, then miracles, then gifts of healings, helps, administrations, various kinds of tongues. 29 All are not apostles, are they? All are not prophets, are they? All are not teachers, are they? All are not workers of miracles, are they? 30 All do not have gifts of healings, do they? All do not speak with tongues, do they? All do not interpret, do they? 31 But earnestly desire the greater gifts. And I show you a still more excellent way (1 Cor 12:27–31).

This list is especially interesting because of the way it mixes a number of spiritual gifts that many believers accept as ongoing with other spiritual gifts that some believers say have ceased—the revelatory, miraculous, and prophetic gifts, that is, the gifts the charismatics tend to emphasize. Our focus, however, is limited to some observations about the gift of speaking in unknown languages (i.e., tongues). Cessationism is the belief that many gifts are irrelevant. This was discussed in the former chapter, but here we want to focus on another extreme—the reason many Christian believers across this world demand or expect one to speak in tongues. This emphasis has caused extreme division, and perhaps, accentuated the problem that Cessationists have started.

"Miracles, then gifts of healings, helps..." (v.28). While Paul did not mention the gifts of miracles, prophecy, and tongues in Romans 12 or 1 Peter 4, his inclusion of them in this mixed listing affirms their normalcy in Corinth. If there was ever a time Paul could have expressed the temporariness of certain gifts or the limited use of them, this would have been the place. Many Corinthian believers were wrongly using their gifts, hence the long discussion and interjection of Chapter 13 on love. One would think if miracles and healings were only given to the apostles, then they would not be added to the list. Paul and the other apostles were not present in Corinth, but the letter was addressed to the believers there.

To be sure, the apostle did downplay the supreme importance of tongues by placing it last in the lists, but he drops no hints of it becoming useless; instead, he simply includes this gift with other God-given gifts. Furthermore, we must point out that Paul was exercising a sense of priority as he wrote this list (first, second, third (v.28)), giving equipping gifts priority over the other gifts, so we should not consider that Paul was not thinking of a gift's importance. So, although some have improperly attempted to restrain the gift of foreign languages (tongues) to the time the Word of God was not available (before canonization—1 Cor 13:8–11), Paul could easily have alluded to their limited usage. After all, why did the Corinthians so greatly use tongues or find the need for them? Most definitely there were many visiting the city because of the temple at Ephesus—one of the word's chief wonders —but God thought they needed to focus more on the written scriptures than the provision of prophecies and interpretation of tongues because, after all, the Word of God is foundational.

Having defended their presence (in a limited way), we need to follow through with this passage and request all believers to refuse to consider tongues or other gifts as a means for salvation or for a mark of spiritual development. What does Paul clearly state? "All do not have gifts of healings...tongues...interpretations, do they?" (v. 30). The apostle insinuates that some have wrongly insisted on the presence of spiritual gifts, like speaking in other languages (tongues), as a sign of salvation or spirituality (12:28,31). We ought to be wary of these distortions! In chapter 9, we showed that speaking in tongues is not needed in order to show or gain salvation. Instead, the gift of tongues marks the coming of the Spirit of God to the people of God, but following the given outline of the book of Acts, we clearly see that not all speak in tongues nor should they.

Instead, the special highlighting of tongues in Acts affirms the expansion of the Gospel to a new region, proving to the apostles that this was God's genuine work among non-Jews, as He did among those at Pentecost. This is further discussed in chapter 9.

God's people should also not conclude that tongues or other spiritual gifts are a mark of spirituality that implies that those who do not have certain gifts are not spiritual. Are not all gifts from the Spirit? Does this not mean that even those who possess gifts that are non-revelatory are spiritual—such as the gift of administration? This is the conclusion we are to make from Paul's words here. "All do not have gifts of healings... tongues... interpretations, do they?" (v. 30). Surely Paul allows for none of these immature conclusions—"I have this gift so I am more spiritual." All the spiritual gifts are a sign of God's Holy Spirit working in the believer's life. He clearly exhorts the believers that not all have any particular gift, including tongues, "All do not speak with tongues, do they?" (v.29) Why then do so many believers clearly disobey the scriptures, then, by perpetuating the teaching that the gift of tongues is a sign of faith or spirituality?

For example, the habit of some to teach others the gift of tongues is made under the assumption that everyone should speak in tongues. Without this assumption, there would not be the confidence that one could or should teach another to speak so. Even the suggestion to "teach one to speak in tongues" is in error as it implies it is not a gift from the Spirit but taught. Why not let the Spirit teach a person? Once we see evidence of a spiritual gift, then it is fine to coach them on the use of it as in any other spiritual gift.

I sense that part of this problem derives from people claiming that "tongues" does not necessarily need to be a language. We have earlier discussed how poorly translating "*glossa*" into "tongues" in our modern English translations has totally confused this generation of believers and perpetuated myths about *glossa* being able to be words or sounds not commandeered by a grammar. Paul does mention a language of angels in 1 Cor 13:1, but this is still a language, which is communicated as other languages on earth.

This emphasis on tongues associated with various denominations is important to understand. For example, why is so much personal attachment and value put on speaking in tongues where most of the gifts do not lead to such extreme affection or devotion? For example, do we try to make sure everyone has the gift of administration? No. Why do some connect the gift of "languages" rather than the gift of "administration" to be more spiritual? This approach clearly counters biblical teaching, especially as it does not rate in the top four gifts of Paul's list but is listed as last.

There are two aspects to this that must be brought up, one of which I have already briefly alluded to. Some connect speaking in tongues with salvation or the gift of the Holy Spirit. I applaud the charismatics for insisting on the need for the awesome work of the Holy Spirit to work in our lives and generating faith to continue on with the proclamation of the gospel. The Spirit of God is needed for genuine salvation to replace dead religiosity. The Continuationists, in many cases, have been zealously evangelizing where the Cessationists have not. The Gospel is going around to the ends of the world because some believe God still speaks to the believers. This is what we should expect from the truths revealed at Pentecost. God is powerfully working in genuine believers around the world to fulfill His mission. This expectation is correct, but to use the gift of tongues as a sign of the Spirit's presence is unnecessary and unbiblical, a fact that is also seen here in this text. "Not all speak with tongues, do they?" We cannot avoid this unless we see that what Paul is speaking about as totally different from what we see in Acts, but this would produce an inconsistent interpretation. The epistles are clearly linked to the missionary journeys in the book of Acts. The letter to the Corinthians is the same group that Paul met up with in Acts 18.

This is why the former questions pose a critical question (at least to me). Why do some believers center their focus on this one gift of tongues in contrast to other spiritual gifts? Perhaps the gift of tongues is considered as more than a spiritual gift but rather a special spiritual communication with God where they can intimately commune with Him and so grow and thrive. Though we are not denying this intimate relationship, there stands a huge roadblock interfering with this conclusion: it is inconsistent with scriptural expectations.

We have insisted in chapter 2 that every believer has this special communion with God—God lives in each believer through the Holy Spirit (see 1 Cor 2). Those who do not have the Spirit are not of God. Perhaps many believers, and undoubtedly this is true, are not taking the opportunity to closely commune with God, but to insist that one needs to speak in tongues before one communes with God or that it is the optimum means of communing with God counters the New Testament truth that all believers can openly speak and pray to God and dangerously shifts basic scriptural teaching. What does the apostle say? "Pray without ceasing!" (1 Thes 5:17). We are not denying that those who speak in tongues do speak with God; indeed, if it is a true *glossa* gifting. But this should be true for all the saints. 1 Cor 14:2 is sometimes used to affirm this communion with God, but that is pushing the language of the verse and contradicts the foundational teaching above. In any case, we all should be intimately communing with God. This is our heritage as the children of God to speak and hear from God (Heb 8:10–11).

Same Spirit
Same Team
Same Goal

Instead of believing that the gift of tongues reveals a special privilege that enables close communion with God (which can easily lead to pride), we should be glad that all the spiritual gifts are manifestations of the Spirit as the scriptures teach, and that as His children we all are to commune with God. So we do not need to think the gift of tongues as supreme above the other gifts—clearly Paul has spoken against this in these verses, but we can and should heighten our expectation of every believer and all the spiritual gifts.

Let me give an example how this works with other spiritual gifts, such as mine, the gift of teaching. At times, when I wait upon the Lord, the Spirit will insert thoughts appropriate for what I will be teaching on. They come rather regularly, stirring my soul and building up my faith. I seek His teaching so I can properly steer my teaching. These insights or teachings present astounding experiences and closer communion with God, but they are difficult to explain to others. But, though I have this gift, it would be naive and unbiblical to suggest that all should have the gift of teaching in order to commune with God.

The Spirit of God uniquely prompts, guides, gives faith for, warns, etc., all believers so they can properly exercise their gifts. God builds up those who properly use their spiritual gifts; in fact, this edification becomes a motivating factor, in my case, to set apart extra time to prepare to teach. I am not better than another because of these insights, but neither is the tongue speaker nor the man with faith, for we all commune with God as we rightly use our spiritual gifts. We are one body and need each other. The moment we make our experience as the model and compel or hint that others ought to have that same experience, it violates the truth of this passage. Not all have the same gift. Those who share the same gift will probably have common experiences, but this does not mean that others do not have special experiences unique to their gifting. We would expect they do, but we would not want them to impose the expectation that others should have the same gifting and attached experiences. Instead, we gladly delight that all genuine believers have the presence of the Holy Spirit working in their lives, gifting them, and constantly working with them to properly exercise that gift in love.

A Positive Statement of Spiritual Gifts

God uses the Spirit of Christ to uniquely anoint each believer with a special gift to give the believer an opportunity to minister to the body of Christ. No believer lives by him or herself. We are members of one body and are made to serve one another through general love acts and specifically through our spiritual gifts.

1) Communion with the Lord (relationship) always stands as a basic foundation for every believer. In terms of networking, we are all spiritually "wired" to connect to and commune with the Lord. A holy life is a prerequisite to ongoing communion with the Lord. If we are not seeking God's presence and communing with Him, then something is wrong. We do not need "tongues" or any certain spiritual gift or experience to enjoy deep intimacy with the Father. This is the inheritance of His children saved by Christ under the New Covenant.

2) Spiritual gifts mark God's special desire to work in and through the lives of genuine believers. The gifts are part of Christ's gift that He shares with each of us. We are not to compare ourselves with others, insinuating one is better than another. That would be like one piece of a puzzle saying it is more important than the other pieces! What nonsense! But instead, we ought to thoroughly enjoy utilizing our gifts to minister to others and be blessed by the gifts of others.

3) Gifts have a larger purpose then serving ourselves. Anytime we begin to focus on ourselves or our gifting, we need to return to a biblical framework. The gifts are not about us, though they become an opportunity to show our devotion to God and concern for others. The gifts instead reflect God's purposes of strengthening and otherwise

ministering to His people through us. How astonishing to see the Almighty God work through our lives by bringing His love, wisdom, comfort, etc. into the lives of His people!

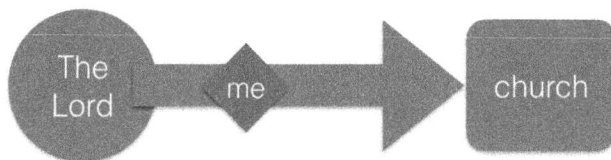

4) Saints on earth may differ in gifting but are required to work together to complete God's redemptive plan. Success never resides in any one individual. Even for the apostles who are "first," they were only part of a greater story. In fact, we find that the apostles, along with the prophets and teachers (and others–Eph 4:11–12), were equipping others so that they too would be optimized for effective service. Everyone serving everyone!

Summary

There has been great zealousness and not a few painful divisions over speaking in "tongues," which is often spurred on by claims of greater intimacy with God. Every genuine believer is empowered by the Holy Spirit and has a spiritual gift to carry out God's greater purposes of strengthening His body. If we do not prioritize God's mission and purpose, it is easy to be distracted with spiritual gifts and our experiences rather than mustering our energies to complete God's purpose for our lives. We are glad God speaks uniquely to some. May it be to all, but it will not be through one particular kind of gifting. God does not sterilize His magnificent operations for the sake of our boasting, but as in Jesus' case, He heals people in diverse ways. So God works in many ways to bring glory to His Name, not our own. Seek Him in your own life and expect great things from God so that the people of God might be built up to complete their service to their gracious Lord. Our spiritual gifts do not establish our favor before God but reveal His involvement in our lives.

Discussion Questions

1. What makes a spiritual gift different from a natural gift?

2. Are any gifts a sign of more spiritual maturity than others? Explain.

3. As a believer, you have at least one spiritual gift. What might be your spiritual gift(s) and the reason you think so?

4. Why might some people treat their own spiritual gift as unique and special, as better than others?

5. What would be the best way for the members of the body of Christ to view themselves with others?

6. What should we do when we or others, though professing Christ, seem to have no faith?

7. What are the biblical reasons given that prove that the gifts of "speaking in foreign languages" (i.e., tongues) or other revelational gifts are not necessary to be a believer or spiritual?

8. Is communion with God linked to any spiritual gift? Explain.

Life in the Spirit!

Section 4: Christian Doctrine: Questions and Theology

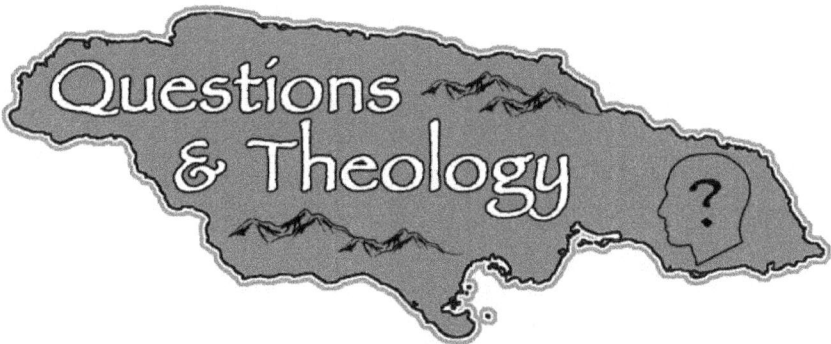

"If I do not go away, the Helper shall not come to you" (John 16:7).

We know some believers really want to reach the island of Christian Doctrine where questions and theology are introduced. But actually, though we want clear answers to tough questions, we want to examine more carefully what the Scriptures actually say about these issues. We will get our "feet wet" with plenty of Scriptures to discover what we really should believe about many of these hard issues, but equally important, we will learn how the Holy Spirit desires to fully engage us in our personal lives to the glory of God and the sake of His people.

#15 The Anointing of the Spirit (John 7:37–39)

Life in the Spirit!
Experiencing the Fullness of Christ

How do you describe a Christian? Here are three overlapping answers: Being like our Heavenly Father, being Christlike, and being regenerated by the Holy Spirit. Each describes how God's grace recaptures the "image of God" that we lost though the Fall. After Adam's sin, the Lord forbade and kept man from eating of the tree of eternal life (Gen 3:24) because He had a better plan: eliminate mankind's guilt and give them eternal life in Christ (Rom 5:16–17).

The Lord uses the new covenant to fashion all of His people into the new temple of God and dwells in us through His Spirit! Though His saving work in our lives is simply awesome, I must assert that we are not qualified to be part of His people, for we have fallen short of His glory (Rom 3:23). Entrance is given only because of His extreme kindness and mercy offered through Christ. His redemption plan forges a great future for mankind through God's good purposes for them in Christ. Let's look in more detail at what God wants to do in our lives from the vantage point of the Holy Spirit's work after a person becomes a believer.

A. The Age of the Holy Spirit (John 7:37–39)

> Now on the last day, the great day of the feast, Jesus stood and cried out, saying, "If any man is thirsty, let him come to Me and drink. 38 "He who believes in Me, as the Scripture said, 'From his innermost being shall flow rivers of living water.'" 39 But this He spoke of the Spirit, whom those who believed in Him were to receive; for the Spirit was not yet given, because Jesus was not yet glorified. (John 7:37–39)

If there be any speculation as to what Jesus was referring to on the last day of the great feast when He invited people to come to Him to drink, John in verse 39 clears away the unclarity. "But this He spoke of the Spirit" highlights that the living water refers to the Holy Spirit. John explained that the offer was reserved for the future as the Spirit was not yet given "because Jesus was not yet glorified" (v.39). He was clearly pointing to a coming time, to those who would yet believe: "Spirit, whom those who believed in Him were to receive," which would include all believers from that time forward.

Jesus clearly identifies the impact that the New Covenant would have on all genuine believers—sealing His people with His blood and securing the pouring out of the Spirit after He ascended (was glorified). The cross would bring forgiveness and reconciliation while Jesus' ascension enabled the Holy Spirit to descend into His peoples' hearts. John's theological conclusion summarizes well everything that has been said of the power of the cross and the indwelling of the Holy Spirit in His people.

"not yet"
Old Covenant

"were to"
New Covenant

Having clarified the deeper meaning of the living water, we can be assured of Jesus' invitation, "If any man is thirsty, let him come to Me and drink." Jesus was not being stingy with His grace, as we see in this open invitation that encourages us all to enter into His abounding grace. Having come to Jesus, we must never forget our dependency upon His grace and favor; we must firmly proclaim that this invitation is only through Jesus and not through any religion or even a membership to Christianity. At the heart of Christianity is belief in Christ.

> *"Do you not know that you are a temple of*
> *God, and that the Spirit of God dwells in*
> *you?" (1 Corinthians 3:16)*

The phrase "From his innermost being shall flow rivers of living water" (v.38) reveals God's intention to immediately, to some large degree, restore the original hope for life that flows from the abundant life instilled in His people through Him. God would not fill a building but His people. At times, His people are called His temple (Eph 2:21; 2 Cor 6:16), probably alluding to the Genesis and Ezekiel temple images where His redeeming goodness flows out like a river (Ezek 47). The New Covenant offers intimacy by dwelling with God, which promises a richer life than that offered in the Old Testament (Heb 8:7–13), at a time when only some could draw near the temple. We need to upgrade our expectations for what God can and will do in the lives of all His believers on earth before reaching heaven's shores.

The following diagram displays the direction that this river of grace takes. God's abounding grace, associated with His presence, comes from above and anoints His people by living among them (i.e., red diamond blocks).

Spirit's indwelling

Outgoing
blessings

God's people

Outgoing
blessings

We are transformed by His kindness and truth and, like running streams pouring over the rough patches of our lives, the arrows represent the healing and hope that flows out from us. This same stream first deeply affects our lives and then continues to pour out, touching the lives of those around us. So we see why Jesus calls us the light of the world (Matt 5:14), for Jesus is the Light, illuminating and otherwise transforming our lives and being displayed in the world. In the end, people see God's glory through our lives and turn to Him!

> You are the light of the world. A city set on a hill cannot be hidden. Nor do men light a lamp, and put it under the peck-measure, but on the lampstand; and it gives light to all who are in the house. Let your light shine before men in such a way that they may see your good works, and glorify your Father who is in heaven (Matt 5:14–16).

Summary

These basic Christian truths should be so readily understood and applied to our lives that each of us is animated and transformed by the fullness of the Spirit of God. We should take up the charismatics' challenge that all believers should have an exciting spiritual life in the presence of God. Jesus' promise was for all believers. It would be wrong to conclude that God, as shown in the Old Testament, merely comes upon this or that person or, as in the New Testament, that He only comes onto those speaking in "tongues." We—all His genuine followers —have become His temple! Inner waters flow out from our lives only after they have first gushed through ours, performing their awesome transformation!

It is a shame that God's people are not all thriving in their relationships with the Lord. There could be numerous things that hinder a deeper intimacy with the Lord, including unbelief, but before going on, let me clarify that I am not speaking of special miraculous encounters but rather the general awe of living in God's presence that occurs when we believe in Jesus Christ.

Some believers are held back because of unconfessed sin. We shouldn't make room for open rebellion in our lives but instead, through repentance and confession move on! Paul rebukes the Corinthians (though not all of them) for continuing to act as a baby (1 Cor 3:1–2). They needed to move forward into the fullness for which God made them. Who would be happy with a soccer game without a ball, a sailboat without a sail to fly over the waters? So we believers need to seek the Lord for His abounding grace and not assume that a profession of Christ or regular attendance at a church defines the Christian life. The opposite is true.

If we find ourselves confused because of the lack of the Spirit's presence, we should focus on the basics of salvation until this is largely resolved.[24] Salvation leads to God's presence, the residing of the Holy Spirit in our lives (i.e., a pledge or down deposit Eph 1:13–14), which leads to holiness and in turn gives occasion for the fullness of God's Spirit. Let us not stop too long to admire our personal experiences but allow the Spirit to further prod us onward into kind actions and regular use of our spiritual gifts. Our whole Christian life should be energized by God's Spirit in us!

If we seek a deeper life with the Lord, that is good. Our whole lives should be so occupied with a deeper longing for the Lord's presence; this is good and natural. This quest should not be an anxious search, fretting about how the Lord does not appear to be doing anything about our request but should rather possess a calm assurance of God's timely and good plan to meet us in His special way.

Salvation => God's presence => Holiness

Being: adopt God's holy standards
Doing: conform our actions to His will

The Spirit's work can be summarized in several steps. The salvation experience, defined by our faith in Christ's saving work, brings us into God's presence while His Spirit dwells within us. From that close association with God, we will develop a genuine love for holiness and a hatred of sin and injustice. This intimate relationship in God's presence

---

[24] God, at times, brings us through very traumatic times that reshape our lives. Instead of doubting our salvation, we should quietly but confidently focus on God's hand in our lives, resting in the love of God found in Jesus' work on the cross and resurrection.

importantly shapes our behavior and thoughts, bringing about the necessary doing (i.e., good works 1 Tim 6:18). The Lord shapes and empowers us to accomplish His purposes for our lives.

All of this is quite extraordinary, not only because of the fact that we do not deserve His kindness but also because He is willing to work in and through our inferior lives. What patience! We will discuss this further as we consider the meaning of the anointing of Jesus and of believers.

B. The Spirit's Anointing of Jesus (Luke 4:17–21; Is 61:1–2)

The anointing of Jesus has important implications for the Christian believer, even though it is rarely connected. We will first clarify the significance of Jesus' anointing and then relate it to the believers.

"The book of the prophet Isaiah was handed to" (v.17) Jesus, and He stated that the Isaiah 61:1-2 prophecy was filled that day: "Today... fulfilled in your hearing" (v.21), which connects the Old Testament prophecy to Jesus.

> And the book of the prophet Isaiah was handed to Him. And He opened the book, and found the place where it was written, 18 *"The Spirit of the Lord is upon me, because He anointed me to preach the gospel to the poor. He has sent me to proclaim release to the captives, and recovery of sight to the blind, ate set free those who are downtrodden, to proclaim the favorable year of the Lord."* 20 And He closed the book, and gave it back to the attendant, and sat down; and the eyes of all in the synagogue were fixed upon Him. 21 And He began to say to them, "Today this Scripture has been fulfilled in your hearing" (Luke 4:17–21; Is 61:1–2).

> And it came about in those days that Jesus came from Nazareth in Galilee, and was baptized by John in the Jordan. 10 And immediately coming up out of the water, He saw the heavens

opening, and the Spirit like a dove descending upon Him (Mark 1:9–10).

"The Spirit of the Lord is upon me" (Luke 4:18) refers to the way the Holy Spirit came upon/anointed Jesus at His baptism. "The Spirit like a dove descending upon Him" (Mark 1:10) convincingly teaches the anointing and ensuing ministry of the Holy Spirit were seen in Jesus. Believers often confuse Jesus' powerful ministry with His divinity, but Philippians 2:3–11 clearly states that Jesus did not utilize His divine powers but depended on the Holy Spirit's powerful anointing. Hebrews 4 reveals how Jesus' coming enabled Him to identify with the believer (i.e., priest) and to encourage us as followers to be similarly faithful with the aid of the Holy Spirit.

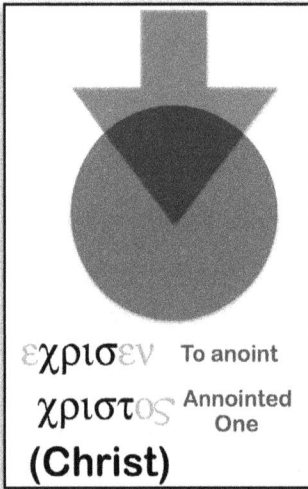

εχρισεν To anoint

χριστος Annointed One

(Christ)

"He anointed me" (Luke 4:18) largely defined Jesus' life and ministry. The word "Christ" comes from the Greek word here for anointing (*crio*). The Old Testament term for anointing, *messiah*, is transliterated as Messiah, and is written in English as *Christ* (John 1:41), God's anointed One. There are four Greek words that can be used for anointing, and the word for the religious or sacred one was used here. The three mundane words (e.g., rub) are used in other places. The picture here is of God's Spirit being poured out on His Son to imbue Him with the necessary gifts to carry out God's special saving purposes.

"To bring good news" (4:18) generally describes how the Holy Spirit imparted vision and empowered Jesus with the mission to publicly preach and teach God's Word, which was often accompanied by the signs of the Spirit (e.g., blind recover sight, 4:19). What happened to Jesus is important because the Holy Spirit's work in Him is what is replicated, though in a lesser way, in the lives of His people.

C. An Anointing for Christians (1 John 2:20,27)

> But you have an anointing from the Holy One, and you all know (1 John 2:20, emphasis mine).

> And as for you, the anointing which you received from Him abides in you, and you have no need for anyone to teach you; but as His anointing teaches you about all things, and is true and is not a lie, and just as it has taught you, you abide in Him (1 John 2:27, emphasis mine).

> Now He who establishes us with you in Christ and anointed us is God (2 Cor 1:21, emphasis mine).

The above verses clearly show that Christ's anointing was similar to that which the believers receive. Was it fully the same? That can be debated, but it appears that we should link the Father's anointing of Jesus with the empowering presence of the Holy Spirit leading to the transformation of the believers.

"But you have an anointing from the Holy One" clearly connects the anointing of the believers with the anointing from God via Christ (remember Christ literally means 'anointed' One: cristos–Christians). The anointing comes from one's faith rather than a reward for some performance, for John was speaking generally to the believers there. Moreover, "Have an anointing" again uses the same religious/sacred word that was used for Christ (noun form: crisma).

"But you have" (2:20) and "for you" (2:27) both refer to all the believers in the local church and not just to selected leaders (1 John

<u>1:3-4</u>). So this anointing, then, is something common to all believers, which is what we would expect after reading Paul's earlier letters to the Romans and Corinthians. "The Spirit Himself bears witness with our spirit that we are children of God" (<u>Rom 8:16</u>). "Now we have received, not the spirit of the world, but the Spirit who is from God, that we might know the things freely given to us by God" (<u>1 Cor 2:12</u>). The teaching and communication of the Holy Spirit taught in the Pauline passages above is affirmed by John, "His anointing teaches you" (John 2:27), again, clearly drawing a connection between the Spirit that anointed Jesus and the one that anoints believers.

"You received" (2:27) affirms that this anointing has happened for believers in the past and associates it with our newfound faith in Christ, an anointing similar to that which Jesus received. Having "received from Him" (2:27) reminds us that we have not earned this anointing but that it is a gift given from God the Father, part of the package of salvation. Regeneration (<u>John 3:3,7</u>), then, does not only show itself when a person is born of the Spirit but also when he lives by the Spirit, having gained a new life through faith in Christ.

"Abides in you" (v.27) confirms this interpretation, in case there is any debate over the meaning of anointing. The anointing is associated with God living or abiding in His people through the Holy Spirit's presence. The Spirit is not just there for a one-time event but abides in us, that is, dwells in us in an ongoing way.

So God's people are anointed by the Spirit in the same way Jesus was and thus can intimately commune with God through Christ and the Spirit just as Jesus did. They are set apart, like Christ, to do God's will, and nothing needs to hinder them from accomplishing the godly tasks that have been appointed them (<u>Eph 2:10</u>). Because of the Spirit, we have God's power, wisdom, and grace. We only need to abide, or commune with the Lord through the Spirit to assure us of these blessings, which again emphasizes the importance of our daily quiet times with the Him and our communion with Him throughout the day (pray without ceasing, 1 Thes 5:17).

> *God's anointing of believers reveals His*
> *expectation for believers to carry out Christ's*
> *life and mission, leaving us no excuses.*

Summary

This anointing for all believers is another way of confirming the characteristics of a genuine believer (the being) and the expectation of the work of the Holy Spirit in the believer (the works). Similar to Christ's anointing, we have our own glorious communion with God and the ability to busy ourselves in carrying out the Father's ministry. Jesus came to do the will of the Father, and having accomplished it (John 19:30), He has given His children the special anointing from the Father for the same purposes. This perfectly fits into the image of Christ being the head and the church being His body. We are poised and equipped to do His awesome will.

D. Sealed by the Holy Spirit (2 Cor 1:21–22)

"Sealed by the Spirit" is used three times (Eph 1:13; 4:30; 2 Cor 1:22). The word "sealed" draws parallels to the authority marking, often in wax, on a document that officiates the content. A king, for example, might use his seal on a certain document to signify that it belongs to him and that no one should dare tamper with it. God has sealed His people with His Spirit, thus declaring that their lives, washed in the blood of the Lord, belong to Him and declaring that Satan better not tamper with them.

> In Him, you also, after listening to the message of truth, the gospel of your salvation--having also believed, you were sealed in Him with the Holy Spirit of promise (Eph 1:13).

> And do not grieve the Holy Spirit of God, by whom you were sealed for the day of redemption (Eph 4:30; also: Rev 7:5,8; 9:4).

> Now He who establishes us with you in Christ and anointed us is God, 22 who also sealed us and gave us the Spirit in our hearts as a pledge (2 Cor 1:21–22).

God's work in His people by His Spirit occurs in an ongoing way. The phrase "establishes us with you in Christ" (v. 21) is based on three past Spirit events including this sealing.

> (1) "Anointed us is God" (v.21)
> (2) "Who also sealed us" (v.22; Rev 7:5,8; 9:4)
> (3) Who also "gave us the Spirt in our hearts as a pledge" (v.22).

Points (2) and (3) are considered one event, the securing of our lives to Him through the Spirit's work.

Summary

As the Spirit anointed Jesus, so the Spirit anoints all His people. God's people are in time sealed by the Spirit as a pledge pointing us to the

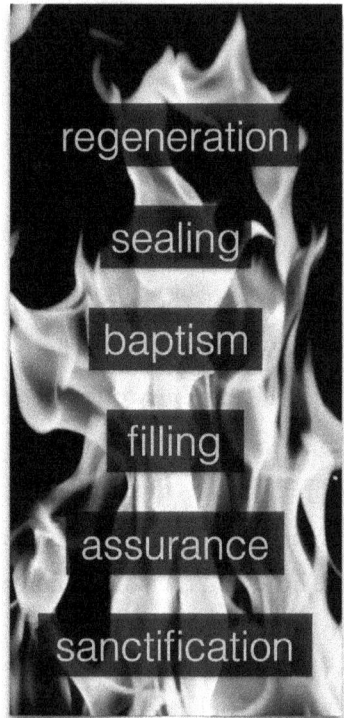

distant richer fulfillment of God's blessings, but let us not forget the Spirit's present work of creating and presenting the church of God to Himself.

Conclusion

Although the anointing Jesus received at His baptism was affirmed with special signs, there is no indication that a dove should descend upon us when we receive the Holy Spirit. As believers, we have, like Christ, received a special touch of God's grace in the form of the Holy Spirit in our lives, who stirs and guides us, beginning with our salvation and taking us right to heaven's shores. The success of our Christian lives largely depends on the degree of our reliance upon the Holy Spirit, living in constant communion with the Father, and so faithfully carries out the tasks God our Father puts in our hands to do.

> In whom the whole building, being fitted together is growing into a holy temple in the Lord; in whom you also are being built together into a dwelling of God in the Spirit (Eph 2:21–22).

Discussion Questions

1. Is it too bold to suggest that every genuine believer has an anointing from the Holy Spirit? Explain.

2. What does the word "anointing" literally mean? Explain its physical and spiritual meaning.

3. What does that anointing look like? What would you expect to happen from that anointing?

4. What is it that Christians tend to disagree about regarding an anointing from the Spirit?

5. What indication of this anointing do you see in your own life? What more do you think you should experience? Why?

6. How is the New Covenant associated with the anointing of the Holy Spirit?

7. What are the implications that God's Spirit lives in the believers, forming us into His holy temple? How does this relate to the local church?

#16 Special Experiences of the Spirit

℣ife in the Spirit!
Experiencing the Fullness of Christ

Two looming, ongoing problems face the church:

(1) Why does the church appear so dead?

(2) Why aren't more Christians filled with God's Spirit (Rev 2–3)?

Christians typically desire for God's love and truth to have a bigger impact on the church and society and have difficulty explaining and resolving the church's unhealthy phenomena. Instead of denigrating theology or the church, let us strengthen our faith by a firmer understanding of the Holy Spirit's life-changing work in the church and ourselves.

The clearer we are regarding the Spirit's work, the less of a problem we will have. But theology is not everything! Some of the deadest churches have great theology! The church in different cultures at different periods tends to swing to intellectualism while minimizing experience or pushing experience while deemphasizing reasoning through the scriptures. Jesus Himself raised these issues (Rev 2–3) so that we would connect our theology (biblically driven perspectives) to our lives. Our aim attempts to present and hold a good balance of these two.

On the one hand, we will center our attention on the need for the Spirit to effectually work in our lives, not just to be saved but to live out godly lives. People rightfully wonder: "Do God's people indeed have the Spirit of God?" and, "What would it look like for God to live in a person's life?" Such questions are asked because of the immorality, lack of integrity, and general lack of passion for the things of God. People confess to being God's people but don't display Christ! Quests to discover answers to these questions have become sources for some to sadly reject God, the Author of Life. People, like God, are rightly opposed to hypocrites! Unfortunately, some professors of faith are comfortable with having inconsistent lives. There are others, however, who are trying to grow and admit that the power and love of the Holy Spirit seems to be missing from their lives. Of course, the possibility is that they are not really the people of God, though please, do not conclude from this that genuine believers can lose their salvation. John says that those, like Judas, who once confessed Christ but later rejected Him, were not really believers in the first place (1 John 2:19).

A. The Need for the Spirit's Work

Following along with the previous chapter, we remember that the fact that "The Spirit was not yet given" (John 7:39) points to the cross, when God redeemed His people. Having gained forgiveness through Christ's work on the cross, God moved into His people to commune with them because His wrath was appeased (1 John 2:2). We want to identify some questions that tend to confuse believers and provide terse answers. Later on, we will look at some of the reasoning and doctrines behind our answers and on how special experiences fit into this. Let's first look at how two passages confirm our pursuit of that balance: experiencing the Spirit and maintaining good biblical teaching. This precious balance will help keep us close to God throughout our lives.

First, Paul in his Ephesians 3 prayer sows great hope for our lives, especially considering that we were once spiritually dead and blackened with the devil's darkness (Eph 2:1–2)! What a long journey that the Lord intends for each of us to make in this life before we meet Him face to face.

> That He would grant you, according to the riches of His glory, to be strengthened with power through His Spirit in the inner man (Eph 3:16).

The apostle helps us imagine the celebrated work that God is doing in our lives with this awesome picture: "according to the riches of His glory" (Eph 3:14–20). Note that we are not to focus on God's glory but the riches of this glory. It is as if we are to imagine the greatest thing we could ever dream of, with the help of all sorts of sounds, sights, and amazement, but then, we are to leap above that level. The riches should draw our minds to the spectacular nature of it all and how it can, in some ways, be transferred to our earthly experiences. Make sure you add this to your definition of a Christian. I believe it will change how you think of yourself! He has gloriously strengthened us.

Paul continues on with the next pregnant phrase, "with power through His Spirit," which restates the assurance that God's people can overcome the world. The power is the strength to live as we ought while maintaining God's mission for our lives clearly in view. We can do all that He desires for us. This is not because of our natural capabilities (Eph 2:1; 6:10–12) but through the Holy Spirit's constant and empowering work in our lives. We hope to further define this work as we continue through this chapter.

Lastly, we must remind ourselves that the majority of the effects of the Spirit are in the "inner man," that is, our new life within our old bodies. The outcome of this inner work will necessarily affect our lives and choices, but we must first cultivate the inner life if we are to grow strong as believers. Right thinking that possesses the right biblical perspective leads us to connect what is really happening in our lives with God's purposes so that we can, so to speak, cooperate with the Spirit's work, having Him more deeply affect our lives. This next passage, likewise, causes us to think greatly of the work of the Holy Spirit in our lives.

> For our gospel did not come to you in word only, but also in power and in the Holy Spirit and with full conviction; just as you know what kind of men we proved to be among you for your sake (1 Thes 1:5).

"Our gospel" is God's saving message that is used by the Spirit of God to bring about astounding changes in our relationship with God that begin the transformation of our lives. The preached word should bring about the Holy Spirit's power and conviction just as we saw in Acts (Acts 2:37). This is just what the Lord did through Paul's preaching in Thessalonica and can do in your own city, town, and heart. The point of stating all of this is to give us an understanding of the special, though common, gifts the Spirit delivers to our lives. Again, Paul uses the word "power" to highlight the great changes that come into our lives. "Conviction" has more to do with the means or the way the Spirit uses God's Word to challenge our minds and thought processes by highlighting our intense need to conform to God's will. This conviction is an important part of the process of winning our souls over to the great love of God and acceptance of His Gospel truth to our lives.

We only can and should conclude that the church as a body is meant to powerfully live out the love and truth of the gospel through the quickening work of God's Spirit in our lives. Having somewhat defined our expectations, let us pursue some often-raised questions.

Important Questions:

- Does the Holy Spirit come to stay with every genuine believer? Yes, indeed He does. The anointing or baptism of the Spirit is for every believer, bringing us an assuring peace that God's Spirit is always with us.

- But can we not lose the Holy Spirit? Some take David's prayer, "And do not take Thy Holy Spirit from me" (Psalm 51:11) as proof that the Spirit can leave a believer. Two main considerations need to be brought up for a proper interpretation. First, in the Old Testament, the Spirit came upon people differently and was not promised to remain with them. David saw this with King Saul just prior to him, "Now the Spirit of the LORD departed from Saul, and an evil spirit from the LORD terrorized him" (1 Sam 16:14). The Spirit left King Saul because of disobedience, leaving a vacuum for the evil spirit to trouble him. David had a genuine concern for he had just committed murder and adultery!

Second, in the New Testament, the Spirit's presence is linked with salvation rather than some special office, task, or appointment. Those who think they can lose their salvation often equate this with the loss of the Spirit, but the scriptures differently identify the issue. First, if the Spirit does not dwell in a person, it is because they do not know the Lord (1 John 2:19). Second, the believer can lose closeness with God because of sin, thus grieving the Spirit (Eph 4:30), and this will restrain God's work, but as God's people, we remain the temples of God. This is the reason, even after we sin, we are pointed to ways of cleansing and forgiveness (1 John 1:9). The genuine believer cannot lose his salvation or the presence of the Holy Spirit, but the effects of the Spirit might be quite dismal.

- Will the Holy Spirit always fully manifest Himself by filling us? The Spirit does much initiatory work in our lives at salvation,[25] but the command "be filled with the Spirit" (Ephesians 5:18) clearly teaches us that spiritual growth is conditional upon our response to His promptings. Our lives, desires, and pursuits will affect the way the Spirit works in our lives. Prayer has a lot to do with our communion with God, His way of pointing out His will, and our way of seeking Him for what we need.

- Should the believer seek a post-salvation second blessing of the Spirit to fully live out the gospel (e.g., laying on of hands, slain in the Spirit, etc.)? The idea behind this, and a lot of things going on in different past and current movements, is the assumption that there is a needed Spirit-engendering experience after our salvation. Clearly, this is not true. When we have the Holy Spirit, we have what we need, that is, we have Him dwelling in us! The greater problem is not the Spirit's presence but our ignorance and disobedience. Some Christians unacceptably misinterpret Acts to back up their approach. In an earlier chapter, I explained this was not needed. This understanding denies the special anointing of the Spirit on all believers' lives. Even the carnal Christians of Corinth were called the temple of God where the Spirit dwelt, "Or do you not know that your body is a temple of the Holy Spirit who is in

[25] I like to think of it like a computer's operating system, which is what enables the computer to be fully used.

you, whom you have from God, and that you are not your own?" (1 Cor 6:19). The problem partly stems from believers who are not regularly filled with the Spirit, thus clouding the glorious work of the Spirit in our lives. The problem is exacerbated by traditional churches producing many professing believers that, though baptized as infants and assumed to be Christians, did not have God's Spirit clearly working in their lives. Special experiences are not necessary to living a life filled with the Spirit, but sometimes they are given.

What we genuinely believe about the Holy Spirit shapes our lives. What do you believe? How important is it to you?

- Shouldn't the believer seek for the Spirit to fully manifest His power, presence, love, and wisdom in our lives and the lives of others? This is definitely the right question to help direct us to where we need to be going. The Christian life is portrayed as a growing relationship, which we will look at later when discussing John 15. Each day provides many opportunities to open your heart to God's Spirit and His work in your life—with your family members, spouse, neighbors, colleagues, fellow students, etc.

- Is it possible to blaspheme the Holy Spirit? This question is a bit more involved, but briefly, believers do not need to fear this blunder of blasphemy as it is impossible for believers to deny the very source of their life. The problem of "blasphemy of the Spirit" largely originates from Jesus' rebuke to those who had hardened their hearts against God even though they saw His miraculous work.

Therefore I say to you, any sin and blasphemy shall be forgiven men, but blasphemy against the Spirit shall not be forgiven. And whoever shall speak a word against the Son of Man, it shall be forgiven him; but whoever shall speak against the Holy Spirit..." (Matt 12:31–32).

True believers born of the Spirit (John 3:5–6), enlivened by the Spirit (John 6:63) cannot commit blasphemy of the Spirit. Jesus' words are not directed toward confused or erring believers but to those who saw the mighty works of Jesus done by the Spirit and yet still repudiated Christ's claims. These people cannot find forgiveness for they have shut the door to God's work of the Spirit, the door to salvation.

Summary

What we genuinely believe about the Holy Spirit greatly shapes our pursuit of Him in our lives. What do you believe? If you quench the Spirit's work in your life because of some sin, then repent from your sin. Doubts multiply when we hold onto unconfessed sin in our lives, which in turn counters the faith necessary to depend on God for strength. Satan uses all sorts of means to confuse God's people and to keep unbelievers from a strong faith. These questions are important to resolve because the answers allow the bright rising sun of truth to dissipate the clouds of doubt that still hang about the morning. But we want to go one step further to fortify our faith, which is what we will do in the following point.

B. Describing the Terms for the Spirit's Work

By carefully defining the biblical terms associated with the Spirit's work, we avoid much confusion and are able to concisely grasp the Holy Spirit's work as it relates to our lives. There are numerous reasons for confusing the Holy Spirit's work in believers' lives:

- The term "spirit" is often confused with "Spirit" (the term Spirit or spirit is used 519 times in the Bible).

- References to the Spirit's work literally span from Genesis to Revelation (Gen 1:2; Rev 22:17).

- The Spirit has worked in various ways at different times, depending on whether it was before or after the cross, i.e., before or after the establishment of the New Covenant.

- The Holy Spirit is invisible, and His invisible nature makes Him hard to understand. Try explaining the wind!

- False understandings pop up everywhere, even in the devious New Age movement![26]

- The plethora of false teaching on the Holy Spirit is misleading and always confusing.

- The absence of good biblical teaching on the Holy Spirit is terribly troublesome (especially since Jesus tried to clarify His role in the Upper Room Discourse in John 14–17).

- The enemy counterfeits the genuine to purposely lead God's people astray.

- Disobedience arises from disbelief.

- The believer's belief that the world offers more than the life God promises us. The spirit of worldliness doubts the goodness of God.

Biblical Terms Describing the Holy Spirit's Work

We have outlined six biblical definitions that describe the Holy Spirit's work. When we assert what has been spoken to us in the scriptures, we

---

[26] "New Age Spirit" http://new-age-spirit.com

can ward off the counterfeits and deepen our delight in the Spirit's presence and work. The first three listed below all happen at the same time during what is called salvation.

Regeneration (Titus 3:5; John 3:7, i.e., "born again") is the one-time spiritual life-giving operation by the Holy Spirit that animates God's people, which is seen in His presence, power, and love. It starts with the Spirit's new life that generates marks of God's saving grace in the heart and life of the believer.

Sealing of the Spirit (2 Cor 1:22; Eph 1:13) refers to the one-time spiritual marking of a believer at salvation, forever establishing him or her as God's own. In Revelation, this sealing is only seen in the spiritual world (Rev 7:3, 9:4) and is set in contrast to the mark of the world (Rev 13:16; 14:11; 19:20). Interestingly, the word for sealing (i.e., putting an official security seal of authority) is used in Paul's letters as well as in book of Revelations, all of which carry a tone of finalization. See the prior chapter for a fuller description.

Baptism of the Spirit (Luke 3:16; Acts 1:5, 2:38, 10:47) is generally spontaneous rather than sought for, signifying a noticeable work of God in a believer's life that flows from regeneration. The universal experience of God's presence in believers' lives was initiated after the New Covenant (literally means 'will') was put in effect through Jesus' blood and verified by Christ's resurrection seen in the coming of the Holy Spirit (Acts 1:4-5). See a fuller description in chapter 9.

Filling of the Spirit (Eph 5:18) reminds us of the ongoing responsibility and opportunity for all believers to be fully influenced by the Spirit's presence and work in their daily lives. Filling of the Spirit reminds us of the potential for each believer to be fully changed by the Holy Spirit's reach into their hearts and minds. This filling describes the intensity of the Spirit's influence on our lives sourced in the Spirit's presence since our salvation.

Assurance of the Spirit (Rom 8:16) speaks of the special revelation of the Spirit, persuading God's people that they belong to the Lord forever. This assurance grows over time and through various experiences, but the message is the same—we are forever His!

Sanctification of the Spirit (2 Thes 2:13; 1 Peter 1:2,15-16), i.e., holiness, refers to the experiential process of increasingly being shaped in life and character by the Spirit in order to be holy like God. The word "sanctified" is also used but in the past tense, referring to a one-time action (1 Cor 1:2; 6:11), more like the sealing, where God's people are set apart (literally "made holy") for Him. This sanctification process is gradual and, with time through diverse experiences, draws God's people closer into His presence, which requires a shedding of selfish and sinful behavior as well as unhealthy attitudes.

Summary

The "Sanctification" chart (reading from bottom to top) represents the interrelation of the biblical descriptions of the Holy Spirit. Salvation is seen at the bottom where the Holy Spirit's work: saves (regenerates), seals (keeps),

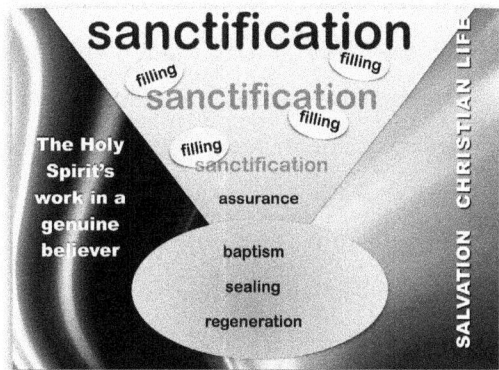

and baptizes (anoints) for ministry. Once believers have all the things necessary for living out a godly life (1 Peter 1:2–4), believers then "work out" (Phil 2:13) their salvation as they deepen their confidence in the fact that they belong to God and consistently obey the Lord. This is seen in the upward and expanding inverse triangle in the chart above. Obedience is important to growing in sanctification because it sets our hearts, minds, and bodies closer to our Holy God, enabling us to be more intimate with Him and allowing us to distance ourselves from the distracting and harmful lures of our flesh, the world, and the evil one.

A proper ability to rightly describe the Spirit's work in believers' lives enables God's people to concisely and carefully present key theological insights for themselves and others. We are trying to understand what it would look like for the Holy Spirit to live in our lives. Our first hurdle is crossed when we are able to find some good, terse answers to relevant questions, but a second is passed when we gain a clear understanding of the biblical terms that describe the Spirit's work that helps lay a good foundation to understand the special experiences that God's people have —which is what we will now carefully look at.

C. Describing the Special Blessings (John 15:7–8)

With a solid understanding and appreciation of what the Bible says about the Holy Spirit's work in our lives, we can go on and better apprehend the special experiences of the Holy Spirit God's people sometimes experience. While some believers overemphasize these experiences, and others categorically dismiss them, we join with Moses, Jesus, Paul, John, and others who recognize that our glorious God at times chooses to powerfully display His grace through His Spirit. Some of these experiences—and this is to be carefully noted—are blatantly bogus, but others are genuine. The Apostle Paul, as an example of the later, in 2 Cor 12:1–2 states that he was taken on an unexplainable trip to the third heaven (in the body or not, he did not know).

Some have combined the general deadness of church members and the special work of God in others to conclude that there needs to be a second experience of the Spirit apart from salvation for a person to live in the fullness of the Spirit. Let us take a look at a few verses to look at this topic once more but from a different angle. We will start with Jesus' stimulating words that tell us that we should be asking much more from our Heavenly Father.

> If you then, being evil, know how to give good gifts to your children, how much more shall your heavenly Father give the Holy Spirit to those who ask Him? (Luke 11:13)

The phrase "give the Holy Spirit" describes the manner in which the experiential presence of the Spirit of God comes upon His people. But we must be careful. Counterfeits abound. Our own fleshly desires can be aroused and cloud our understanding. While Paul spoke about visions and revelations, he only did so to keep the Corinthians from running after false apostles, not to present them as a typical model for others (2 Cor 12:1–2, 12). But again, the Holy Spirit is seen as a very good gift from God that should positively impact our lives.

Of course, these words can confuse us. The first thing we should notice is that this is pre-cross and that the New Covenant was not fully in effect. Besides, the phrase "your heavenly Father" seems to indicate that Jesus was speaking to His disciples who knew Him rather than for those seeking salvation. So, although, this verse is not a clear verse that helps us definitely understand how we should be affected by the Spirit, it still does teach us several important points:

- The Holy Spirit's work should be seen as one of the greatest blessings we can receive.

- Our communion with God will always involve the Spirit's work in our lives.

- God likes for us to seek Him for His best gifts like the Holy Spirit —"To those who ask Him." The Lord's gifts are personal, must be requested, and unique. Further intimacy with God is always to be sought within the biblical parameters of love, forgiveness, obedience, and humility.

Christians are rightly frustrated with the general deadness of many church members and understandably seek a special work of God in their lives to awaken them. Many of them, however, need a new life; they haven't had a first genuine saving experience. Below is another statement in which Jesus vividly highlights the Spirit's anticipated work in the lives of His people.

> If you abide in Me, and My words abide in you, ask whatever you wish, and it shall be done for you. By this is My Father glorified, that you bear much fruit, and so prove to be My disciples (John 15:7–8).

Jesus alludes to what I would call both a usual and special experience with God through the Spirit. Every experience of the Spirit is special. The Almighty God uses His Spirit to commune with His people, but this should be normal for God's people, so we teach all the young believers to pray and read God's Word. Although special experiences come and go, believers are to live in an abiding relationship with Christ directed by God's Word. Jesus speaks of a constant communion or abiding with Him and His words in us. This is typical!

Once we start focusing on the need for some special experience like the "laying on of hands" (Acts 8:18–19), we lose focus on the truth of God. Some, for example, insist on the need to find an anointed preacher and be "slain in the Spirit," but they have forgotten the teaching of the Spirit above. We have all that we need at salvation. God lives in our lives as John 15 above indicates. (Besides, the loss of control of our physical body and minds is biblically unsupported.)

Special experiences of the Holy Spirit have and will come upon God's people at times, but they are not necessary for being filled. If we confess all of our sins, nothing stops us from being filled with the Spirit and living in communion with our Lord. It is wrong to look for special experiences to build our foundational relationship with God. Instead, if a special experience comes, then make sure it does not supplant what is clearly taught in the scriptures and is squarely understood in relationship with the main salvation teachings.

Below I have noted three strong men of God who, though having a deep understanding of God's Word, had special experiences from God. You can listen to Martyn Lloyd-Jones describe these three special experiences of God at the footnoted web reference, the start time being noted below.[27]

- John Flavel [Time: 19:35–22:10]

- Jonathan Edwards [Time: 22:16–24:34]

- D. L. Moody [Time: 24:35–27:10]

What did you note as the common thread? First, they all were fully devoted to the Lord. They were settled in their faith. Second, we see that it was unexpected and unplanned for. Though they might have sought to know the Lord more, as D. L. Moody set out to do, they were already living for the Lord. These special experiences were all characterized by an intense sensitivity to God's presence and certain truths, such as His love.

---

[27] http://www.mljtrust.org/search/?q=further+reflections

Seek not an experience, but seek Him (Christ). Seek to know Him. Seek to realize His presence. Seek to love Him. Seek to die to yourself and everything else that you may live entirely in Him and for Him and give yourself entirely too. If He is at the center, you will be safe. But if you are simply seeking an experience, ...thrills... excitement, well then you are opening the door to the counterfeit and probably receive it (Martyn Lloyd-Jones T:34:11–34:48.[28]

So, we should see that special experiences of the Spirit can, and at times do, come upon the people of God in wholly unexpected ways, but they are always consistent with the Word of God and work in parallel to the sanctifying progress of the individual; in other words, speeding up the process. The Holy Spirit shows us that we too can grow in our relationship with the Lord, to be more sensitive to His truth and thus find further transformation in our lives.

Two Important Conclusions

Two important conclusions must drive our perspectives: (1) Believers do not need another new experience of God's Spirit to be filled with and otherwise led by the Spirit of God, and (2) Some believers have been powerfully moved of God by special Spirit-initiated experiences, often heightening the believer's sensitivity to the things of God, enabling their service of ministry to be more productive and ongoing (John 15:1–15).

Historical Perspective

Before closing this point on special experiences, it would be helpful to briefly cast a historical perspective on the church's overall approach to the Holy Spirit and these special Spirit experiences. Because of the great excesses around us, now and before, we tend to be extremists–running after one and opposing the other, or vice versa.

---

[28] Ibid.

Puritanism originally represented a reform away from the sterile and unbiblical developments found in Roman Catholicism. They insisted on preaching freely from God's Word rather than reading a prayer book dictated by others. They led the way to open their minds and hearts to the Word of God, that is, to God Himself. But Puritanism suffered from the same test of time and temptations of the evil one, and so there became two large reactions within Puritanism. Martin

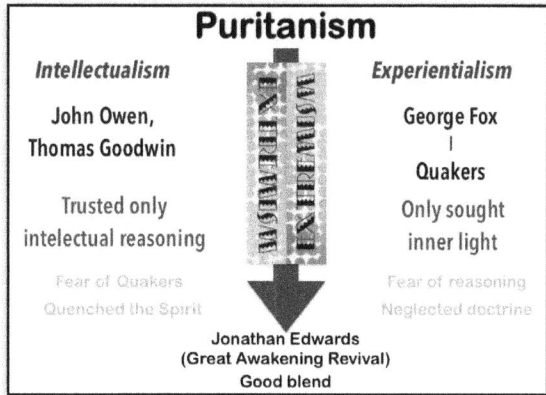

Lloyd-Jones in the talk cited above presents the two extremes (see "Puritanism" chart): Intellectualism, represented by John Owen and Thomas Goodwin, and experimentalism on the other side, represented by George Fox and the Quakers. The intellectuals were fearful of the Quakers and so focused on rational thought, and yet were influenced too much by the world. Fox didn't think theology in and of itself summarized the Christian and so focused on seeking inner illumination. But without a commitment to the Word of God, he lost his grip on the truth of God.

Jonathan Edwards, however, as shown in his book *"Religious Affections,"* as well as other books, clearly brought these two threads together to strengthen the church of God, insisting on both theological perspicuity as well as an experiential understanding of God. This is our point: we must retain a strong commitment to the Word of God and the Spirit's work in the church so to be fully attentive to the Spirit's work in our lives.

Summary

It is important to seek experiences consistent with the Bible where we are not merely looking for spiritual experiences but those which come from abiding in Christ, whose fruit lasts (John 15:16). Doesn't even the term "fruit" speak volumes on our expectations of what will happen when we regularly commune with our Lord through the Spirit (cf. Gal 5:22-23)?

D. Seeking Revival

The introduction of revival is vital to the work of the Spirit of God. Revival is the outpouring of God's Spirit upon believers in such a way that the work of God is pushed forward in their lives so that many others come to know the Lord.

There is no doubt that the present scene in North America and Europe presents a people who are begging for a revival of God's truths. The need is here, but few are crying out against the sin or for God's truth. The church is slowly dying out while the hostility against Christian teaching and practice is growing in unthinkable ways, even though the enemy's reasoning is wholly unreasonable and unproven. God's people, however, must remain on high alert. Note how the saints fervently prayed for their imprisoned Apostle Peter: "So Peter was kept in the prison, but prayer for him was being made fervently by the church to God" (Acts 12:5). God's people can, if in a concerted effort, bring about change through prayer (Acts 12:12–17). In the end, Peter was released by an intervening angel.

The invasive darkness has all but swallowed up the godly family. Like the Psalmist, we sincerely cry, "Help, Lord, for the godly man ceases to be, for the faithful disappear from among the sons of men" (Psalm 12:1). Our families and churches are deteriorating before our eyes and should raise great concern within God's people to cry out for revival, pleading to our saving God to strengthen the church in such a way that God's people become keenly aware of His presence and truth that can bring about immediate—and usually surprising—changes to their lives, and therefore, to the communities around them.

I will provide two quotes here on revival, one from Jonathan Edwards and the second speaks of George Whitfield. Both are in reference to the First Great Awakening in 1734–1735.

"The town," says Mr. Edwards, "was never so full of love, nor so full of joy, nor yet so full of distress, as it was then." Whenever he met the people in the sanctuary, he not only saw the house crowded, but every hearer earnest to receive the truth of God, and often the whole assembly dissolved in tears: some weeping for sorrow, others for joy, and others from compassion. In the months of March and April, when the work of God was carried on with the greatest power, he supposes the number, apparently of genuine conversions, to have been at least four a day, or nearly thirty a week, take one week with another, for five or six weeks together.[29]

George Whitfield's (1735) "great and sudden fame had preceded him and he was in immediate demand. He began preaching in Philadelphia at once and thousands flocked to hear him. The population of the town did not exceed 12,000 souls, yet his initial audiences numbered from 6,000 to 8,000!"[30]

---

[29] –CHAPTER VII. Remarkable revival of religion, in 1734, and 1735 (From Vol 1 of The Works of Jonathan Edwards).

[30] www.revival-library.org

Seek revival not only for yourself but for those around you, that God's glory might be further displayed in the places that darkness now appears to rule. The prayer that God has given me is that the Lord, Jesus the Groomsman, would amazingly work among His people and prepare His bride, dressing us in spectacular white wedding garments of holiness, for His spectacular return.

Conclusion

Here are some concluding points:

- At salvation, all of God's children gain what they need to live out the gospel by the Holy Spirit.

- Many professing believers are dead-like because they were never genuinely saved.

- We should not seek a second "post-conversion" experience but be further amazed at what God has already done in our lives through faith in Christ.

- Remember that the Lord works in His people in unique ways through His Spirit for His own purposes. Be excited over how He specifically works in you.

- We should seek a fuller and deeper walk with the Lord for all by seeking God's greater works in our own lives!

God's people are the temple of God. If they are filled with God's Spirit, then people will eagerly seek God's truth (though there are always distortions to mislead us). Big questions should arise in our hearts if, when we speak about joy in the Lord, we do not experience this joy, or if when we speak of God's love but don't exercise that love, or when we teach on God's holiness but inwardly despise His holiness by preserving secret places for our sins and actively question His will. May we repent and seek God for His greatest good in our lives!

Discussion Questions

1. Do you sense that the church is missing something? Explain.

2. Explain the role that the Spirit of God plays when a person becomes a believer.

3. How do you discern between the genuine and bogus work of the Spirit of God in the lives of His people?

4. Regeneration often takes place in a flash so why does it seem some people take so long before believing?

5. Do you long for a second experience or relish God's presence to work in you?

6. Do you sense a need for a revival for the church today? Why? What would you want to see happen? Do you pray for this?

7. In what ways could you better prepare for when Christ returns? Be practical and seek those changes in your life today.

Life in the Spirit!

#17 The Person of the Holy Spirit (John 14:26)

Life in the Spirit!
Experiencing the Fullness of Christ

The constant confusion regarding the person of the Holy Spirit is understandable (Acts 19:2) because of the huge gap between the Spirit's nature and ours. This, perhaps, explains why people more commonly describe the wind by what its currents do: "Such a strong wind today.; look at the branches move." Christians likewise typically focus more on the Spirit's function rather than His person. A good understanding of the Spirit's personhood, however, really helps us in our Christian growth at several levels. Instead of feeling distant or that He is some vague force or source of energy, He comes, lives, and operates in us!

The Spirit is not an impersonal force; He is personal, having His own authority, opinion, and purpose. Many misunderstandings pop up when we try to understand Him only by what He gives or brings. Let us think back to Jesus and remember how He healed the ten lepers. He praised the one leper who came back and thanked Him, the one who understood the person behind the healing and, rather than being consumed with what he had received, went to give thanks. The Spirit is invisible; we can't see Him. And though the Spirit is like the wind in some ways, He differs as He is personal and engages us on an individual level. Even if the wind became visible, we still could not focus on it as we do a person because it is so grand and dispersed, being moved rather than commanding itself. Let's further ponder on the person of the Holy Spirit.

A. The Coming Change (John 14:26)

> But the Helper, the Holy Spirit, whom the Father will send in My name, He will teach you all things, and bring to your remembrance all that I said to you (John 14:26).

> He shall glorify Me; for He shall take of Mine, and shall disclose it to you. (John 16:14)

A quick glance at Jesus' description of the Holy Spirit brings a great upsurge in our understanding of the Spirit. That which has been very unclear, even with the Bible in hand, all of a sudden, becomes much more straightforward. This chapter will focus on the implications of the Spirit's personhood and character while other perplexities within the Godhood will be further explained in the following chapter.

First, we need to clarify the intricacies of what is said in John 14:26 regarding the personal nature of the Holy Spirit. In the Greek (the NT's original language), the neuter adjective should typically follow the noun for the word 'spirit', since by definition it is neuter (as opposed to masculine or feminine grammatical declension).[31] Each of us would understand this for the wind has no association with a gender, being neither male or female. But halfway through the verse Jesus uses a

---

[31] *ekeinos* is a Greek pronoun here in the masculine form and denotes a person, which can be translated as 'he' or 'that one'.

pronoun in the masculine form, forcing us to conclude that, like the actions that follow, the Holy Spirit is not a mere force—though powerful—but is a person. The Holy Spirit is not an "it" but a "He." Jesus in 16:14 again uses the same masculine adjectival form, emphasizing the fact that Jesus used the descriptive word intentionally.

Although a few passages like Acts 2, i.e., the Spirit's association with force and wind, might lead some to conclude that the Spirit is but a force or power that comes and goes, we instead find that He has characteristics of a person, having His own will, thoughts, dislikes, and actions. The Holy Spirit, then, can teach and remind the disciples. The Spirit is not a man but is one who possesses a personal nature not so different from ours that enables Him to teach us. The Spirit is not just a spiritual network but the person on the other side communicating with us.

The Spirit's personhood greatly shapes the manner in which we relate to Him, which forms one main theme of this book. For example, we do not treat inanimate objects as though they have their own personalities. I do not care whether my blanket wants to be on the bed covering me or folded in the drawer; the blanket does not have preferences. The wind, though strong and forceful at times, does not get its feelings hurt when we close our windows to shut it out. The Spirit, however, can be spoken and listened to. When He stirs us, He is purposely doing it to fit us for God's master plan. The spiritual gifts He imparts are not accidental but designed and intentional, and He grieves when we "shut the window" to His wishes.

So, let us step back to the Old Testament where we find many actions of the Holy Spirit that emphasize His holy nature. The term "Spirit of the Lord" is used 28 times, whereas the "Spirit of God" is used 24 times in both Old and New Testament combined. The "Spirit" belonged to or was otherwise connected to God, but their relationship in the Old Testament was not clear. In the New Testament, and particularly in John, we find much clarity on the topic. For example, the phrase, "The Helper, the Holy Spirit" (14:26) shows how He stands by our side in lieu of Jesus. The Holy Spirit, unlike Jesus who was subject to an earthly body, can be in multiple places at once, bringing wisdom, strength, knowledge, etc., to all of God's people as they go out into the world making disciples (Matt 28:19-20). Surely, if Jesus was on earth we would want Him to be with us; however, if He was with me, then He couldn't be with you unless we were all together. The spirit nature of the Holy Spirit allows Him to be with all the believers simultaneously. So it is said that Jesus dwells in us and animates us through the Holy Spirit. At times in joint worship, do we not sense the Spirit of God lifting all of our spirits in praise and adoration? If He is doing this in our local churches, we can be sure that He is doing the same great work in churches around the world in India, China, and Nigeria, for example. The implications of the Spirit's full work in believers is not reserved for a certain geographical place. Jesus, through the Spirit, lives in all of His people; thus, the Spirit is Jesus' assistant.

The translation "Helper" of the Greek word *paraklete* is acceptable but greatly limits the original meaning for the actual Greek word used here. Only John uses *paraklete* in the noun form and always in reference to the Holy Spirit (though it is sometimes translated as "Counsellor" and "Advocate") (John 14:16, 26; 15:26; 16:7).

In John 14:26, Jesus asks for the Helper to come: "And I will ask the Father, and He will give you another Helper, that He may be with you forever." Notice the continual presence of the Spirit. Remember: Jesus spoke all of this in anticipation of His own death and ascension. He would not physically return right away because that would bring about the end of the world; instead, Jesus would live through the Spirit in our lives. This is why we can still be Jesus' disciples though we do not see Him.

In John 15:26, Jesus relates how the Spirit will affirm Jesus to us as believers, "The Spirit of truth, who proceeds from the Father, He will bear witness of Me." John 16:7 reminds us that Jesus had to leave so that the Spirit of God could come, while 1 John 2:1 also calls Jesus the Helper or Advocate, "And if anyone sins, we have an **Advocate** with the Father, Jesus Christ the righteous." Here, *paraklete* only refers to Jesus Christ who, like a defense lawyer, presents the case that we are shielded by His death and life on our behalves and therefore are not guilty as charged (1 John 2:1-2).

The Spirit of God is involved in many activities after conversion. He comforts (Acts 16:7), builds up, strengthens (Acts 9:31), encourages (Acts 15:31), and exhorts (1 Cor 14:1-3). The Spirit's work ranges from comfort to exhortation. The Spirit, like Jesus, who also is our *Paraklete*, leads us forward but also comes to our side to bring the right word to help us move forward. How does one move the weak forward? By a comfort and a gentle pull. How does one lead the insensitive one? By clear instruction, rebuke, etc.

John's repetitive use of this word reflects the personal nature and work of the Holy Spirit. As the Counselor, the Lord Himself through the Spirit brings encouraging words pertaining to our particular needs.

An increased understanding of the Spirit's work in our lives will greatly enrich our delight in the intimate way He seeks to work in and through our lives. The Holy Spirit has no physical body and no limitations on where He can be and can use all of God's help, wisdom, strength, and comfort to edify our souls.

B. Attributes of the Holy Spirit (John 3:8)

In the examination of John 14:26, we looked carefully at one verse and how one word in particular, the Spirit's title *Paraklete*, helps us better understand the nature of the Holy Spirit. In this section, we will expand this biblical search to clarify the other characteristics of the Spirit. We will observe the things that the Holy Spirit does and how they might reflect on His personal nature in the way He interacts with us. Let us start with Jesus' use of the wind to describe the Spirit.

> The wind blows where it wishes and you hear the sound of it, but do not know where it comes from and where it is going; so is everyone who is born of the Spirit (John 3:8).

The wind is likened to the Spirit of God (3:8). This analogy goes deeper than this verse for the Hebrew and Greek words for (s)Spirit also can be translated and used as air and wind (see chapter 1 for more details). We can tentatively conclude that the Spirit of God is invisible, omnipresent, and powerful like the wind. It might be difficult to comprehend the Spirit, but an understanding of the wind helps fill in some gaps of our knowledge.

The wind, however, much like the picture of the Spirit in the Old Testament, does not give us an image of personhood, does it? The wind seeps into houses and brings cold drafts during the winter; it is inanimate, driven to and fro, not choosing where to go. The Spirit of God similarly is driven by the Father's will, but we also learn in the New Testament that the Spirit of God is personal, quite contrary to religious terms like "Atman" (the Hindu concept of world soul), the Force in the

Star War movies, or even an impersonal understanding of God who is in all.

In the Old Testament, the personal nature of the Holy Spirit cannot be clearly discerned. The phrase "The Spirit of the LORD came upon" is regularly used (Deut 34:9; Judges 3:10; 1 Kings 18:12; 2 Chr 24:20), but whether it is a force or the person of God is not clear. There is no doubt that some extraordinary change came upon the person, as though suddenly God were with him or her, but the personal nature of the Spirit cannot be discerned and only later is powerfully communicated.

> Then the LORD said, "My Spirit shall not strive with man forever, because he also is flesh; nevertheless his days shall be one hundred and twenty years" (Gen 6:3).
>
> And I have filled him with the Spirit of God in wisdom, in understanding, in knowledge, and in all kinds of craftsmanship (Ex 31:3).
>
> But they rebelled and grieved His Holy Spirit; therefore, He turned Himself to become their enemy, He fought against them (Isaiah 63:10).

A number of verses refer to the Holy Spirit as speaking to or telling a person something.

> And the Spirit told me to go with them without misgivings (Acts 11:12).
>
> Therefore, just as the Holy Spirit says, "TODAY IF YOU HEAR HIS VOICE" (Heb 3:7).
>
> And the Holy Spirit also bears witness to us; for after saying (Heb 10:15).
>
> Paul had spoken one parting word, 'The Holy Spirit rightly spoke through Isaiah...'" (Acts 28:25).

The Spirit also is said to communicate intelligent messages just like one person would communicate a message to another, like a prophecy or defense (bear witness).

No prophecy was ever made by an act of human will, but men moved by the Holy Spirit spoke from God (2 Peter 1:21).

And it is the Spirit who bears witness, because the Spirit is the truth (1 John 5:7).

He who has an ear, let him hear what the Spirit says to the churches (Rev 3:22).

The Spirit Himself bears witness with our spirit that we are children of God (Rom 8:16).

The Holy Spirit is signifying this, that the way into the holy place has not yet been disclosed... (Heb 9:8).

...The Holy Spirit solemnly testifies to me in every city, saying that bonds and afflictions await me (Acts 20:23).

By this you know the Spirit of God: every spirit that confesses that Jesus Christ has come in the flesh is from God (1 John 4:2).

Note how the Spirit has a moral and theological perspective.

The Spirit of God acts in ways that imply a personal nature.

- Reveals: "For to us God revealed them through the Spirit" (1Cor 2:10).

- Searches: "For the Spirit searches all things, even the depths of God" (1 Cor 2:10).

- Seals: "Having also believed, you were sealed in Him with the Holy Spirit of promise" (Eph 1:13).

- Affirms: "God has sent forth the Spirit of His Son into our hearts, crying, "Abba! Father!" (Gal 4:6).

- Leads: "For all who are being led by the Spirit of God, these are sons of God" (Rom 8:14).

- Decides: "For it seemed good to the Holy Spirit and to us to lay upon you no greater burden..." (Acts 15:28).

- Makes holy: "That my offering of the Gentiles might become acceptable, sanctified by the Holy Spirit" (Rom 15:16).

- Enables faith: "For we through the Spirit, by faith, are waiting for the hope of righteousness" (Gal 5:5).

- Lives in: "Do you not know that you are a temple of God, and that the Spirit of God dwells in you?" (1 Cor 3:16).

- Gives life: "Not of the letter, but of the Spirit; for the letter kills, but the Spirit gives life" (2 Cor 3:6).

- Guides in prayer: "With all prayer and petition pray at all times in the Spirit" (Eph 6:18). I never liked the "in the Spirit" translation and much prefer the "by the Spirit" translation which more clearly shows how the Spirit aids us (Luke 10:21).

- Preaches the gospel: "Who preached the gospel to you by the Holy Spirit sent from heaven" (1Peter 1:12).

The Spirit of God responds as a person:
- Grieves: "Do not grieve the Holy Spirit of God, by whom you were sealed for the day of redemption" (Eph 4:30).

- Quenches: "Do not quench the Spirit" (1 Thes 5:19).

- Is filled with: "Do not get drunk with wine, for that is dissipation, but be filled with the Spirit" (Eph 5:18).

- Fellowships: "The grace of the Lord Jesus... and the fellowship of the Holy Spirit, be with you all" (2 Cor 13:14).

Some verses allow a vagueness about the Holy Spirit's personal nature even in the New Testament, but the Spirit's personal nature is further clarified by the many ways He works, which allows no other conclusion than that He has a will and can associate with us as a person. Even at the end of the New Testament, the last two references to the Holy Spirit in Revelation, we see a willingness to allow various understandings of the Holy Spirit. Perhaps this is more important in some verses so as not to conflict with roles of the Godhead. After all, there is only one God, "Hear, O Israel! The LORD is our God, the LORD is one!" (Deut 6:4)

> And he carried me away in the Spirit to a great and high mountain, and showed me the holy city, Jerusalem, coming down out of heaven from God (Rev 21:10).
>
> And the Spirit and the bride say, "Come." And let the one who hears say, "Come." And let the one who is thirsty come; let the one who wishes take the water of life without cost (Rev 22:17).

The way the Spirit works in Rev 21:10 by carrying John away is most readily seen as an impersonal force doing the will of God. In just the next chapter, however, the Spirit is seen alongside the bride, welcoming the return of Jesus, the Bridegroom. The first usage does not preclude a personal nature of the Spirit but only doesn't make it clear. The last verse apparently serves as a deliberate theological point to show the Holy Spirit's eager anticipation for the return of Jesus.

Earlier (John 16:7), we read that the Holy Spirit could only come once Jesus ascended. Revelation 22:17 sets us up to anticipate the changes that will happen upon Jesus' return. My guess is that this arrangement of the Holy Spirit on earth is only for a brief period. When the church is transformed and brought to share in Christ's full glory, a whole new arrangement will be made. This does not mean that the Holy Spirit will not be present, but it does mean that He will no longer need to live among sinners and sinful believers.

Summary

The personal nature of the Holy Spirit has been made quite apparent in the New Testament through verses that mandate the essence of a person. The advantage of the Spirit of God working as He does is that He can work and live in all of God's people at once. He spontaneously carries out God's purposes and wonderfully works in the lives of God's people, ever expanding the kingdom of God. Because of the Spirit's perfect submission to the Father's will, we do not observe His own opinions and will expressed, just as one wave boundlessly joins another, resulting in one larger wave.

C. The Implications of the Personal Nature of the Holy Spirit

Lastly, we want to apply what we now know of the personal nature of the Holy Spirit to those who call themselves Christians and to seek God's fullness in our lives through the Spirit. Perhaps, the first step is to clarify what the Holy Spirit is not and then move onto clarifying who He is.

Mixed Understandings of the Spirit

The popularity of South and East Asian religions with their pantheistic and atheistic influences has stirred confusion into people's understandings about the Holy Spirit. It is largely true that there has been very little taught on the Holy Spirit except that which is connected with healing, gifts, and renewal. We will, however, never understand the gifts of the Holy Spirit if we do not understand the Holy Spirit Himself, along with His purposes. The sweeping popularity of the New Age movement has encouraged departure from the scriptures and treats the Spirit as a force of God, or more particular, an impersonal higher force that we, humans, can tap into or control.

It's no doubt that the heart of this understanding, whether found in yoga, mantra chanting New Agers, or the religious martial arts, largely stems from Atman, the spirit of Hinduism, which is called the World Soul, a being who abides in all living things. The Sanskrit word "*Atman*" interestingly is much like the Hebrew (*ruwach*) or Greek (*pneuma*) word, which means "breath or spirit." One can see why many religious disciplines focus so much on breathing during various stages of meditation.

This is why we have a whole chapter devoted to proving and explaining the difference between a personal and impersonal nature of the Spirit. Although it first seems insignificant, the ramifications are huge. The teaching of an impersonal spirit warps our understanding of evil and denies any Father or Creator God and only admits to an eternal existence. Consider how a New Ager would think about morals. If God has no personal will, then there is no moral right or wrong. However, with our biblical understanding, everything changes because we know Christ and because the Holy Spirit lives in us.

A Sanctifying Spirit

The Holy Spirit is a sanctifying Spirit who continually shapes us into God's likeness. These personal "updates," defined by the holy character of the Holy Spirit, affect our lives through the change of our hearts, instilling in us what is described as a new life. The personal nature of the Holy Spirit, then, brings not only power to our lives but a love or affection for the things of God. This is why John powerfully concludes that no genuine believer will persist in living in open sin (1 John 3:6). When anointed by the Spirit (1 John 2:27), our deepest self-centric lives shift into a diametrically opposed orientation, becoming other-centered or truly loving (1 John 3:11, 3:23; 4:7, 11-12). A mere force or power only pushes or shoves and has no concern for the decisions we make. God, however, is concerned about the way we treat others (think love); He cares even about the motivations by which we treat people. The Holy Spirit's presence, indeed, is God's presence in us, helping us think like Jesus and be like God. When we see love, we can know that they are of God. The personal nature of the Spirit enables these particular attributes of God to be rooted into our lives (Eph 3:17).

A Communicative Spirit

The Holy Spirit is a communicative Spirit. This has been clear from very near the beginning of this study, but let us consider this along with the concept of the personal nature of God's Spirit. In order to appropriately investigate the implications, we must first consider what kind of "voice" we might hear if it was only an expression of the impersonal universe. That impersonal voice or sound would not be personal and would lack meaning as it only unknowingly discloses its presence, much like gravitational waves signify its force known as gravity. There would be no intelligence behind the voice and therefore would consist of mere noise and sounds. There cannot be any messages unless an intelligent being shapes the sounds so as to communicate knowledge. (People search for UFOs and aliens rather than mere objects because they want to have genuine communication.) God, on the other hand, communicates wise messages to us. The most noticeable are recorded for us and are called God's Word. The scriptures are inspired by the Spirit of God (2 Tim 3:16-17), bringing the message of salvation, directing our belief, but also providing life and encouragement. A person resistant to the faith, on the other hand, forfeits the network necessary for faith and life, leaving him or her to wander elsewhere for direction, becoming very susceptible to the devious messages from the evil one.

Many of the actions of the Holy Spirit have to do with speaking. While some are messages designated to a certain group of the seven churches in Revelation (Rev 2-3), there are many specific instructions that we are meant to understand and are helpful for living godly and productive lives. The word *paraklete* means to exhort or counsel, inferring that the Holy Spirit brings particularly helpful words to our minds for comfort and to otherwise strengthen our souls. For example, the worshiper can be encouraged by the preacher's message from God's Word because the Author of the Scriptures, the Holy Spirit, illuminates the believer and uses that truth to specifically help him or her. The Spirit takes the Word of God and brings it to our attention so that we can find strength and direction for our lives. This is why we should never underestimate the value of regular spiritual disciplines. The message might have been for all, but the Holy Spirit, who knows our individual needs, also knows the mind and will of the Father and can help us be positively charged and changed by the truth.

God our Father speaks to us individually through the Spirit. While God often uses general messages of His Word to direct us, He also uses the "still small voice." The Spirit goes beyond the conscience, which only tells us when we have done something wrong, by empowering us to work right along with directing us in the way to go. We can think of these implanted words by the Spirit as individualized messages that often arise from conversations with the Lord.

Summary
The existence of the Holy Spirit's personal nature, as opposed to being only a force, is critical for our Christian lives. It is through the Holy Spirit that God empowers us, creates a new spiritual life, and develops an ongoing intimate relationship with us. Instead of feeling inferior

because we believe in God, we should send out a hundred Hallelujahs to our God for arranging the way He kindly works with us through the Holy Spirit, giving us things that we otherwise would never have. Jesus did leave us but did not leave us as orphans but powerfully accompanies us through the Holy Spirit.

> And I will ask the Father, and He will give you another Helper, that He may be with you forever; that is **the Spirit of truth**, whom the world cannot receive, because it does not behold Him or know Him, but you know Him because He abides with you, and will be in you. **I will not leave you as orphans; I will come to you.** After a little while the world will behold Me no more; but you will behold Me; because I live, you shall live also (John 14:16-19).

Discussion Questions

1. What attribute of the Holy Spirit most amazes you?

2. Share an experience where you grieved the Spirit of God. How did you work through it?

3. How have you seen the Holy Spirit help you?

4. What is one step you can take to be more attentive to the way He wants to help you in your daily life?

5. How might you persuade another believer that the Holy Spirit is not just a power but a person (of the Trinity)?

6. Is it important to argue with unbelievers about the person of the Holy Spirit? Why or why not?

#18 The Spirit of the Trinity (Matt 28:18-20)

Life in the Spirit!
Experiencing the Fullness of Christ

Understanding the Trinity is much like humans trying to understand the beginning of time. We can only go back so far–within a few seconds to after creation, perhaps, and then all attempts to comprehend what happened at the beginning of time break down. An attempt to grasp the mystery of eternity is also similar to our futile endeavors to understand the Trinity and quickly ushers us to a point of incomprehension. Some have likened this to an ant trying to understand a person who gazes at it. As much as the ant tries and regardless of how long it tries, it will not ever rightly perceive, let alone know for certain, this human being. Though the ant's comprehending faculties are operating normally, its inherent abilities—even with an endless extension of time, prevent it from properly apprehending us because of our vast differences.

In the same way, man can understand God, His Maker, as man carries some of the traits of God because God designed it to be so. "And God created man in His own image, in the image of God He created him;

male and female He created them" (Gen 1:26-27). There definitely are similarities, but these exist along with our differences; namely, we being the created and He the Creator. Though the inscrutable mystery of God's nature is impossible to grasp, the similarities cause us to seek and understand God at some intersecting points. In a sense, this chapter starts with an admission of failure to comprehend God and to design a description of His holy person in the Trinity. It's no wonder so much of Christendom has varying ideas on this topic!

However, though God's nature stretches beyond our comprehension, we hope to take time to contemplate the Trinity and describe the Indescribable so that this great mystery of God—as much as we can grasp at it—sets us trembling, fills us with fear, and yet gently overwhelms us by revealing His great eternal wave of undeserving love.

Our poor thoughts of God are embarrassingly numerous. We lack a true fear of God and so treat Him as one of us. Beyond these errors stands the foolishness of thinking that God is pleading with us, treating Him as a beggar. Or, even worse perhaps, is the immature way we treat His mercy by demanding kind treatment when all we really deserve is judgment. Or consider the way we adamantly tell others what God is like—as if we can be thoroughly clear in our minds. If we understood God, surely we would be greatly humbled in our hearts. There would be no room left for bragging.

Many Old Testament verses speak of the danger of seeing God. Samson's father rightly discerned, "We shall surely die, for we have seen God" (Judges 13:22). And yet his wife also rightly perceived, "If the LORD had desired to kill us, He would not have... shown us all these things, nor would He have let us hear things like this at this time" (Judges 13:23). Something else is going on here that enables

God's sinful creatures to seek Him and rejoice in His presence all while God's wrath can engulf us.

Our counter-thoughts demean God into something like a voodoo doll that we can control and manipulate (Deut 5:6-9). Our understanding of God greatly affects the way we think of the Spirit of God—for good or ill. It is possible that the teaching on the Holy Spirit has not been more clear to somewhat disguise God's glorious person behind a cloud of His glory. Doctrinal truth (from our vantage point) is only helpful when it permeates our thoughts and belief system and solidifies the foundation of our spiritual lives, animating us to be filled with His Spirit.

As a whole, we have focused on how the Holy Spirit relates to the believer during these studies. However, having said that, through our search in the scriptures, we come to no different conclusion as the saints of old as recorded in the ninth question of the shorter catechism:

> Q. How many persons are there in the Godhead?
>
> A. There are three persons in the Godhead, the Father, the Son, and the Holy Ghost; and these three are one God, the same in substance, equal in power and glory.[32]

In this chapter, although primarily discussing the Spirit's relationship to the other persons in the Trinity, we will aim at further understanding the relevance of the Spirit to our lives.

A. The Trinity Functions as One

The easiest place to begin to understand the concept of the Trinity is by the way the three persons of the Trinity—the Father, Son, and Holy

---

[32] Shorter Catechism: https://reformed.org/master/index.html?mainframe=/documents/fisher/q0006.html

Spirit (older versions use "Holy Ghost"[33])—function together. So, although they have their wills, they work together perfectly, having one will. The Athanasian Creed states, "We worship one God in Trinity, and Trinity in unity; neither confounding the persons nor dividing the substance."

Perhaps an example of blended wills is seen in a good marriage, when a faithful wife, also a helper, supports the work of her husband in whatever way she can. The Spirit will never contribute the disagreement that a wife might as He always conforms His decision to the Father and Son. There is only perfect harmony, blended as one will, the will of the Godhead, and yet there be more than one person.

This truth of oneness can be seen in the ways each person of the Godhead works together in creation, redemption, God's Word, salvation, and communication. For instance, God the Father "created the heavens and the earth" (Gen 1:1) and yet the "Spirit of God was moving over the surface of the waters" (Gen 1:2). Colossians 1:16-17 fills in Christ's part by stating:

> By Him all things were created, both in the heavens and on earth, visible and invisible, whether thrones or dominions or rulers or authorities--all things have been created by Him and for Him. And He is before all things, and in Him all things hold together (Col 1:16-17).

Although we know each person of the Trinity has a distinct role, we can also in profound simplicity proclaim: "For thus says the LORD, who created the heavens (He is the God who formed the earth and made it, He established it and did not create it a waste place, but formed it to be

---

[33] The "ghost" of the old term for the Holy Spirit, i.e., Holy Ghost, does not reflect the spooky or ghastly understanding of today but the invisible nature of the Holy Spirit.

inhabited), "I am the LORD, and there is none else" (Isaiah 45:18). God made the world, and both the Spirit and the Son played a key role.

This is true for salvation too. We can, without a doubt, announce, "Truly, Thou art a God who hides Himself, O God of Israel, Savior!" (Isaiah 45:15) But when we look more carefully at the scriptures, the roles that the Father, Son, and Holy Spirit play in salvation are quite different, providing a wonderful masterpiece of provision upon which we can meditate.

> But when He, the Spirit of truth, comes, He will guide you into all the truth (John 16:13).
>
> Then the LORD said, "My Spirit shall not strive with man forever, because he also is flesh; nevertheless his days shall be one hundred and twenty years" (Gen 6:3).
>
> And I will put My Spirit within you and cause you to walk in My statutes, and you will be careful to observe My ordinances (Eze 36:27).

Although we have great confidence in God's foreordained redemptive work as described in the scripture (Eph 1:3-4), we must remember that we are not defending or describing the Trinity here but amplifying the Holy Spirit's unique role.

Perhaps, we can proceed by thinking about the Spirit of God's function during Jesus' baptism.

> And after being baptized, Jesus went up immediately from the water; and behold, the heavens were opened, and he saw the Spirit of God descending as a dove, and coming upon Him and behold, a voice out of the heavens, saying, "This is My beloved Son, in whom I am well-pleased" (Matt 3:16-17).

On one hand, the Father, through the baptism, announces Jesus as His Son. God the Father spoke and released His full blessing upon His Son, Jesus Christ—the baptized One—as the Spirit of God descended as a dove upon Jesus. The perfect blend of this marvelous work is so clearly expressed:

> Now the Lord is the Spirit, and where the Spirit of the Lord is, there is liberty. But we all, with unveiled face, beholding as in a mirror the glory of the Lord, are being transformed into the same image from glory to glory, just as from the Lord, the Spirit (2 Cor 3:17-18).

Let's think about this anointing from a broader triune perspective from the Old Testament, for the Holy Spirit who crafted the Old Testament scriptures was the same as the one who brought together the New Testament. Each illustration of the Trinity reminds us that we are treading on very difficult ground regarding the Holy Spirit. The teaching of the Trinity is perhaps the most difficult topic to comprehend and relate to our lives. The Holy Spirit is invisible and holy, yet we are visible and sinful. Could there exist a greater impasse between any two parties? The Spirit is eternally omnipresent while we inhabit a tiny space for a short time on earth. The Trinity delightfully boggles our finite minds when we vainly attempt to grasp the eternal persons of the Trinity. Each attempt of the finite to present these eternal truths abash us not only through the inadequacy of words to describe these splendid truths but also in our shamefully unholy lives imperfectly reflecting these holy truths.[34] Perhaps God will bless our attempts to systematize the Old Testament with the New Testament truths by lifting us a few degrees closer to knowing God's infinite person.

---

[34] I wonder at what point will a fuller apprehension of His glory overpower my ability to write anything, causing me only to gaze at the glorious beauty of His righteousness.

Now to Him who is able to keep you from stumbling, and to make you stand in the presence of His glory blameless with great joy, to the only God our Savior, through Jesus Christ our Lord, be glory, majesty, dominion and authority, before all time and now and forever. Amen (Jude 1:24-25).

There are numerous studies on the Servant, i.e., the messianic prophecies in the later part of Isaiah. Through the Servant Songs, the character of the Messiah, the coming, person, and work of Christ, slowly comes into view. But when pondering the first Servant Song (Isaiah 42:1-4), the character of the Trinity comes into view and is later amplified and affirmed in the New Testament. Let us note the interplay of the triune persons in the One greater redemption plan below.

Behold, My Servant, whom I uphold; My chosen one in whom My soul delights. I have put My Spirit upon Him; He will bring forth justice to the nations (Isaiah 42:1).

God the Father (the One speaking) designates His Son as "My Servant." He is the Father's chosen one: "in whom My soul delights." The Father has put "My Spirit" upon this one. Does this not perfectly reflect the scene at Jesus' baptism with the heavenly dove descending upon and anointing Jesus? So the cryptic Old Testament reference to the Trinity's action, "I will put My Spirit upon Him" comes alive in the saving process of mankind, forming a critical part of the New Covenant and in total agreement to the other scriptures. The Father directs and decides while the Son obeys and goes out like a spoken word (John 1:1-2). Meanwhile, the Holy Spirit is the Divine One, strengthening and empowering the One serving the Father. Since we are in Christ, the Spirit liberally anoints us as God's people.

Though the Spirit worked generally in the Old Testament, it was prophesied and later, in the New Testament, affirmed that Jesus would be anointed by the Holy Spirit but also serve as the faithful servant, obeying and carrying out the Father's will perfectly.

B. The Triune Name (Matt 28:18-20)

There are numerous scriptural references that compel us to entertain the theory of the Trinity. Although we call it doctrine, we are using clues and logical deductions to guess what this mystery might mean. Through the verses given, we are encouraged, if we dare, to step toward the conclusion that the Trinity is our best explanation of the Godhead. The Lord knew beforehand how cults and other religions would accuse Christians of having three gods when there is but one, but He considered the hints important enough to help us keep our balance and anticipation of knowing Him. I do not consider it proper to argue about the Trinity with unbelievers. If they are interested in understanding, the first step is to embrace the gospel. But, for believers, we relish in the ability to know and commune with God.

The Trinity was not the starting point of this book! Instead, we started with a believer's earliest experiences and understanding of the Holy Spirit. This discussion of the Trinity is reserved for those who genuinely seek further understanding in their quest to know God. The existence of the Trinity is hinted here and there within Scripture, and it takes a regular reader to notice these disclosures. Our purpose, then, is to better understand and relish the more refined aspects of the Holy Spirit within the Trinity. Let's explore three references to the Trinity below.

Matthew 28:18-20

> And Jesus came up and spoke to them, saying, "All authority has been given to Me in heaven and on earth. 19 Go therefore and make disciples of all the nations, baptizing them in the name of the Father

and the Son and the Holy Spirit, 20 teaching them to observe all that I commanded you; and lo, I am with you always, even to the end of the age" (Matt 28:18-20).

Matthew depicts the persons of the Trinity in one short breath under one Name: Father, Son, and Holy Spirit. This singular usage of "name" (28:19), though having three parts, matches the pattern in Genesis 1 where the plural Elohim is rightly and repeatedly translated as God the Creator but irregularly takes a singular verb (usually plural noun takes plural verb). The Bible affirms throughout that there is but one God (Deut 6:4; Mal 2:10, 1 Cor 8:6; Eph 4:6; 1 Tim 2:5). These words of Jesus have certainly shaped our understanding of our commission to go out in the full knowledge that God is mysteriously at work in His people on their way to fulfilling this Great Commission. Each person in the Trinity is of equal status, having a divine nature and sharing one name. They work as one. There is, then, one commission, and nothing will stop the full purpose of God's Divine purpose to fulfill it, even through the church is weak and frail.

1 Peter 1:2

Peter condenses the amazing work of the triune God in an amazing compacted sentence that can take a book to explain.

> According to the foreknowledge of God the Father, by the sanctifying work of the Spirit, that you may obey Jesus Christ and be sprinkled with His blood: May grace and peace be yours in fullest measure (1 Peter 1:2).

Each person of the Trinity plays an important part/role in the salvation process: the Father chooses and exercises His will; the Spirit lives in God's people, setting them apart for the Lord; and Jesus, the Son, offers His blood as the atonement for sin.

John 14:26

> But the Helper, the Holy Spirit, whom the Father will send in My name, He will teach you all things, and bring to your remembrance all that I said to you (John 14:26).

John 14:26 was discussed earlier, but for extra support regarding the Trinity, we turn again to Jesus' words that allow us to see the transition —not like in modalism where God, like a butterfly's transformation, is thought to become a new person: Father to Son to Spirit, and thus are separate and do not relate to each other. Jesus, however, clearly identifies the perfect cooperation within the Godhead. The Spirit is not substituted for Jesus but instead lives in us, carrying out some of the duties of Jesus, such as teaching and guidance, while Jesus continues to exist (and intercede for us) while the Father (as we see in other places) teaches the Spirit what to say.

(1) To the foreknowledge of God the Father	**No accident, God-controlling**
(2) By the sanctifying work of the Spirit	**God is drawing us closer to Him**
(3) That you may obey Jesus Christ and be sprinkled with His blood	**Guidance & salvation**

Isaiah 63:8-10

> For He said, "Surely, they are My people, sons who will not deal falsely." So He became their Savior. 9 In all their affliction He was afflicted, And the angel of His presence saved them; In His love and in His mercy He redeemed them; And He lifted them and carried them all the days of old. 10 But they rebelled and grieved His Holy Spirit; Therefore, He turned Himself to become their enemy, He fought against them (Isaiah 63:8-10).

Isaiah 63:8-10 hints at all three persons of God: (1) The Father: "He said" or the one that claims the Israelites as His people; (2) The Son: Savior, angel of His presence; and (3) The Spirit: "grieved His Holy

Spirit." This notion of grieving is picked up in the New Testament, clearly depicting the Spirit as a person with a will and purpose that has been rejected.

Romans 15:30 and 2 Corinthians 13:14

The last two verses are similar in how they describe the part that the Holy Spirit plays in God's sanctifying and unifying work.

> Now I urge you, brethren, by our Lord Jesus Christ and by the love of the Spirit, to strive together with me in your prayers to God for me (Romans 15:30).
>
> The grace of the Lord Jesus Christ, and the love of God, and the fellowship of the Holy Spirit, be with you all (2 Cor 13:14).

In this last verse, it is helpful to remember the basis of the common benediction, "The fellowship of the Holy Spirit be with you all." The rich meaning of the word fellowship clearly shows the way the Holy Spirit, indeed God Himself, intimately works within us.

Summary

The three persons of the Trinity are repeatedly and variously referred to as One, whether in the Old or New Testament. If there was not a Trinity, these verses would not be written to lead us to these conclusions. We are not speaking about one or two vague texts but many texts, some of which have been briefly listed above. Instead, such verses purposely lead the careful mind to understand the Holy Spirit as one who lives in us is, God Himself, a person of the Godhead. Although some have stated that the Trinity is a man-made teaching, it is the scriptures that compel us to carefully draw a different conclusion, that guides us to consider God in His grandiose state. Jesus was not just some created being who died for us; He is God. The Holy Spirit is one who lives in us, a personable force that is also God with whom we are to fully reckon with. Do not these truths leave us increasingly astonished with how God the Spirit lives in our lives to carry out His purposes?

C. Place of Doctrine

What are we to conclude from all of this? Was doctrine shaped by history (detailed and recorded experiences in time) or did doctrine shape the event? Both are true, are they not? The doctrine we believe was shaped by the very events that were recorded in time in the faithful scriptures. God uses the events to affirm and clarify abstract truths.

Doctrine consists of stated truths that provide guidance on how we are to comprehend and instruct others. A variance of doctrine in essential areas means we are denying or otherwise restating events and the significance of those events differently than we were meant to conclude.

> Therefore having been exalted to the right hand of God, and having received from the Father the promise of the Holy Spirit, He has poured forth this which you both see and hear (Acts 2:33).

> When the Helper comes, whom I will send to you from the Father, that is the Spirit of truth, who proceeds from the Father, He will bear witness of Me (John 15:26).

Doctrine, though, if we think about it on a deeper level, also shaped the events that illustrate and teach us (2 Tim 3:16-17). The very teachings we believe in did not arise from the events of history but are an outworking of what was true all along. In this case, we are speaking of the truth of the Trinity. The surrounding facts of the three persons of the Trinity are eternal who, in time, touched down on earth, enabling us to find and believe in the Lord through Christ.

D. Our Response to the Spirit of God

The Spirit of God has a holy mission. When we understand and respond to the Spirit, we are living in agreement with God's will; however, when we fail to prioritize what He instructs us to do, we bring grief to the Spirit (Isaiah 63:10; Eph 4:30). Hebrews 10:29 captures this disregard of the things of God by the phrase "insulted the Spirit of grace."

> How much severer punishment do you think he will deserve who has trampled under foot the Son of God, and has regarded as unclean the blood of the covenant by which he was sanctified, and has insulted the Spirit of grace? (Heb 10:29)

The book of Numbers records the foolishness of hardening our hearts against God's directive by constantly diminishing the importance of the words of the prophets. Yes, because the Spirit is invisible, it is easier to pay more attention to one's senses, as Samson did, rather than the prompting of the Spirit. While it's easy to follow the large swath of disobedience scattered through the scriptures, let us, in hope, focus on what it means for us to properly entertain the Spirit's presence in our lives.

The Lord seeks those who walk in the Spirit. Like Joshua, the Spirit of God ought to be noticeable in our lives. "So the LORD said to Moses, 'Take Joshua the son of Nun, a man in whom is the Spirit, and lay your hand on him'" (Num 27:18). Although the church tends to emphasize the gifts of the Spirit, perhaps we should note the way we can display the Spirit's fruit through a change of character. It is unfortunate that some speak much about the Spirit of God yet have an ulterior motive, seeking to bring attention to themselves rather than glory to God, thus revealing a basic flaw in attitude; the Spirit of God always brings glory to the

Father. For this reason, we need the Spirit of God to worship, "But an hour is coming, and now is, when the true worshipers shall worship the Father in Spirit and truth; for such people the Father seeks to be His worshipers" (John 4:23). Or again, "We are the true circumcision, who worship in the Spirit of God and glory in Christ Jesus and put no confidence in the flesh" (Phil 3:3).

Some might assume that if God lived within people's lives, then they would never suffer sickness and trouble, but the example of Christ, filled with the Spirit, has otherwise instructed us. Even in our most difficult times—such at Stephen's stoning—the Spirit of God delights to dwell in His people, making sure that we lack no needed thing. "But being full of the Holy Spirit, he gazed intently into heaven and saw the glory of God, and Jesus standing at the right hand of God" (Acts 7:55). "If you are reviled for the name of Christ, you are blessed, because the Spirit of glory and of God rests upon you" (1 Peter 4:14).

Summary

This book is a careful recording of the Spirit's work in a Christian's life. Some chapters, such as this one, are deeper, out of reach except for those who faithfully seek God. Faith and understanding of the Holy Spirit come slowly. Even in Acts the believers did not comprehend the person and actions of the Holy Spirit. In a sense, we all sense the import of Jesus' instruction for them to stay put until they were filled with the Spirit (Acts 1:5). When they waited, they were thoroughly transformed. Our Christian growth runs parallel to our understanding of the Holy Spirit's work in our lives. While doubt chips away at the faith that is essential for our growth, our singular belief that the fruit of the Holy Spirit is supremely better than what the world offers will dash many attempts of the devil to seductively fling the world's temptations before our eyes.

The Holy Spirit finds a home in every genuine believer, who becomes a part of the body of Christ, the temple of God's dwelling. We are unworthy vessels because of our horribly stained sinful lives, but through Christ's redemption, we can daily commune with the Spirit of the one and only Holy God and take part in His divine will so that His purposes might be fully accomplished in our lives.

Let us, however, not be like stubborn Samson, who, though he had the Spirit and brought limited help to the people of Israel through his amazing superhuman strength, had to be led along through his sinful passions (Judges 14:6-7). God in His infinite wisdom used Samson, despite his sinful lusts, to complete His grand redemptive plan, but it was not to Samson's profit. Yet consider our rich opportunity to welcome the Spirit of God to mightily move in and through our lives! Instead, we can be like Joshua who, through faith, led the people of God into the Promised Land. This aspiration will lead us into greater obedience and faith, allowing more of the Spirit's awesome work to be done through our lives for His glory and purposes. This is the very fear of the evil one when any believer, let alone many at once or all in one place, awaken to a desire for and delight in God's divine purposes that are fully manifested in his or her life through the Holy Spirit (Acts 16:26).

Observe what happened when God's people were in agreement in Acts 1-2 at Pentecost. Or observe how the Holy Spirit spoke specific words through prophecy in Acts 13:1-5, which led to the sending out of a missionary team that brought the Gospel to the lost, and so the missions of the church expanded the Kingdom of God to reach the

Gentiles. These one-time events are preserved in the Scriptures so that we, the Church in the following ages, would aspire to be part of God's great redemptive program that is even now expanding to the ends of the earth. The anointing of God's people announces their appointment to be both His kingdom and priests and reminds us of the Holy Spirit's anointing on our lives that designates us for His greater purposes. "And He has made us to be a kingdom, priests to His God and Father; to Him be the glory and the dominion forever and ever. Amen." (Rev 1:6).[35] God's extreme grace is shown to us in order to display the mighty glory of God's work throughout the world. So let us allow the Holy Spirit to fully remove everything that impedes us from being fully swayed, moved, directed, empowered, encouraged, and warned to display the glory of God in our lives.

---

[35] 1 Peter 2:9-10 in full agreement states, "But you are a chosen race, a royal priesthood, a holy nation, a people for God's own possession, that you may proclaim the excellencies of Him who has called you out of darkness into His marvelous light; for you once were not a people, but now you are the people of God; you had not received mercy, but now you have received mercy."

Discussion Questions

1. What are the chief teachings of the Trinity?

2. Why is it that Christians believe in a Trinity? Support your reasons with Scripture.

3. When was the teaching of the Trinity first declared to be a main teaching of the church (you might need to look this up)? How did it come about?

4. What are the implications of having the Holy Spirit working in our lives?

5. Would you say that a person needs to believe in the Trinity to be a believer? Why or why not?

6. How should a believer respond to the presence of the Holy Spirit working in his or her life?

7. Examine your life for those things that hinder the Spirit's full work. Confess and eliminate those things and invite the Spirit to more powerfully move in your life.

Conclusion

Even though the same wind has blown through the world for millenniums past, we are far from being considered its master. The same is true for God's people who fail in their every attempt to harness the power of the Spirit for their sinful purposes. I am sure that if I was in charge of that sailboat on that Florida lake (which I mentioned in the introduction), I would have smashed it, even though there were no other boats nearby! Many today sadly try to gain control of the Spirit with large-scaled activities, highly financed schemes, and even worship power. Congregations have become dependent on loud instruments to create adrenaline uplifts to produce a chemically induced excitement and have become blind to the Spirit's quiet way of working (though the Spirit is not always quiet!).

As we progressed through this book, we have highlighted how the Spirit of God, step by step, seeks to interact with our lives. Although He brings power and enlightenment, He is a God who seeks our personal allegiance. He reveals His will so that we will seize the opportunity to affirm our loyalty to Him. Start where you are today and become decisive in carrying out God's will for His glory. Become overwhelmed by how this Holy God would want to indwell and empower you to carry out His purposes. Yes, we have differing gifts and opportunities, but His design for working in each one of His children is the same: to work together to bring glory to the Father.

The Spirit of God leads us along in life that we might join Him in His great operations, securing the great purposes God has for our lives. Open up the sails of your life to respond to the Spirit's winds by complete obedience to the Lord. Dedicate yourself to be men and women of His Word; dare to obey God's Word and follow the Spirit's leading, then watch the amazing feats of the Lord!

Each of us has a sail that is unfolded by obedience.
Be like Jesus and step into the life of humble obedience to the Father.

Appendix 1: Exercise #1 Discerning Spirit from spirit

The original biblical languages had no letter case differentiation. How do the translators know when to use a capital "S" for the Holy Spirit or a small "s" for spirit? Only by the context. I edited each mention of the spirit in the following verses to have a small "s" so that we could better experience what translators experience when trying to discern whether they should capitalize the "s" or not.

Exercise #1: Circle each mention of "spirit" that should be capitalized and underline the correctly lowercased mentions (those with a small "s").

Gen 1:2—And the earth was formless and void, and darkness was over the surface of the deep; and the spirit of God was moving over the surface of the waters.

1 Sam 16:15—Saul's servants then said to him, "Behold now, an evil spirit from God is terrorizing you.

1 Sam 30:12—And he ate; then his spirit revived.

Psalm 143:10—Teach me to do Thy will, For Thou art my God; Let Thy good spirit lead me on level ground.

Matt 12:43—Now when the unclean spirit goes out of a man, it passes through waterless places, seeking rest, and does not find it

1 Cor 6:17—But the one who joins himself to the Lord is one spirit with Him.

_____ More samples below _____

Gen 41:38—Then Pharaoh said to his servants, "Can we find a man like this, in whom is a divine spirit?"

Num 5:14—...if a spirit of jealousy comes over him and he is jealous of his wife when she has defiled herself, or if a spirit of jealousy comes over him and he is jealous of his wife when she has not defiled herself,

Judges 14:6—And the spirit of the LORD came upon him mightily, so that he tore him as one tears a kid though he had nothing in his hand; but he did not tell his father or mother what he had done.

1 Sam 16:15—Saul's servants then said to him, "Behold now, an evil spirit from God is terrorizing you."

Psalm 143:4—Therefore my spirit is overwhelmed within me; My heart is appalled within me.

Prov 25:28—Like a city that is broken into and without walls is a man who has no control over his spirit.

Isaiah 11:2—And the spirit of the LORD will rest on Him, the spirit of wisdom and understanding, the spirit of counsel and strength, the spirit of knowledge and the fear of the LORD.

Eze 36:27—And I will put My spirit within you and cause you to walk in My statutes, and you will be careful to observe My ordinances.

Matt 22:43—He said to them, "Then how does David in the spirit call Him 'Lord,' saying...."

John 3:5-6—Jesus answered, "Truly, truly, I say to you, unless one is born of water and the spirit, he cannot enter into the kingdom of God. That which is born of the flesh is flesh, and that which is born of the spirit is spirit."

Romans 8:2—For the law of the spirit of life in Christ Jesus has set you free from the law of sin and of death.

Romans 8:14—For all who are being led by the spirit of God, these are sons of God.

1 Cor 2:12—Now we have received, not the spirit of the world, but the spirit who is from God, that we might know the things freely given to us by God,

Gal 3:2-3—This is the only thing I want to find out from you: did you receive the spirit by the works of the Law, or by hearing with faith? Are you so foolish? Having begun by the spirit, are you now being perfected by the flesh?

Eph 2:22—...in whom you also are being built together into a dwelling of God in the spirit.

Phil 4:5—Let your forbearing spirit be known to all men. The Lord is near.

Appendix 1: Exercise #1 Discerning Between Spirit and spirit

1 Thes 5:23—Now may the God of peace Himself sanctify you entirely; and may your spirit and soul and body be preserved complete, without blame at the coming of our Lord Jesus Christ.

1 John 4:1—Beloved, do not believe every spirit, but test the spirits to see whether they are from God; because many false prophets have gone out into the world.

Question

What makes it easy or hard to decide which spirit has a capital and which has a small one?

Appendix 2: Exercise #2 Activities of the Holy Spirit

Who is the Holy Spirit and what does He really do? Let's take a look at what the Bible says!

Exercise #2: The following Bible verses contain references to the Spirit of God ("Spirit") and help us identify different activities of the Holy Spirit. After each verse, use the space by each verse to write down one or more verbs that describe the Spirit's actions found in that verse.

Judges 14:6—And the Spirit of the LORD came upon him mightily, so that he tore him as one tears a kid though he had nothing in his hand...

Isaiah 4:4—When the Lord has washed away the filth of the daughters of Zion, and purged the bloodshed of Jerusalem from her midst, by the Spirit of judgment and the Spirit of burning,

Isaiah 11:2—And the Spirit of the LORD will rest on Him, The Spirit of wisdom and understanding, The Spirit of counsel and strength, The Spirit of knowledge and the fear of the LORD.

Eze 3:12—Then the Spirit lifted me up, and I heard a great rumbling sound behind me, "Blessed be the glory of the LORD in His place."

Haggai 2:5—'As for the promise which I made you when you came out of Egypt, My Spirit is abiding in your midst; do not fear!'

Matt 1:20—Joseph, son of David, do not be afraid to take Mary as your wife; for that which has been conceived in her is of the Holy Spirit.

Matt 3:11—As for me, I baptize you with water for repentance, but He who is coming after me is mightier than I, and I am not fit to remove His sandals; He will baptize you with the Holy Spirit and fire.

Luke 2:26—And it had been revealed to him by the Holy Spirit that he would not see death before he had seen the Lord's Christ.

Luke 4:1—And Jesus, full of the Holy Spirit, returned from the Jordan and was led about by the Spirit in the wilderness.

Luke 12:12—...for the Holy Spirit will teach you in that very hour what you ought to say.

John 3:5-6—Jesus answered, "Truly, truly, I say to you, unless one is born of water and the Spirit, he cannot enter into the kingdom of God. That which is born of the flesh is flesh, and that which is born of the Spirit is Spirit."

Acts 1:8—...but you shall receive power when the Holy Spirit has come upon you; and you shall be My witnesses both in Jerusalem, and in all Judea and Samaria, and even to the remotest part of the earth.

Acts 1:16—Brethren, the Scripture had to be fulfilled, which the Holy Spirit foretold by the mouth of David concerning Judas, who became a guide to those who arrested Jesus.

Acts 11:12—And the Spirit told me to go with them without misgivings. And these six brethren also went with me, and we entered the man's house.

Acts 13:52—And the disciples were continually filled with joy and with the Holy Spirit.

Romans 8:26—...The Spirit also helps our weakness; for we do not know how to pray as we should, but the Spirit Himself intercedes for us with groanings too deep for words;

2 Tim 1:14—Guard, through the Holy Spirit who dwells in us, the treasure which has been entrusted to you.

Rev 3:6—'He who has an ear, let him hear what the Spirit says to the churches.'

Question:
Which activity would you like to know more about? Why?

Appendix 3: Difficult Passages

(1) What does John 20:22 mean? What are the implications for the average Christian believer today of this special impartation of the Spirit?

> And when He had said this, He breathed on them, and said to them, "Receive the Holy Spirit" (John 20:22).

John 20:22 is a difficult passage to interpret. But, because the verse was directed to the apostles after the cross but before the Day of Pentecost, it very well can be concluded that this incident is a one-time special event, making Jesus' action largely irrelevant to God's people today because genuine Christians all have the Spirit of God.

Jesus used His breath, the word, which stands for the Spirit, and anointed them with the Holy Spirit.[36] This was a pre-Pentecost event, before the Spirit of God was poured out upon His disciples to specifically impart the Holy Spirit to guide them through the fifty days leading up to the Spirit's coming. It definitely is not linked with a special unction that all of us should seek but only as a temporary measure before the Holy Spirit came upon them all. Up to this time, Jesus was otherwise shielding and protecting them from Satan (John 17:15; Luke 22:31-32) and now does the same through the indwelling of the Holy

---

[36] Notice the connection between Jesus' "breathed" here and God's "breathed," which took place early after the creation of mankind, "Then the LORD God formed man of dust from the ground, and breathed into his nostrils the breath of life; and man became a living being" (Gen 2:7). God is interested not only to keep our bodies alive but to have His Spirit fill and rule our lives.

Spirit. The work of the Spirit here is not different in nature but is a special provision to protect God's work in His people during a special time.

(2) What does it mean that God's people will be "baptized with the Holy Spirit" (Acts 1:5)? Please note that the filling of the Holy Spirit was linked to the baptism of the Spirit as predicted by John the Baptist: "He will baptize you with the Holy Spirit and fire" (Matt 3:11; Mark 1:8; Luke 3:16). This is discussed in detail in Chapter 4, The Birth of the Spirit, part C.

(3) Speaking in tongues, even its meaning, has sadly divided the modern church even though it unified the early church in the Book of Acts by bringing the various Christian groups under one umbrella and the apostles' oversight (See Chapter 9, Part B: The Filling of the Spirit). The Holy Spirit will at times equip God's people with the spiritual gift of tongues (i.e., speaking in unknown foreign languages, 1 Cor 14:27-32).

(4) Why are some believers so antagonistic to being filled with the Spirit even though Christians are commanded to be so (Eph 5:18)? This critical spirit largely arises from abuses of "being filled," but perhaps other disappointments, misunderstandings, and teaching with insufficient instruction on basic Christian living all form part of the resistance to appreciating this instruction. Chapter 9 speaks more about filling of the Spirit.

(5) If being filled with the Spirit is a command (Eph 5:18), then we ought to obey it. However, the whole concept seems very complicated. How does an average believer become filled by the Holy Spirit? This verse hints that there really is no such thing as an 'average believer'. God dwells in every genuine believer and desires to fully enable each Christian to carry out God's will by filling him or her. The context is

very important because the apostle draws a contrast between being filled and influenced by alcohol and being filled and influenced by the Holy Spirit. Paul goes on and describes this communion with God as evidenced in singing, giving thanks, and properly getting along with each other (Eph 5:18-21), which is explained in more detail in Chapter 9, "The Filling of the Spirit." The point is that all believers can and should be wonderfully helped and otherwise influenced by the Spirit in their lives.

(6) Why is it that some people insist that today there are no miracles or gifts, such as speaking in tongues, even though the Bible speaks of them? The question is a good one. There are two schools or general approaches to this topic: Cessationism and Continuationism. They are discussed in more length under Section B of Chapter 13, Spiritual Gifts (1/2).

(Feel free to email me with further questions.)

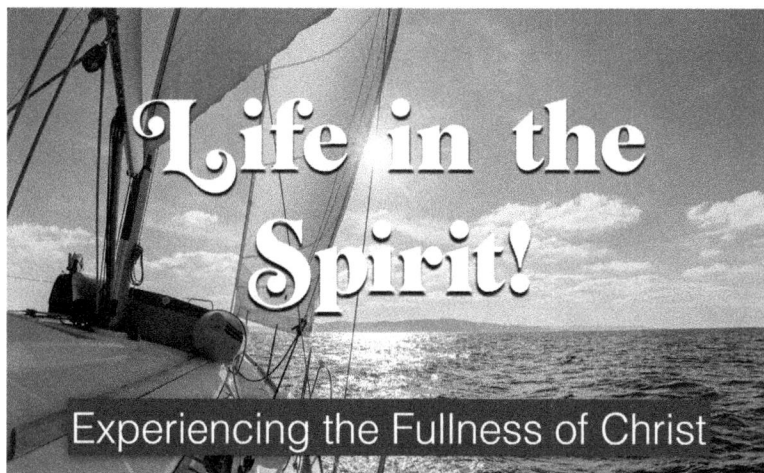

Life in the Spirit!

Experiencing the Fullness of Christ

About the Author

Rev. Paul J. Bucknell, an active author and international instructor, has written more than twenty books on pertinent Christian training topics. Paul worked as a cross-cultural church planter in Taiwan during the 80's, pastored at a Chinese church (largely in English) in the 90's, and started this writing ministry in 2000. His books are written with the conviction that the more we build our lives on the truth of God's Word, the stronger and more vibrant our faith and lives will be. Paul's international training seminars take God's Word and apply the truth therein to different aspects of Christian living for pastors and Christian leaders.

As the founder of Biblical Foundations for Freedom, Paul provides printed and digital media along with video training courses and an ongoing website ministry. Paul with his wife, Linda, have eight children and presently delight in having five grandchildren.

(More on Paul, Linda, and the ministry)

About *Life in the Spirit!*

I have been a believer for around fifty years, most of which have been spent in ministry. Through the years I, like yourselves, have seen the misunderstandings and ignorance of the Holy Spirit lead to many frustrated Christians. How tragic and unnecessary! *Life in the Spirit!* is a biblical theology of the Holy Spirit that dives deep into the scriptures to explore all that the Bible has to say about the Spirit; but it is also much more than that. We begin this study from the perspective of a typical believer who, starting a new faith, would be introduced to the person and work of the Holy Spirit. We journey from one topic of the Holy Spirit to another, making sure the foundational teachings are well understood before moving on. Step by step, we explore the main teachings of the Holy Spirit and carefully apply them to our own Christian lives. Discussion questions at the end of each chapter help us practically and theologically engage in the chapter's content personally and with others.

What about the tough questions and all the different viewpoints? I hope that this book serves as a bridge, or at least the foundation of a bridge, that provides a unified understanding of the Holy Spirit. With careful attention to the scriptures and an understanding of the divisive viewpoints, we should be are unafraid to live out the fullness of the Spirit, eager to work with others with varying viewpoints, and able to explain our biblical position.

May the rich love of Christ be poured out through the Spirit in each of our lives and our congregations throughout the earth. Isn't that what our Father wants? Why be satisfied with less when our Lord desires that we experience the fullness of Christ today?

Join us in this adventure of experiencing the fullness of Christ's Spirit!

www.ingramcontent.com/pod-product-compliance
Lightning Source LLC
Chambersburg PA
CBHW062148080426
42734CB00010B/1608